CHATTEY'S ISLAND

James Ehmann

CHATTEY'S
ISLAND

Ticknor & Fields
New Haven and New York
1982

Library of Congress Cataloging in Publication Data

Ehmann, James.
  Chattey's island.

  1. Economic development projects — New
York (State) 2. Erie Canal (N.Y.) 3. New
York (State) — Economic policy. 4. Chattey,
Nigel. I. Title.
HC107.N7E39   338.9747   82-5598
ISBN 0-89919-126-6   AACR2

Printed in the United States of America

Q 10 9 8 7 6 5 4 3 2 1

Book design by Ann Schroeder

For Sarah

"Take a look at history. Revolutions always begin on the waterfront. We could make this a crusade."

— Patrick Sullivan

CHATTEY'S ISLAND

THEY DESCRIBED NIGEL CHATTEY, variously, as a snake-oil salesman, an itinerant Pakistani cavalryman, too much of a gentleman, too much of an Englishman, a swashbuckler, an enlightened technocrat, an authentic visionary, a lunatic. Without argument, he was a man of ideas, and one of his notions was a lot bigger than the rest. In 1978, New York State officials offered Chattey, who needed the money desperately, almost a quarter of a million dollars in fees and services to further develop the concept. Chattey all but went berserk before he walked out on them, affronted.

"You could see a volcano there, and he was trying not to explode," recalled Bernard Lawson, one of the state's attorneys, "but at the end of the meeting, he exploded. I kept my words very measured, because he was looking for a fight, and I wasn't going to give it to him."

The offer, as Chattey saw it, was preposterously small, "a sham, a downright insult in light of what I'd put into the idea," he said. "My fury was something to behold, and it shocked the hell out of them. These pontifical lawyers just aren't used to a guy losing his cool like that, but there was nothing else for it. I think they thought they could steal me blind." A plan to save so much of the world, he said, was going to cost more.

Chattey had a demonstrable talent for conceiving solutions before other people so much as recognized the problems, but if he was indeed a visionary, he had blind spots. He plainly had no precognition, back then, of the ways in which others would respond to his offer of salvation, one of the grandest ideas of the age.

FREED OF HIS THREE-PIECE WALL STREET DUDS, Chattey wandered in gardening garb around his rolling acre of yard on a cool morning in April of 1980. He spoke fondly of the dormant treasures set soon to awaken and make an Eden of the place — the squill and amanda blanda, the late Darwin tulips, the jonquil and impatiens and narcissi, the exotic azaleas. The centerpiece of the property was a hillside water garden, where a three-foot falls of Chattey's design spilled over a 400-ton flow of metamorphic rock. The reflecting pool below was aimed to bounce its image of upended oaks between the branches of an interposing purple maple and on through the family's kitchen window. Chattey leaned against a dogwood and shared with me his glee in *Scilla siberica* and chionodoxa, already blooming blue and violet through the mud and the lingering snow, then imagined the fuller spread of color mid-May would bring. Neighbors knew him as a bulb-and-seed genius, a landscaper summa cum laude.

"When the spring garden comes in, the display is magnificent," he said. "People come and walk through the yard. We find total strangers out back saying 'Isn't this beautiful?' and I don't know how to respond, whether to say 'I am *so* glad you are pleased' or 'Will you *please* get off of my property?' "

Beneath the talk of snowdrops and iris, however, beyond the gardening blab and tales of errant tourists, Chattey's true concern that morning was strictly political: he wondered about how to seduce, or failing that, how to ambush, the Honorable Hugh Carey, governor of the State of New York.

Redesigning a fair piece of the world was no simple affair, and Chattey wanted the governor's help. Mere approval of his idea by the state's chief executive would go a long way, Chattey reckoned, toward convincing private industries and public agencies to pay the millions of dollars needed for a detailed study of the plan's feasibility. Governor Brendan Byrne of New Jersey had called for the funding of such a study. So had Ed Koch, mayor of New York City. But after years of attempted persuasion in Albany — and despite the lesser officials' offer of a quarter of a million dollars in funding — Hugh Carey remained a mum governor.

The piece of the world Chattey planned to save, in the narrow view, included the entire tri-state region of New York, New Jersey and Connecticut. More generally, the plan promised beneficial ripples from New York north to New Hampshire, south to Kentucky and west to Montana. Intending no hyperbole, Chattey said the idea might well begin in the United States a second industrial revolution.

The plan remained unstudied and untested, however, and more than a few apparently respectable critics thought Chattey was full of muffins. For Governor Carey to link his name to so controversial a proposal early on, his aides assured me, would be a political risk of enormous proportion. Chattey proposed a public works project of a scale seldom seen since the Chinese built the Great Wall, and the project's epicenter was the State of New York.

Chattey seemed insufferably pleased with himself, and I could understand why, when he first listed for me the project's potentials: to reduce air pollution, to eliminate the ocean dumping of sewage sludge and toxic wastes, and to productively dispose of hundreds of millions of tons of municipal garbage; to cripple a principal cause of inflation, to strengthen the dollar overseas and to dramatically improve the nation's balance of trade; to rebuild the failing industrial base of the Northeast and the Midwest; to lower the costs of gasoline and home heating oil; to create real-work jobs by the tens of thousands, in a time of high unemployment, for people generally believed to be unemployable; to allow for the sensible distribution and use of domestic fossil-fuel supplies, particularly the coal of Appalachia, Montana and Wyoming; to ensure domestic economic stability by providing optimal flexibility in energy supply; and just maybe to prevent an American oil war in the Middle East.

The project was even designed to pay for itself. Oil imports might be reduced by as much as 25 percent, a million or more barrels a day, and the cost of remaining imports, at least another million barrels daily, would plummet. Chattey's rough calculations, in 1980 dollars, indicated that the plan would save New York, New Jersey and Connecticut alone, in energy costs alone, something like $20 million every twenty-four hours, about $7 billion a year. "You can build one hell of a facility with that kind of money," he said.

Additionally, and some people thought more importantly, embarkation on so fantastic a plan was just the thing to convince Americans that their nation had not lost its spirit and spunk, its élan. Chattey dared not put a dollar value on that.

Despite his disinclination to say so in public, the awesome significance of the scheme was not lost on Governor Carey. His formal endorsemant, risky or not, was all but in hand, in fact, back in 1978. In a press release which was never released, Carey said the plan "would appear to be, if achievable, of immense importance to the entire Northeast and to offer significant benefits to the nation as a whole." But at the last minute, the governor's blessing was withheld. Nigel Chattey's dealings with Bernard Lawson and others of the governor's minions fell apart, because a handful of wonderfully intelligent men failed at some rather elementary communication, misunderstood one another horribly, then got mad and hurt each other's feelings.

Hence no endorsement, no funding, no "important benefits" for anybody.

Chattey tried other approaches to the governor, but by 1980 Carey had other things on his mind. In the months before the Presidential nominations, he left the running of the state largely to subordinates so that he might campaign — and he did so tirelessly — for Senator Edward Kennedy. Carey, at the time, was reported to be courting one Anne Ford Uzielli, who had made it known that she had no intention of settling in Albany. Political observers in the state capital widely believed that Carey wanted a new job in a new place — that his hope, were Kennedy to be elected President, was to be given an ambassadorship, to Ireland, say, or perhaps to be selected for the vice-presidency itself.

Chattey had no idea how to get his attention.

"If you can grow browallia well, it tells you a lot

about the climate zone you've achieved," the gardener told me, showing off the hothouse he had built in an oversized closet off the living room of his home in Irvington-on-Hudson, New York. Inside were grape hyacinths, variegated ivies, bromeliads, primula and three varieties of flowering cactus. "The bloom in there in early March was absolutely incredible," he said. Geraniums were a special pride. "Last year we had thirteen blossoms on a single plant. That has to be a record."

Chattey had long intended to enlarge the green room, but he could not afford the expense. A horticulturist by avocation, he was by profession an industrial consultant with expertise in economics and engineering, geography and geopolitics, and he had earned very well. But he had not earned much since he gave up his business in 1975 to promote his idea full time, and his savings — for recreation, for home repairs, for his daughter's education, for his own retirement — had gone into the effort. "There is no question," he told me, "for a family man, I have extended myself further than the limits of prudence would dictate." In 1980, Chattey was fifty-two years old.

The plan for solving everybody else's problems was not hard to understand, just big. The leviathan of civil engineering had two parts:

In ocean waters off New York City, say twenty miles out, roughly equidistant from Long Beach on Long Island and Long Branch on the Jersey shore, all but out of sight of the coast, Chattey imagined new land. He wanted to sink in the ocean an artificial island, a sweeping cluster of dikes enclosing a network of protected waters — "polders," the Dutch called them — forming a complex perhaps half a mile square. Longshoremen at work on new quays would unload vessels carrying domestic coal to fuel a power plant built on a barge and floating within one of the polders. At a second, able-bodied seamen on a ship holding liquefied natural gas would pump their explosive cargo into a floating regasification station. Off a third, tug operators would guide to mooring a crude oil carrier four times too large to enter the Port of New York, too large in fact to call at any port on the American East Coast. Engineers in a central operations building would then send to the mainland energy in whatever form — electricity, oil or gas — through undersea cables and pipelines. Elsewhere in the complex, small tankers carrying municipal and industrial wastes would pump their toxic cargoes into the body of the island for environmentally sound, and permanent, disposal.

And that was just for starters. Over the course of a decade, polder after polder might be added, some holding protected waters, some supporting dry land, all radiating from the initial cluster until a monstrous scarab of a complex, with secondary, wave-baffling dikes reaching out like the great insect's legs, lay off the Port of New York. Chattey envisioned an ultimate island of between eight and twenty-five square miles (in the latter case, the size of Manhattan itself), room enough for the region's noxious or dangerous, but essential, industries — fossil fuel power plants, garbage-burning power plants, oil and gas stripping stations, oil refineries, petrochemical plants, solid waste reduction units and the like. The complex would also offer modern transshipment facilities where foreign-flag vessels would load American coal, to meet their nations' energy needs, and American grain, to feed their peoples.

The second part of the plan called for the creation of a major new system of transport, an energy-efficient commercial connection between the new superport and its hinterland — the industrial cities, the farmlands and the mines in the heartland of America. Coal from the West and grain from the Midwest would follow the system, and industry, fed by raw materials cheaply shipped, would thrive along its path. Chattey wanted to modernize America's first great public works project. He hoped to re-dig the Erie Canal.

"Sure, I get it," said a radio talk-show host. "And your next project, I bet, will be to re-dig the canals on Mars."

The facetiousness was understandable. A group of New York State senators learned of the idea in 1978 and said its implementation would constitute nothing less than the largest single act of construction in the history of the world.

"If this is such a damned good idea," asked Steve Galante, a friend of mine who in 1980 worked as news editor of a *Wall Street Journal* weekly publication, "how come I've never heard of it?" I had only recently learned of the project myself, and I was asking myself the same question.

THE GOVERNOR'S SILENCE on so important a matter "seemed to me wholly inexcusable," wrote New York State Senator J.D. Hammond. "Was it not his duty, as governor of the state, to have officially advised us of his opinion on the matter? If he was in favor of it, he should have so declared himself. If against it, he should have warned us not to adventure on the measure. There was a timidity (may I not say a littleness?) in thus evading the question, unsuitable to the character of an able, honest and independent statesman."

Hammond, long dead now, served in the state senate in 1817. The "measure" he spoke of was De Witt Clinton's plan to cut a ditch across the State of

New York — "a navigable communication," as Hammond put it, between the tide waters of the Hudson River and the Great Lakes frontier. The senator was saddened and angered by the refusal of Daniel Tompkins, who was then the governor, to commit himself concerning the proposed construction of the Erie Canal. Tompkins believed, however, that taking a stand on either side of so controversial an idea would be a political risk of enormous proportion. His caution was soon rewarded. Later that year he was elected to the vice-presidency of the United States under James Monroe.

NIGEL CHATTEY HAD SLEPT WITH CAMELS, for warmth, in the deserts of India. He had argued petroleum prices with Sheik Ahmed Zaki Yamani. He was once nearly drowned after losing his ketch to a storm in the English Channel, once nearly frozen to death in a Himalayan pass after being chased out of China by a platoon of communist cavalry. He had hitch-hiked, ship by ship, across the South Pacific. He had led patrols to intercept gold smugglers crossing from Afghanistan into Pakistan. He had mapped remote Asian frontiers so forbidding "that I don't think anyone had ever been there before," he said, "and I doubt anyone's found reason to visit since." He had worked in executive capacities for oil companies, shipbuilders, grain distributors. He had worked independently for dozens of other industries in Indonesia and Guatemala and Germany and Iran, in twenty countries all told. Chattey had a sometimes wild-eyed understanding of the relationships between time and space and size and resources, a talent he credited to his education; he grew up as part of the last generation of Englishmen bred to sustain the Empire. He had been an American for twenty-five years by 1980 but, hardly a typical citizen, he remained a difficult man, a very difficult man, for his home-grown countrymen to comprehend. I do not think he realized, at first, that in promotion of his new idea he was out to accomplish, all but single-handedly, a task to which government would have assigned a thousand workers. Still, he knew that to move the plan at all he would need allies. He selected two.

One was Constantine Sidamon-Eristoff, an engineer, an attorney and a politician, a member of New York's Metropolitan Transportation Authority and the former highway commissioner of New York City. The day I met him I asked about the plan's general lack of renown. "Maybe we're just bad salesmen," he said, gently forgiving what I would come to think of as scandalous behavior on the part of state and federal officials. "And maybe part of the problem," he added, "is Nigel Chattey himself. He is such a *flamboyant* British personality. That is what has fascinated me from the start, but I suppose it could be turning a lot of people off."

I could relate to that. I met Chattey late in 1979 at Hancock International Airport in Syracuse. I was working for the local newspaper, and he had flown in to discuss his project. The mellifluous mid-Atlantic patois left me instantly suspicious. Then there was his habit of talking about one thing while seeming to think about something else altogether. Then there were the deep, clear eyes which appeared to see through solid matter and tended from grey to either green or blue, depending on their target, a change spookily accentuated by Chattey's all but complete absence of eyebrows. Then there was the black felt Robin Hood hat. No feather, thankfully.

Chattey was a striking man, tall and solidly built; the angles of his face were sharp, the forehead high, the fine chestnut hair in distinguished recession, greying at the temples. He looked to me a little like an actor or an airline pilot, a little like a con-man, a little like a madman — I could not decide which, though I leaned toward the latter possibilities when he tried to rent a car with his American Express Card and the clerk explained that his account was frozen for non-payment of bills. Slowly and with consummate authority he said, "That is not possible," and then he demanded that she double check, re-scan the computer, find her boss, call New York, do whatever was necessary to clear up the problem *right now*, thank you very much.

She did. He was right, and we were both relieved. In a restaurant soon afterwards, Chattey began at once to tell me of the project's geopolitical potentials. When the waitress interrupted to take our orders, he shifted easily into delightful small talk — approving her laments about the weather, sympathizing with her complaints about her head cold, asking her opinion about the relative merits of American and Canadian bacon — in a matter so gracious and engaging I feared she would think it flirtatious. Whatever she thought, she warmed to him instantly, and so did I. Then she left to deliver the orders and he was suddenly all business again, telling me about tons of this and volumes of that and the shape of the world in the year 2000. Intriguing stuff.

"Some people think weeks ahead, or months. Some think in terms of years. The trouble with Nigel Chattey is he thinks in terms of decades," I was told later by Chattey's other partner in promotion, John Petty, former assistant secretary for international affairs of the U.S. Treasury Department. "His concepts are good but his timing is bad — he's always *years* ahead of the crowd.

"I recall in the mid-sixties," Petty said, "Chattey was on a lecture tour as a petroleum economist, and we sat down one night, like old friends will, to solve the problems of the world. He described his view of how the world monetary system was going to evolve, and he said the principal determining factor at some point in the future would be where the oil reserves were, that we were going to have a currency based upon, almost supported by, oil — an 'oil dollar,' or 'petrodollar.' That was the first time I ever heard the phrase." Chattey went on, in 1964, to advise Petty that by the early 1970s petroleum would become a political weapon for those who controlled the reserves and to suggest that the United States move full-speed toward energy self-sufficiency. An oil embargo was likely, he forecast, by 1972. The projection was off by a year.

In 1980, John Petty was president of the twelfth largest bank in America, Marine Midland, a job he assumed in 1976 shortly before he heard Chattey's plan for the island and the canal. He grasped it quickly. "I am struck by it every day," he told me in his office on the third floor of the bank's tower in lower Manhattan. "I go up to the fifty-first floor for lunch, and I sit there and watch the river and count the ships that go by, and I think what a shame it is to have the greatest natural port in the world dying of apathy."

Petty convinced other Marine Midland officials to underwrite the expenses of promoting the Chattey project in the amount of $10,000 a month. He believed marvelous opportunities for the bank would accompany a regional revitalization. Marine Midland had branches in New York City, in towns up the Hudson to Albany, and from there across the state to Buffalo, on the route of the old Erie Canal.

"And when the tide comes in, *all* the boats are going to rise," Petty said.

By 1980, others could see the potential. A January editorial in the *New York Times* read in part: "This grand proposal, attacking at once the high cost of New York fuel and the difficulty of siting unwelcome industries, is so complex that it will cost millions even to study it. But De Witt Clinton's plan to build the Erie Canal was equally dynamic. At a time when too many of us think of contraction and reduction and of the joys of becoming poorer, it is heartening that some neighbors dare to think big."

GEORGE WASHINGTON HIMSELF was among the first to note the topographical advantages of New York, natural blessings which later inspired De Witt Clinton and later still captured Chattey's fancy. "Would be to God we have wisdom enough to improve them," Washington wrote in 1784 after touring the lands of the Mohawk. He knew that without some improvement, all of young America — the cities and towns and villages along the eastern seaboard — would remain economically and politically land-locked forever, blocked from easy access to the rest of the continent by the great Appalachian chain. Only New York had the natural capacity to breach the barrier mountains, thus the chance to become "the seat of empires," Washington wrote.

(In a more parochial moment that year, the commander-in-chief entreated the governor of his native Virginia to survey immediately the best canal route between the James and Potomac rivers, in hopes of diverting to Old Dominion the western trade "which otherwise at no distant period will be attracted to the state of New-York.")

Clinton recognized the advantages a generation later. First, New York City enjoyed an enormous protected harbor. Second, the harbor lay at the mouth of the Hudson River, a tidal fjord navigable for 160 miles into the continental interior. And third, the river led to the mouth of the Mohawk Valley — the only break in the flank of the Appalachians, anywhere from the Longfellow Mountains of Maine to the southern terminus of the Blue Ridge in Georgia, low enough to allow construction of a canal to the west.

New York City was a fifth-rate seaport in those days, a laggard behind Boston, Baltimore, Philadelphia and New Orleans. "Yet the superiority of New-York is founded in nature," Clinton wrote in 1817, "and if improved by the wisdom of government, must always soar above competition." He imagined the "empire state" Washington had predicted. A canal to the Great Lakes would channel the incalculable wealth of a developing continent across New York's central tier, down her principal river and into her principal port. New York City, which was still heavily wooded as Clinton wrote, "will in the course of time become the grainery of the world, the emporium of commerce, the seat of manufactures, the focus of great monied operations. Before the revolution of a century, the whole island of Manhattan, covered with habitations and replenished with a dense population, will constitute one vast city."

No century was required. Business for New Yorkers expanded exponentially. In 1826, the first full year of canal operation, more than five hundred new firms opened in the city, and more new houses were built there than stood at the time in Albany. By 1840 tonnages moving to and from the New York waterfront surpassed those of Boston, Baltimore and New Orleans combined, and Philadelphia was ruined as a port. Baltimore, which commanded the mouth of the National Road, had formerly handled the bulk of the western trade; financiers there were so panicked by the instantaneous loss of commerce that they pooled their resources in 1828 to create a competing mode — the nation's first railroad, the Baltimore & Ohio.

An abundance of cheap energy was the single factor that allowed the B&O and railroads that followed to eventually undercut the canal's commercial preeminence. Cheap energy in the form of wood and coal gave rail companies the competitive edge shortly after the Civil War, and later, cheap energy in the form of diesel fuel enhanced the superiority. After World War II, that same cheap energy, fueling trucks, fostered the railroads' decline.

Everyone knew it, though not everyone liked to hear it, when Chattey explained that history had fully circled. "There *is* no more cheap energy," he said at scores of promotional presentations. "That era is over."

Nobody argued. A barrel of oil which cost two dollars in 1973 cost thirty-two dollars in 1980, and economists predicted prices of sixty dollars per barrel by 1990. "Now we have to ratchet the whole system back a notch," Chattey said. "We have been moving by air what ought to move by truck, by truck what ought to move by rail, and by rail what ought to move on barges." The relative economies were obvious. According to the Army Corps of Engineers, one gallon of gasoline, fueling an airplane, would move a ton of cargo four miles. The gallon would move the ton sixty miles by truck, about two hundred by rail. Fueling a barge, a gallon would move a ton five hundred miles. Such mode-by-mode statistics varied somewhat, depending on the source, but the proportions were always the same.

"But in order to build water transportation systems, you've got to have bulk commodity flows," Chattey said. "Well, I suppose we have the Arabs to thank for this, because now that commodity has emerged. It is coal."

So it would seem. In 1980, experts from thirteen

industrialized countries, in a study sponsored by the
Massachusetts Institute of Technology, concluded that
coal was the only fuel that could meet the extra energy needs of the world through the year 2000, indeed
was the only source of energy that could ensure the
survival of the Western economic alliance. Soon after
the World Coal Study appeared, leaders of seven countries that relied on OPEC oil, including the United
States, vowed to reduce imports by 50 percent in the
decade to come, principally by using coal instead of
oil to generate electricity. The object was obvious:
every five minutes, the Free World's debt to oil-pro-
ducing nations increased by more than $1 million.
President Carter then asked Americans to double their
annual production of coal to 1.6 billion tons by 1985,
both for domestic use and for export. According to the
MIT study, the United States held about one-fourth of
all the economically recoverable coal in the world,
some 171 billion tons of it, solid hydrocarbons containing more than twice the energy value of all the
known reserves of liquid hydrocarbons in the Middle
East. "If we want to get out from under OPEC, we've
got to shift to coal," Chattey said. "Everybody's been
saying it, but nobody else — and I mean *nobody* — has
come up with a practical way to do it."

There was a hitch or two. America's traditional
Appalachian coal reserves were 4 percent sulfur in
content. Sulfur dioxide, emitted from utilities using
the coal, combined with moisture in the air and then
precipitated as dilute sulfuric acid. Acid rainfalls had
already killed all the fish in some 170 lakes in the
Northeast and Canada, and scientists were only beginning to measure its long-term effects on forest
ecosystems. Despite new federal regulations, utility
operators resisted the installation of flu-gas
desulfurization units, called "scrubbers," because of

the expense. The emission reduction devices could account for more than 10 percent of the cost of building and operating a power plant.

At the same time, legendary labor unrest in the Appalachian fields put American producers at a lasting disadvantage, when bidding for long-term contracts, because they could never guarantee delivery.

At the same time, burgeoning export demands had so overwhelmed the nation's principal coal port, Hampton Roads, Virginia, that foreign colliers often lay at anchor for three weeks, at an average cost to each shipowner of $15,000 a day, awaiting a turn to load. The delays effectively added about six dollars to the cost of every ton of coal, putting American producers at a still greater disadvantage vis-à-vis their competitors overseas.

Worse yet, more than a third of America's coal reserves, and by far the cleanest of the reserves — coal four times as free of sulfur as coal in Appalachian seams, just the stuff for utilities in the Northeast, in Europe, in Japan — lay in the Powder River region of Montana and Wyoming, nowhere anywhere near where it was needed. The East Coast and its ports were still blocked by mountains, and high rail rates in 1980 made it far cheaper for New England utilities to import coal from South Africa or Poland than from sister states in the West.

For all coal's potential as the fuel of the future, the facts remained that there were few safe places to burn it, few simple systems for moving it, no efficient way to offer it for sale overseas. Thus some 20,000 miners were out of work in 1980, and industry officials — especially in the West, where they lacked the most basic of Yankee necessities, a buyer — complained of a production overcapacity of 100 million tons a year.

"Yet the optimal logistics system for moving Western coal to the East, a distance of 2,200 miles, is already 85 percent in place," Chattey said, tracing the route on a map of the United States, one of the two dozen story boards he lugged from presentation to presentation. Unit trains of the Burlington-Northern Railroad ran from the Powder River fields to the new Ortran coal port at Superior-Duluth, on Lake Superior. The modern Bel-River class of coal ships loaded there and ranged over the lakes as far east as Detroit, and could easily sail on to Buffalo. If vessels could reach Albany, they could follow the Hudson to New York and Chattey's island, and from there low-sulfur coal could be distributed throughout the Northeast and transshipped to the rest of the world. The only missing link in the system was the 350-mile stretch traversed by Clinton's Folly, the Erie Canal.

Chattey maintained as well that Western coal, even after cross-continent shipment, would arrive in New York competitively priced with Appalachian supplies. "Production in the Appalachian fields is fifteen tons per man-shift and going down," he said, "while production in Western fields is 150 tons per man-shift — and going *up.* Nowhere else in the world have I seen a variance by a factor of ten in a single commodity. Western coal is going to move, all right." The variance affected price, of course. In 1980, Eastern coal sold at the mine mouth for an average of about $25 per ton. Western coal ranged from four to seven dollars.

No single commodity could pay for a new canal, Chattey knew. He foresaw many others, foremost among them the vast quantities of grain he believed North America would have to produce to feed the peoples of the Eastern Hemisphere in the years to come. A spokesman for the U.S. Department of Agriculture later told me that export demand for grain was increasing by 6 percent per year, and that the trend was expected to continue, more than doubling the overseas sales of 1980 by the year 2000.

Chattey envisioned a new canal with a draft, at most, of twenty-nine feet, consistent with the shipping lanes of the Great Lakes. That was a lot to consider, of course. Digging a statewide channel of such depth would produce an incredible volume of spoil, some 460 million cubic yards of it, enough rock and dirt to fill both towers of the World Trade Center one hundred times, enough to bury the Panama Canal, twice, or to cover New York's bureaucracy at Empire State Plaza in Albany to a depth of two miles.

"No problem," Chattey said. "The first elements of the island form a pilot project, holding perhaps a receipt facility for liquefied natural gas and a number of power plants burning Appalachian coal barged up from Hampton Roads or Newport News. You build that cluster with sand and gravel dredged from existing deposits on the floor of the ocean, to provide an immediate tactial solution to the energy problems of New York. That much could be in place and operating within two years of permits. Then, if after all the studies you want to, you dig the canal and use the spoil to make the complex bigger. It's that simple. I can do it."

"Wait a minute," said a television newsman during a broadcast interview in Syracuse. "If you dump all that dirt in the ocean, it seems to me all you'd get is a lot of muddy water."

"That is a very good question," Chattey said. "Let me explain."

The reporter listened, and he watched as though he expected Chattey next to climb to the roof of the building, announce that he could fly, and step off.

THE PRESIDENT REACTED THE SAME WAY. "You talk of making a canal 350 miles through the wilderness? It is little short of madness to think of it," Thomas Jefferson said. Canal advocates approached him in 1809 to ask for federal financing of the scheme. Jefferson refused. "The idea is one hundred years ahead of its time," he said. "You might as well try to build a ladder to the moon."

Undaunted, New Yorkers built the canal without federal help. Even before it was finished end to end, commerce on interior stretches assured colossal success, and Jefferson, with an elegance characteristic of the man, ate his words. He maintained that his prediction of failure was reasonable, but he conceded that he had made the forecast one hundred years too late.

THE IDEA OF AN OFFSHORE ISLAND first surfaced in New York soon after the canal was completed. During several years in the 1830s, city officials advanced a plan to build in the middle of the Hudson River a giant breakwater, two hundred feet wide and as long as Manhattan, to provide surface and cellar storage space for the port's swelling volumes of cargo. That plan listed and sank, but other island-making notions, proposals to create more of Manhattan itself, survived and were implemented, year after year for generations, until virtually the entire rim of the island had been extended into the East and Hudson rivers. On the East Side, for example, ships once docked at Pearl Street. Then Water Street was added, then Front Street, and finally South Street, where the great clipper seaport was built.

New Yorkers a century and a half later were not quick to recall what first brought their city to greatness. Gone were the days when thousands of canal boats, lashed six abreast and moored for the winter between Pier No. 2 and Pier No. 10 on the East River and at Brooklyn's Atlantic Basin, constituted floating suburbs of the city. New Yorkers late in the twentieth century, faced with the most calamitous economic conditions in the region's history, were too busy trying to survive to remember. "Down-the-drain statements were the ones you usually heard," said John Petty, the banker. Then Nigel Chattey appeared in the midst of the doomsayers.

"At the turn of the nineteenth century, New York was no larger than Charleston, if as large," he began presentations to civic leaders, industrialists, politicians, scientists, longshoremen, businessmen, environmentalists, bureaucrats, construction workers, engineers, reporters and anyone else who would listen. "It was not until De Witt Clinton took advantage of three geographical assets" — the protected harbor, the Hudson River, the Mohawk Valley — "that New York was catapulted into predominance among the port cities of North America, creating the base for commerce and industry, then banking and service, which would serve this nation for 150 years. Now that has come to a halt. The growth has stopped and we've done nothing about it. Industry is leaving and we do nothing to hold it. What was once the most prosperous region in the Western Hemisphere has become the welfare capital of the world."

Nobody argued. Like all the cities of the Northeast and Midwest, New York had big trouble. Industries were moving south like rats behind a piper, flocking to the tune of cheaper land, cheaper labor, cleaner air, a better tax climate, better weather and, among the foremost, less expensive energy. About 60 percent of the state's electricity was produced by burning oil, and 95 percent of that oil was supplied by OPEC, earning for New York the highest utility rates in America — two and one-half times the national average. Wattage that cost sixteen cents in Seattle, forty cents in San Francisco, fifty-six cents in Chicago and sixty-four cents in Philadelphia cost one dollar in New York.

The regional tax base was in tatters. The U.S. Census Bureau reported that industrial relocations cost the Northeast 900,000 jobs during the 1970s. Three million people followed those jobs, accounting for the first regional population decline in history. "If we do nothing to reverse the trend," Chattey said, "the Northeast is destined to become nothing but a Social Security satrapy of the Sunbelt."

But Chattey was an optimist. Also a geographer. He hoped to re-exploit the natural advantages Washington and Clinton saw and to add to them three more: the Cholera Bank, the Hudson Trench, and the downwind location of both. Taken together, the six offered "an economic opportunity of order-of-magnitude proportions, a potential unique in all the world," he said.

Though Chattey sometimes teased reporters, telling them the idea had come to him as inspiration, in a flash, in fact he had nursed it through years of development. In 1971, the Mobil Oil Corporation hired Chattey's consulting firm to scout the East Coast for a place to build a new generation of oil refineries and petrochemical plants to serve the eastern United States. The Clean Air Act of 1970 had precluded the expansion of existing facilities, most of which were located on the coast between New York and Philadelphia. That corridor was so polluted that not even new storage tanks could be built because of the bleed-off of gasoline vapors, and the Hess refinery in eastern New Jersey was soon to close for that very reason. Chattey searched for six months and concluded that there were *no* environmentally acceptable sites, "not one, nowhere from Key West, Florida, to Goose Bay, Labrador," he said. Nowhere onshore, at least.

Offshore, he discovered a possible site. Between twelve and twenty-five miles south of Manhattan, under seventy-five feet of water, lay the Cholera Bank (so named because ships carrying passengers infected with the disease were quarantined there in Clinton's time). The near-level submarine plateau was the largest formation of its kind on the continental shelf of the eastern United States and of a geological structure "which would support anything man might want to build out there," Chattey said.

What he hoped to build, first off, was a small honeycomb of polders, 63-acre patches of water protected from ocean swells by massive surrounding dikes — elongated and truncated pyramids, each 120 feet high, 1,500 feet long on a side and a mile wide at the base. Industries built on barges could float safely at anchor within the polders, or the water could be pumped out, allowing for construction on the seabed itself.

("I think he thinks he's Jules Verne," I heard one state worker say to another as Chattey explained dike-and-polder technology during a presentation in Albany. Both men laughed, but the suggestion of science fiction was sadly uninformed. Dutch engineers, using thousands of windmills as pumps, had been reclaiming land from the sea in exactly that fashion since thirty years before Columbus set sail. I later asked the quipster if he knew what all those windmills in Holland were for. "Sure," he said, guessing badly, "they grind grain.")

Chattey called the cluster of polders ICONN, an acronym for Island Complex Offshore New York and New Jersey. "You could burn the dirtiest and least expensive fuels in the world out there," he said, clearly delighted, citing as examples high-sulfur Eastern coal and Boscan crude, a high-sulfur Venezuelan oil barely half as costly as supplies from the Middle East. According to the U.S. Weather Service, winds at the proposed site of ICONN blew offshore 85 percent of the time. Stack emissions would be carried out to sea, where, Chattey hypothesized, resulting sulfuric and nitric acid rainfalls would be neutralized by the alkaline waters of the Atlantic, with no adverse environmental impact. Officials of the Environmental Protection Agency told me the theory was sound. (As a matter of fact, mankind's industrial activities were gradually increasing the ocean's salinity; the acid rainfalls stood, if anything, to help to restore the water's natural pH balance.) When the wind shifted onshore, island industries would switch to secondary boilers designed for cleaner fuels — sweet crude, low-sulfur coal or natural gas.

"Do you see what this means?" Chattey asked his audiences excitedly, watching for some sign of "eureka!" in their eyes. Some saw. Many did not. Economics was not a fun subject, and energy economics was even less fun — largely, I suspected, because of the numbers involved. People generally conceived of any number over 10,000 or so as simply one hell of a lot, a zillion maybe. Few imagined the imports of low-sulfur Persian Gulf oil, between 4 and 8 million barrels a day, in terms of actual barrels — enough in the latter case, if laid end to end, to reach from New York to San Diego, with a sufficient remainder to run a spur up the coast to Seattle and still have barrels left over. ICONN might eliminate the daily use of oil in barrels stretching from New York to St. Louis, but few people thought of the $7 billion annual savings as a stack of one-thousand-dollar bills twice as high as the Empire State Building.

People understood easily enough that coal provided the Btu equivalent of oil at between one-fourth and one-third the cost, but few comprehended the implications. Facts remained. The chairman of New York's Power Authority told me that converting a single 700-megawatt power plant from oil to coal, even with the cost of scrubbers figured in, would generate an annual savings of $200 million. New York had an installed capacity of 31,000 megawatts, and about half of that could be converted to coal-firing, the power official said. Were all those conversions to occur — and supplies of low-sulfur coal were a key ingredient in the recipe — the annual savings would exceed $4 billion. And that was just for New York. New Jersey and Connecticut had a stake in the plan, as did all the United States. In 1980, Americans surrendered more than $80 billion for foreign oil. To sit atop that pile of one-thousand-dollar bills, a man would need oxygen.

"I'd stay out of this if I were you," one of John Petty's corporate friends told him when the promotion began. "The environmentalists will kill you."

Chattey begged to differ. He maintained that the net environmental impact of the complex in fact would be positive, and officials of the National Wildlife Federation agreed. "There is almost nothing you could do on the Cholera Bank that would be worse than what we're doing right now," one told me. "What we're doing now is not far short of cholerous," Chattey said. Each year, cities in New York and New Jersey dumped into the ocean 10 million cubic yards of dredge spoil contaminated with heavy metals and PCBs; 8 million cubic yards of sewage sludge; 4 million cubic yards of non-toxic acids; and 1 million cubic yards of "cellar dirt," the debris of razed buildings and other failed dreams onshore. That was 80 percent of all wastes dumped in American waters, all dumped in a single location — enough poison and filth to cover every street in Manhattan knee-deep, every year.

"We have the dubious honor of generating more solid waste than Tokyo, Paris and London combined, which may say something about New Yorkers," Chattey said. "Even our sewage sludge is peculiar; we can't use it for the normal purpose, which is reduction for use on the land, because ours is contaminated with mercury and cadmium. Why, we don't know — but that may tell us something else about New Yorkers. For *fifty years* we have used those waters as the dump for the metroplex, creating the most polluted body of ocean water in the world, with the possible exception of the inland Sea of Japan." Then he offered a remedy.

"The interesting thing about industries built on barges is that they don't really care what they float in," Chattey said. He suggested that wastes currently dumped in the ocean might be pumped instead into wet polders. After a time, solid and near-solid pollutants would filter to the bottom (and so long as the water level inside the polders was kept lower than that of surrounding seas, outward seepage would be impossible). Then industrial barges might be towed to new polders, and the contaminated water pumped after them for more filtration, leaving the drained polders to be filled with earth, burying the settled pollutants forever and providing dry sites for other island industries.

The western edge of the undersea bank upon which the complex might be built fell away into another geologic anomaly, another natural blessing — the Hudson Trench. Eons earlier, the Hudson River had cut the canyon, more than 150 feet deep, before a primordial Atlantic rose to swallow the mouth of the river. Even the largest commercial vessels in the world — coal carriers of 250,000 deadweight tons, oil tankers of 450,000 — could sail on the course of the submerged canyon and directly into ICONN, with no significant channel dredging needed. Chattey figured that was big news.

At the best of times, New York's harbor bottomed out at forty feet, preventing entrance of ships of more than 80,000 tons, and continual dredging was needed to maintain even that. An official of World Scale Associates, the indexing firm for world shipping rates, told me that crude oil transported in those smaller vessels cost $2.30 per barrel for delivery to New York from Ras Tenura, the principal Saudi Arabian port, in 1980. For crude carried in supertankers, the delivery charge would be only $1.20, which meant that were Chattey's island to function as nothing more than a deepwater harbor for the Northeast, where half the nation's oil imports were used, a daily savings of between $2 million and $4 million would result.

But Chattey imagined much more than an oil port and a site for power plants and waste disposal. On the eventual ICONN he envisioned facilities to clean and blend and export coal, to export grain, to produce synfuel and to process methanol, to strip and refine and distribute crude oil, to receive and regasify liquefied natural gas and liquefied petroleum gas, to reduce sewage sludge, to produce fertilizers and petrochemical feedstocks, to make steel from imported iron pellets, to refine ores for the production of zinc, mercury and lead — to do all of those nasty or stinking or hazardous things that nobody wanted done in his own backyard. Barges carrying coal and grain to the island would back-haul agricultural and industrial raw materials, moving up the Hudson and through the canal to the American "North Coast," the 6,000-mile shoreline of lakes Erie, Huron, Michigan and Superior, encouraging the revitalization of economies through the Midwest. The ICONN-Erie Project might take ten or twenty years to complete, Chattey said, creating along the way millions of man-years of work "which, with the wisdom of government, might be given to the region's hard-core unemployed. Most of it is digging dirt and pouring concrete. You need no very special skills for that."

Chattey, I must mention, did not want to rush out and build ICONN-Erie right away. "Just now, I cannot honestly say for sure that it *should* be built," he told me. He was, after all (and sensing the irony, he smiled as he said it), a conservative man.

All he wanted was for someone to fund an exhaustive feasibility study, a proper examination of the financial, environmental, technological, social, economic and legal ramifications of the plan — to affirm its practicality, or not, once and for all. Chattey was no executive with a corporation to back the venture, however, no government employee with an agency to follow through. He was a private citizen, self-employed, and he knew nobody was likely to come asking for the plan. He therefore put his business on the shelf and his future on the line one day in 1975 and stepped from his door, determined to beat a path to the world.

Some years later, he and I sat in his living room, checking the location of something or other in one of the many atlases he kept stacked beside his volumes of Goethe, Aesop, Plato, Plutarch, Shakespeare, Bacon, Steele, Swift, Kipling, Tennyson, Churchill, Terkel and Nash. His youngest daughter, Mimi, bounded bright-eyed and gorgeous between the three-foot statues of Hanuman and Rama, which stood sentry at the door, to announce that she was off on some sort of teen-age adventure. She had recently been accepted to

Johns Hopkins University, though Chattey confessed, after she left us, that he had no idea how he would pay the tuition. Had he known back in 1975 the personal and financial costs of beating a path to the world, he told me, he would have stayed home and kept the idea to himself.

ONLY A LUNCHEON WAS NEEDED to sell the idea to Constantine Sidamon-Eristoff. By training, he was a geological engineer and an attorney, so he understood both the technology and the legal ramifications. By profession, he was a transportation specialist, so he understood the economics. By avocation, he was a politician, so he understood the mechanisms that might advance the project. By inescapable circumstance, he was an environmentalist. His wife was a board member of the National Conservation Foundation and a trustee of the American Museum of Natural History. His sister was the legal director of New York's Environmental Control Board. His brother-in-law was president of the New York Zoological Society.

Most of all, though, "I was attracted to the 'blue sky' " of the project, he said. "The normal person in the Northeast hears about this and says, 'Well, that's terrific, but you'll never get it done. It's visionary, it's far out, it's impracticable — an *island*, for God's sake?' But just *think* what you could do out there," he said, looking past me toward tomorrow. "You'd have your power production, your fisheries, your solar collecting. You could build a line of windmills sufficient to keep Grumman (Aircraft Corporation) working for ten years. ICONN would be the place for all sorts of experimental technology."

When Eristoff heard the proposal, "The first thing he said was 'You better write it down,' " Chattey recalled. "Easiest damn thing Connie ever said." The effort took Chattey four months. "For a country whose economic growth has been built on virtually limitless land," he wrote, "to find that this resource is in fact finite is a milestone in economic history."

Chattey told me he "hoped simply to do the best piece of work this human being is capable of doing." So he gave up his Park Avenue office to work on the report and set to ciphering in a ten-by-ten-foot windowless room in the basement of his home in Irvington. How much would new land cost to create, and how much would it be worth to potential users? How much was needed, based on the number of industries which had tried but failed to locate in the New York area since 1970? How much would the waterway cost, what were the possible routes, and for each, where were the toughest terrains? How many jobs for "under-skilled and under-literate workers" might be created? What was the balance of capital payments and construction costs? How much could local and general governments expect to collect in taxes?

"He hated putting that together, that Black Book, we called it," Eristoff told me. "Nobody was paying him to do it. Nobody was paying me, either, but I saw for myself a nice fat client if we could get the studies going. I wanted to do the legal work." To be in a position to do it, Eristoff established a new Manhattan law firm: Sidamon-Eristoff, Morrison, Warren, Ecker & Schwartz, a bipartisan outfit. The cable address was "Nonpareil."

With Black Book in hand (there were only four copies — the inventor feared industrial theft), Chattey and Eristoff sought reactions and advice from the Northeastern Energy Institute, the Woods Hole Institute, the New York Sea Grant Institute, the Natural Resources Defense Council, and from dozens of people each knew in industry and government. The idea evolved. The possibility of connecting the island to the mainland by an undersea rail tunnel was rejected as too expensive. Use of the island as a site for nuclear plants was rejected as too shortsighted. They considered the sound of the thing, as well. By midyear 1976, the plan was no longer "The Chattey Project" (too personal), no longer "Atlantis" (a portent of doom), no longer "Offshore/Canal Concept for the Economic Advancement of the Northeastern U.S." (OCCEANEUS was unwieldly on the one hand, bad spelling on the other). The tighter plan was ICONN-Erie ("and you can call people who don't like it ICONNoclasts," a friend joked). Then Chattey called John Petty.

Petty, just then, was preparing to move from the capital to New York City. "I said the only two hours I have in the next two weeks is in the car from my farm in southern Maryland to Washington. We can talk on the way," Petty remembered. He read the Black Book as Chattey drove. "What I saw was an opportunity to express a belief in the continuing economic prosperity of the region," he told me. "Good for the bank."

Petty was a sharp, no-nonsense guy, urbane and intellectual, an actor of national and international consequence. His manner was at once soft and omniscient and strictly formal. When first we met I assumed the air of propriety surrounding our discussion was a function of our being strangers, but I may have been mistaken. In meetings with Chattey and Eristoff, he maintained a similar decorum. He was the only man I ever heard Chattey call "Sir" and sound like he meant it.

Few people, including me, ever saw the other side of John Petty. Each working week he commuted between New York City and his Maryland spread. "I'm really a farm boy at heart," he said.

Petty became involved in the Chattey plan

(bravely, I thought, as when he took over Marine Midland the bank was actually losing money) simply "because it makes such good sense," he told me. Coal might form the canal's base load, he said, though he considered grain the more likely commodity, but no matter: "I look at the fundamentals of having a deepwater port in the center of a major urban area, and of having an integrated transportation system, as *basic* in geo-economic terms, as fundamental as the building of wharfs and piers on a waterfront. The basic infrastructure has a regenerative effect: secondary and tertiary industry follows; it feeds upon itself. These are articles of faith with me," he said.

So the ICONN-Erie triumvirate was set: Chattey, the thinker — impatient, rambunctious and fiercely independent, still fit and trim, moving with the assurance of the Royal Commando he once was, sometimes smiling like an overgrown imp; Eristoff, the politican — robust and rounding in his middle years, given to the smoking of pipes, congenial and extremely well met, savvy in matters of government; and Petty, the banker — a slighter man than the others, but one with an understanding of money and power, privy to the financing ways of the world, serene in that knowledge, at home in high places.

Perhaps never had so small a group tackled so prodigious a project, and despite their combined expertise, none of the three knew where to begin. In the metropolitan area alone, there were 1,400 separate municipal, county, state and federal governing authorities, dozens of agencies within each of them, myriad trade and special-interest groups, and thousands of potentially affected industries, all with a conceivable interest in or jurisdiction over the Chattey plan.

Still, neither Chattey nor Petty nor Eristoff foresaw real trouble in selling the concept. The package would sell itself. Here was an opportunity to clean up the environment without freezing economic growth, to exploit energy resources without damaging the environment, to help stop that "financial hemorrhage," as Chattey called it, which was the money America paid for foreign oil. Here was a chance to create jobs without draining the treasury, to assist industry without subsidies or bail-outs, to salvage whole regions of the nation, to ensure domestic security, to restore national confidence and pride. Surely such an idea deserved study. Surely someone very soon would hear of the plan and understand it and offer funding for the feasibility test. Or so the three men believed.

That belief was one of the flaws in their theory. A lot of important and powerful people would not understand it. To understand ICONN-Erie required imagination.

Another problem was one they failed to consider at the time and later could scarcely believe: that so many of the people who *did* understand would applaud the brilliance of the thing, marvel at the possibilities, and then do precisely nothing about it.

Promotion of the project was into its fourth year — its fourth unsuccessful year — when I finally heard of it and chose to go after the story. My preconceptions were not remarkable. I expected to find the feasibility studies blocked by great thickets of red tape, by bureaucracies too monstrously overdeveloped to move, by a lot of highly-placed stupidity. All those were facts of the matter, to be sure, but the real problem was a lot worse than that — and to my mind, a lot more frightening.

11

CHATTEY AND ERISTOFF SHOT OFF THEIR MOUTHS at
every opportunity, opportunities earned for the most
part through Eristoff's efforts, his connections.
("Without Connie, I don't think I'd have gotten in to
see *any*body at first." Chattey said.) They met with
early success.

"The fundamental question is how are we going
to get the energy producing regions of this nation connected to the energy consuming regions in the shortest possible time and at the least possible cost," Chattey said at the presentations. "If you agree with that
premise, then you have no choice but to study
ICONN-Erie."

People agreed. "To do major and great things you
have to make a leap of faith," said Dan Curl of the
New York Chamber of Commerce and Industry, the
first official disciple of the ICONN-Erie thesis. Curl
could offer no funding, but he helped to spread the
word, and government types soon learned of the plan.

Money for preliminary feasibility studies seemed ensured on the first formal approach.

The project had come to the attention of John Dyson, certainly one of the most effective and perhaps the least liked of all the functionaries New York had to offer. He was commissioner of the state's Department of Commerce.

"It really burns the bureaucrats, the way I keep saying that the civil service doesn't do a day's work," Dyson told me, "that they should be smarter, and better, and more considerate, and more thoughtful about what they do. In the departments where I've worked, people who weren't willing to work — they all left. Very quietly you found people resigning. When I got done with the Commerce Department, we had 25 percent fewer people doing three times the work," which naturally left other state agencies, by comparison, looking bad. "There are a number of people in this town who'd like to have me skinned on their wall," he said. I later heard him say this to a labor leader: "Listen, we've got a lot of watermelons in the government. For God's sakes, don't give me a lot of watermelons in the labor movement. If a politician happens to pass by, grab him by both of his collars and say, 'Listen, you jerk, you have been turning this economy off for ten years and we're going to turn it back on and if you don't want to be part of it, get the hell out!' "

Dyson was outspoken and self-assured to the point of obnoxiousness, some said. Also, some said, a genius. His were the brains behind the "I ♥ NY" tourist campaign, one of the few successful economic development programs in the state's recent history. Enemies nevertheless found reason to snipe. Legislators publicly accused him of rank egotism for including a picture of himself in the early "I ♥ NY" newspaper ads. Dyson retaliated with a show of modesty. When next called before the legislature, he testified wearing a Lone Ranger's mask.

To have so controversial a personality on the ICONN-Erie team would be risky, Chattey knew. Still, whatever else he was, Dyson was a doer.

And he loved ICONN-Erie.

"If you try to put the economy of a region back together fifty jobs at a time, the task is not only horrendous but also boring," Dyson told me. "But here's something that isn't pork barrel, it's real, it's a hell of a goddamned good idea. We're in a lot of trouble here, partly because of the stupid things that we did. We could have done this project at the time Empire State Plaza was built," in the late 1960s and early 1970s, "for about the same cost. Instead of paying for the most elaborate office space for bureaucrats anywhere north of Brasília, we could have done something useful."

Dyson's involvement in the project began in November of 1976 with the promise to work toward state funding for the studies and to win strong support from the leaders of the state, especially the support of Governor Carey. Thereafter, his staff and the project principals met monthly. Petty generally dealt with Dyson. Chattey and Eristoff worked with Dyson's executive deputy commissioner, Roy Sinclair; with Mike Curley, the department's legal advisor; and with Bernard Lawson, an admiralty lawyer with the state's Job Development Authority (Dyson was in charge of that, too). Together, they mapped a tentative strategy. The first priority was to secure a letter of endorsement from Hugh Carey. The rest of the thinking went like this:

• The governor's support would inspire the state legislature to appropriate half of the $1.5 million in seed money needed to establish project offices and to complete a study of some discrete island function — for example, the operation of a receiving terminal for LNG, liquefied natural gas.

• The state funding would lead interested industries to put up the other half of the $1.5 million.

• Then the completed study, made possible by joint public and private sector investment, would prompt agencies in Washington to pay the additional millions needed for a complete feasibility test of the ICONN-Erie concepts.

Dyson and Petty believed some federal grant money might be won immediately, and their influence opened doors, so Chattey did his "dog-and-pony show," an hour-long sales pitch with charts and paintings and sometimes movies, for officials of the National Oceanic and Atmospheric Agency and the federal Department of Transportation. Both agencies promised money — contingent on approval of the plan by the State of New York. Then Chattey briefed a few key New Jersey officials, then several trade groups, then a few New York congressmen. Almost everyone liked the idea.

Dyson, meanwhile, took the plan to Governor Carey. John Petty told me later that Carey "was in favor of the project, but he felt that he should not be the leader of the charge at this time." So Dyson drew saber, slapped leather and advanced without him but was stopped in his tracks straightaway. For one thing, Dyson was not popular in government circles. For another, "I have enough trouble explaining to the legislature ultimately simple-minded ideas," he told me. "More complicated ones seem to be almost beyond the politician's ability to grasp."

Hence, a new strategy: they would inspire governmental interest by demonstrating support in the private sector first. In March of 1977, Dyson and Petty co-sponsored a dinner for corporate leaders at the Metropolitan Club in Manhattan. These "times require bold thinking," Petty told the group. "Timid attitudes will not solve the problems of the state and the nation." Then Chattey made the presentation. Contributions totaling more than $50,000 came in that night from a dozen industries, including General Electric, New York Telephone and the Long Island Lighting Company. The money was channeled into Dyson's Job Development Authority to pay Chattey's expenses in revising the prospectus — creating the project Blue Book — and in preparing the federally required Program Evaluation and Review Technique for ICONN-Erie. The PERT diagram was submitted to the Office of Deepwater Ports of the U.S. Department of Transportation, and it was accepted without revision.

Nevertheless, state officials were reluctant to make a commitment. "When you've got an idea of this magnitude," said Mike Curley, Dyson's legal advisor, "you go to some people in government and their eyes glaze over. No matter if you ask them for fifty cents out of their budgets, they react with what I would consider the normal bureaucratic recourse, which is they don't want their names involved. Something like this has so many chances of going up like a skyrocket and down like a stone that they don't want to be *the* guy in their agency that endorsed it."

That did not worry Chattey; he would, he believed, generate so much support for the plan elsewhere that the state could not possibly ignore it. He explained the idea to officials of the Environmental Protection Agency, and they liked it. Next he briefed officers of the U.S. Army Corps of Engineers.

General Robert Moore, who commanded the Great Lakes District of the Corps, said the project appeared to be "entirely feasible." Moore's staff suggested to Chattey that the island be sited over an existing dump on the Cholera Bank, to facilitate the permitting process; also that it be sited beyond the twelve-mile limit, to avoid legal hassles with New York and New Jersey.

No problem, Chattey said. The acid waste dump — an ideal location for ICONN because it both bordered the Hudson Trench and lay between the two least used, most exploitable, New York shipping lanes — began eighteen miles off the coast of New Jersey and almost twenty off the Long Island shore. Moreover, it was twenty-nine miles from the Statue of Liberty, which meant freedom from the jurisdiction of New York's Port Authority, as well. The authority's authority ended twenty-five miles from Liberty Island.

General Moore also voiced support for the second part of Chattey's plan. His Corps district just then was working on a congressionally authorized study of an "all-American waterway," proposed to run between lakes Erie and Ontario across the Niagara escarpment in western New York, roughly parallel to Canada's Welland Canal. Moore confided to a friend that, in his judgment, his people were doing the wrong study. Instead, he said, they should think about re-digging the Erie Canal.

Chattey then made such a Corps study possible. The army's engineers traditionally had difficulty responding to Erie Canal proposals because, strange as it was, half of the system lay in the Corps' Great Lakes fiefdom, the rest in that of New York. While Moore's district studied the "all-American" plan, his counterparts in New York City investigated a separate congressional request, one to determine the best water route between the Great Lakes and the East. The Buf-

falo-to-Albany route was not under consideration,
however, because the New York District's jurisdiction ended in the center of the state, smack in the
middle of the old Erie Canal.

So Chattey surreptitiously composed a scathing
letter to the head of the New York District of the
Corps, outlining the absurdity of omitting so obvious
an alternative. The missive also demanded that the
Corps consider deep-draft possibilities. Dyson's people typed the letter under Hugh Carey's letterhead and
slipped it to the governor. He signed. Whether or not
he read it, Chattey never knew, but that mattered little. It did the trick. The New York District included
the Erie Canal in its studies.

In Albany, meanwhile, Dyson went on with his
lobbying — he had been at it for months — and still
state legislators were hesitant. Chattey became increasingly impatient. Take it easy, relax, the others
told him. Working out the politics of the project would
take time.

"We were proceeding with baby steps," Mike
Curley told me, "because it's such an enor . . . such
a wi . . . I mean, you can imagine what it would be
like if the legislature debated it."

Thus the monthly meetings focused only on
strategy. Dyson suggested that environmental groups
be approached sequentially, "starting with the most
reasonable and ending with the Sierra Club." Petty
advised against briefing the "seven sister" oil companies, the Consolidated Edison Corporation, and any
other firm generally perceived by the public as "evil."
A contribution from one of them "could be the kiss
of death," he said.

Through all the talk, Chattey fidgeted. He ached
to begin. To hear him tell of the sessions was to watch
in mind's eye the pages of a calendar pad riffling, one
by one being blown to oblivion.

In May of 1977, Dyson sent up a trial balloon; he leaked the plan to the press. "We don't know if the scheme will really work out," read a *Daily News* editorial, "but we give four stars to the planners who dreamed it up." NBC News hoped that the studies would be "pursued with enthusiasm." *Newsday* was less enchanted. "Even Dyson concedes this scheme is a little on the imaginative side," the editorial read. "The state needs vision, but not this kind of grandiosity."

Dyson and his subordinates were most wary of such criticism. "Our philosophy was to defuse objections at every step of the road," Curley told me. "You can't just walk into the Mohawk Valley Environmentalists and say 'This is what we're going to rip up your valley to do' and have them sit there and applaud. What we wanted to do was just lay out how to go from A to B to C to D to E. That's the only way we saw to keep the project from becoming ridiculous, from having people laugh at us, or having them say 'It's a wonderful idea,' which a lot of them said — and they yawned and went home. Without something to back you up, you become like a guy who trains dogs to whistle. If you want people to take you seriously, you've got to start weighing their desks down with paper."

The LNG study was to be the first ream. Nine utilities in the New York area wanted to purchase natural gas discovered in 1977 in the Canadian arctic; the question was how to move it to market. A pipeline from southern Canada to the U.S. gas pipeline network would cost $2.5 billion, while only $200 million would be needed to build instead a small dike-and-polder receiving terminal.

Yet the legislators, in part because of the governor's silence, remained reluctant to provide even endorsements, let alone funding, so in September of

1977, almost a full year after talks between Commerce and ICONN-Erie began, Dyson agreed to get the studies started himself. He told Petty that about $325,000 in year-end funding could be drawn from his budget, and he promised that the allocation would come with the governor's endorsement.

The money was considerably less than Chattey had hoped for, but he agreed, then went on seeking major funding elsewhere. He was talking about national survival, after all. "We could do anything in this country, if we'd only *agree* to do it," he said at presentation after presentation, "but we never seem to agree on anything, unless it's to do something on another planet. The only national goal we've achieved since World War II was the creation of a multi-billion-dollar golf cart." He smiled then with feigned naivete, glancing moonward. "And it's still up there."

And later: "Ladies and gentlemen, the sword of Islam is singing in the wind. You talk about the Four Horsemen of the Apocalypse — well, they're thundering down on us out of the desert." He intended no hyperbole. If oil imports remained constant, the OPEC nations stood to collect enough money by 1988 to buy every share of every company on the New York Stock Exchange, even if they never raised the price-per-barrel by so much as another nickel. Worse, if for any reason supplies of imported oil were to stop (a Soviet mining of the Strait of Hormuz in the Persian Gulf would do nicely), then the only question remaining for debate would be how long the American economy would survive. An optimistic estimate was about a month. (This, of course, made for some amusing foreign policy, which included such things as selling American military jets to the Saudi Arabians — because we needed their oil — so that they could shoot down American military jets sold earlier to Israelis, who wanted them in order to defend themselves against Saudis.)

One night at the Yale Club in New York City, Chattey told me, "People worry about the complexity of the studies. Well, I'm not worried about the studies. I'm worried whether we can get the damn thing built in time."

In preparation, he lined up Paul Buiar & Associates as governmental consultants to the project, the New York Sea Grant Institute to do oceanic environmental work, Tippett-Abbett-McCarthy-Stratton (TAMS) as the lead engineering firm, and A.L. Burbank & Company as consultants on the LNG terminal. Eristoff, meanwhile, surveyed relevant international law of the sea, and Petty talked the idea up in the financial community, briefing George Woods of the World Bank and David Rockefeller of Chase Manhattan, among others. The former told Petty, "Stick with it, John."

Back at the Commerce Department, however, governmental and entrepreneurial personalities were making for no perfect marriage. Chattey and Eristoff had either the good sense or the temerity, depending on your perspective, to expect to make some money on the deal. Dyson became suspicious of them both because they thought the state should pay them for the work they had done and the expenses they had incurred while developing the project in 1976 and 1977. (Expenses aside, Eristoff had kept track of the time he had put into the project; based on his pro bono rate of pay as an attorney, he figured his two years of sweat equity in ICONN-Erie were worth about $57,000.) Petty grew more and more angry because for more than a year Dyson had come up with nothing but talk. Chattey and Eristoff, for their part, were offended by Dyson's concern for long-term strategy.

From the State of New York, they wanted only active political support and a healthy contribution. To realize ICONN-Erie they saw need for a private sector, quasi-governmental alliance of state and federal agencies, large corporations, labor unions and major universities — a task force they hoped to command. "It was never intended by anybody on our side that the Department of Commerce should be the lead agency, in toto, for the project," Chattey said. Were it to assume such a role, he feared, he and Eristoff easily might be written out of the project's development beyond the simple LNG study, might be cast over the side and left in the wake of ICONN-Erie.

Commerce officials worried about Chattey's worries. They thought he was losing it. "He was always, throughout the whole process, paranoid that somebody was going to steal his idea," recalled Roy Sinclair, Dyson's deputy commissioner, "like the State of New York was going to come along and rip off this inventor." Chattey made no bones about his personal stake in the plan, a stake he told me he was hell-bent to preserve. In the effort, he admitted, he was capable of belligerence.

"That's what really ticked me off," said Bernard Lawson, the admiralty lawyer. "Man, if there was anybody that was in his corner, it was us. But this paranoia that we wanted to steal the idea made Nigel his own worst enemy."

Mike Curley recalled: "The thing was, Nigel always thought he had a proprietary interest in the idea. We mentioned a few times, 'Nigel, there is no way on earth you can patent an idea,' and he said, 'Well, I know, but there are other ways I can protect it.' "

One way was to be in a better position than anyone else to execute the plan, so Chattey worked month after month on possible canal routes, possible island configurations, economic analyses to justify the costs, all manner of conceptual exploration. "There are many better engineers in the world than I am," he said. "There are probably not many better geographers. There are certainly very few people who are better at both."

Another way was to control a known organization, so he and Eristoff and Petty formed three nonprofit corporations to promote the plan, to solicit funds, and to direct the studies of ICONN-Erie.

Another was to continue to build the alliance, so in January and February of 1978, Chattey and Eristoff engineered invitations to explain the plan to senators Daniel Patrick Moynihan and Jacob Javits, the Long Island Association of Commerce and Industry, the state legislature's committee on canals and ports, New York's secretary of state, the Dome Petroleum Corporation, the Nassau-Suffolk Regional Planning Association, the assistant U.S. secretary of commerce for environmental affairs, the Mitre Corporation, the Coastal Engineering Research Lab of the Army Corps, the National Transportation Policy Study Commission, the Liberian Tankers Owners Association, the Long Island Forum of Technology, and the National Advisory Council on Oceans and Atmosphere. A representative of the Argonne National Laboratory, a federally funded lab which specialized in energy technology, caught an ICONN-Erie presentation in Buffalo and was so impressed that he asked Chattey to brief top Argonne officials in Chicago. They in turn were so impressed that they asked him to get in touch immediately with the U.S. secretary of energy, the chairman of the U.S. Senate Committee on Energy and Natural Resources, the U.S. secretary of commerce, and Jack Watson, assistant to President Carter for intergovernmental affairs, to arrange for a White House briefing.

Yet another way to protect the plan was to monopolize essential intelligence, so Chattey contacted the world-class island makers of The Netherlands' Royal Bos Kalis Westminster Group. He met with Cornelius Stigter, president of the group's hydraulic engineering branch, first in New York, then in Rotterdam, and subsequently put Royal Bos Kalis to bed, selling the group an option on the island-design study for $200,000, with $25,000 to be paid immediately to Chattey's firm — Nigel Chattey Associates — and the balance to come when the group exercised the option. According to a standing agreement, Eristoff got $5,000, 20 percent of the down payment.

Chattey's fear that the project might develop without him was hardly paranoia. There had been a dozen other proposals to rebuild the Erie Canal; there had been other proposals for offshore facilities. In 1968, the engineering firm of Howard, Needles, Tammen & Bergendoff said New York's fourth jetport might be built on an artificial spit connecting Hoffman and Swinburne islands in New York's upper bay. That same year, Chattey suggested an island jetport off the Long Island coast. Between 1970 and 1978, Public Service Gas & Electric of New Jersey spent $350 million on a plan to float nuclear power plants on barges protected by giant breakwaters off the Jersey shore. And in the early 1970s, New York Assemblyman Jerry Kretchmer proposed that a land mass made of municipal garbage be built off Staten Island as a site for coal-fired power plants. For various reasons, each of those plans first listed, then sank.

But no one before had mated the ideas of an industrial island and a new canal, a synergistic union which Chattey believed made all the difference. By the very existence of the other, the benefits of either project would increase by at least a factor of ten, he said. And if people did not realize that yet, they would, by God, before he finished with them.

Still, his fear was sound. "Every great project has to have somebody who ignores common sense and just pushes," John Dyson told me, "someone with the ability to withstand frustrations every single day and yet to still be able to get up in the morning and fight the battle anew. But nobody's indispensable," he said. "Not even Nigel Chattey."

THERE WAS SOME EVIDENCE TO THE CONTRARY, in theory at least. Historians were of the all but unanimous opinion that if not for a single individual, De Witt Clinton, there never would have been any Erie Canal. Clinton alone was willful enough to push the idea, tenacious in the face of enormous opposition, year after year after year. He did not ignore common sense; rather he sought to create new tenets of common sensibility. "It remains for a free state to create a new era in history, to erect a work more stupendous, more magnificent and more beneficial than has hitherto been achieved by the human race," he told New Yorkers in 1816, adding, in what I whimsically thought might be a forecast of ICONN-Erie: "We are fully persuaded that centuries may pass away before a subject is again presented so worthy of all your attention, and so deserving of all your patronage and support."

As governor of New York, Clinton had no fear that the idea might be stolen. Topography made it impossible elsewhere. Besides, the idea was not his in the first place. Cadwallader Colden, surveyor-general of New-York, mused about such a canal in 1724, as did George Washington in 1783. The idea occurred to state assemblymen Christopher Coles and Jeffrey Smith in 1784 and 1786, respectively, and to George Clinton, De Witt's uncle and New York's first governor, in 1791. Gouverneur Morris, the U.S. ambassador to France, wrote to a friend in 1800 that "one-tenth of the expense borne by Britain in the last campaign would enable ships to sail from London through Hudson's river to Lake Erie."

Only when Jesse Hawley had the idea in 1806 did it come to the public's attention. Hawley, a failed flour merchant, occupied a twenty-month term for bad debt in a central New York jail by writing a series of fourteen essays, "Observations on Canals," which were published in a local newspaper under the pen name "Hercules."

"We entertain vast ideas of the destinies of these United States," he wrote, "but to what are we destined? Nations have often mistaken the true path to wealth and greatness by pursuing the phantoms of glory. In early ages they were infatuated with the ideas of erecting monuments of national grandeur. The impious project of a Babel; the renowned Pyramids; the magnificent Hanging Gardens; the stupendous Colossus — ALL were but so much splendid folly." Hawley proposed as a more noble focus of effort something useful, specifically, "the connecting of the waters of Lake Erie and those of the Mohawk and Hudson rivers by means of a canal." He projected the cost of the work at $6 million, and balance sheets tallied twenty years later found his forecast right on the nose.

In 1808, Joshua Forman, the New York assemblyman who approached Thomas Jefferson with the idea, won approval in the state legislature to conduct a survey of possible canal routes. "I most solemnly declare," Forman later wrote, "that the idea of [the] canal was original with *me*, whoever else had thought of it before. I have sat still in the confidence that some impartial historian would discriminate between the importance of *thinking* a thing, and *doing* it."

Richard Wright, who in 1980 was secretary of the New York Canal Society, told me the waterway doubtless had hundreds of inventors. He supposed that every pioneer, dragging wagon and family and livestock behind, who breasted the crest of Onondaga Hill and saw the interminable files of hills still ahead, "probably thought a canal through the valleys would be a wonderful idea."

Not everyone thought so. Critics dismissed Morris' notion as "a romantic thing, typical of the man." Hawley's essays were assailed as "the effusions of a maniac," and the plan as "Quixotic," "a whimsical vaguery" which "would require the revenue of all the kingdoms of earth, and the population of China, to accomplish." Forman's resolution was approved only after a change in wording put the onus for route selection on the surveyor-general, "thus shifting from themselves the responsibility of countenancing so wild a project," Forman wrote. And later: "Judge then my surprise when, after the middle section was completed, all opposition having ceased, a scramble had commenced for the credit of originating the measure."

When Clinton snatched up the standard in 1809, opponents emerged of no less stature than Martin Van Buren, who would become President, and William Seward, who would later take a fancy to Russia's Alaskan territory and have a folly of his own. In 1816, at Union College, "My chef-d'oeuvre in the literary society was an essay in which I demonstrated that the Erie Canal was an impossibility," Seward wrote in his autobiography, "and that even if successfully constructed, it would financially ruin the state." (Following the huge success of the canal, Seward naturally changed his mind. In 1842, in fact, when he sought re-election as governor of New York, the primary plank in his platform was a pledge to modernize the waterway. People thought he was crazy. He lost.)

To bring the canal into being took all of Clinton's political prowess and fifteen years of his time. In 1812, in a broadside aimed at critics of the plan, he wrote: "Things which twenty years ago a man would have been laughed at for believing, we now see. Under circumstances of this sort, there can be no doubt that those microcosmic minds which, habitually occupied in consideration of what is little, are incapable of discerning what is great, will, not unsparingly, distribute the epithets 'absurd,' 'ridiculous,' 'chimerical,' on the estimates of what [the canal] may produce. [We] must, nevertheless, have the hardihood to brave the sneers and sarcasms of men who, with too much pride to study, and too much wit to think, undervalue what they do not understand, and condemn what they cannot comprehend."

But the state legislature, in part because of the governor's silence, was reluctant to make the commitment. Clinton chastized them in his "Memorial to the Citizens of New-York," the highlight of his dog-and-pony show of 1816: "Delays are the refuge of weak minds, and to procrastinate on this occasion is to show a culpable inattention to the bounties of nature; a total insensibility to the blessings of Providence; and an inexcusable neglect of the interests of society."

Clinton's bill became law, and construction began, a year later.

Jesse Hawley, still a man of no means in 1817, petitioned Clinton for work as a mere engineer. By the time the waterway was finished in 1825, Joshua Forman had decided to seek his fortune elsewhere, and he ended up selling real estate in North Carolina. Gouverneur Morris was dead. Clinton, who never made a dime on the project, died in debt in 1829 in the midst of the state's new prosperity. The legislature, in gratitude for his service, appropriated $10,000 to provide for his widow.

"Nigel has committed so much of his resources, both financial and human," John Petty told me 150 years later, "that as an independent consultant, he hasn't in my judgment made adequate provisions for his own retirement. I think his hope is to not be forgotten if the project is funded and built. I don't believe he expects to make a million on it. He just doesn't want to die a pauper."

CHATTEY WAS ALREADY IN DEBT when the State's offer finally was made. The bank's contribution generally was spent before the end of the month, every month. After that, the expense of promoting the project came out of Chattey's pocket, and Eristoff's. Two years of work on ICONN-Erie had drained not only the former's savings but all the money he had managed to borrow on his business, as well. Chattey was hungry, and he began to lose patience with John Dyson and the Commerce Department crew. At the same time, they lost patience with him.

Who would own the island, they wanted to know. How would it be taxed? Could it be financed through tax-exempt bonding? Were there any geological reasons that it could not be built? "And how do you defend it?" Mike Curley asked. "It seemed to me you were extending the sovereignty of the United States twenty miles out into the ocean. There're all sorts of rumors about a Soviet submarine that sits in the trench out there, so, you know, how do you protect the fucking thing? You've got to answer those questions, that being the first thing. Then you estimate the magnitude of the change in trading patterns. Then you begin your design of the island, in gross terms, without having 100,000 people spending 1,000 years at drawing boards. And, you know, you take it step by step.

"I just couldn't conceive of a project like this getting off the ground with somebody running around doing a dog-and-pony show," Curley said. "I don't mean that in a detrimental sense to Nigel personally. He's a lovely man. What I mean is that Nigel would give a speech in the normal course of his duties, and there would be, say, an aide to a congressman there, and the aide would come up and say, 'Gee, that's really terrific. If you ever get down to Washington, I'd like you to brief my boss,' and *bang!* Nigel's gone the next morning on a ten-day round of briefings. What we wanted was for someone to sit down with a real sense of discipline and crank out the next phase. That's what we wanted Nigel to do."

As a matter of fact, privately and when he found time, Chattey was at work on phases to come. Many of Curley's questions would have to be resolved by the feasibility studies, but many others were answered already. Concerning the question about sovereignty, for example: The Cholera Bank just happened to lie in a natural "bight" — those waters inshore of an imaginary line drawn between two contiguous promontories on a coastline. Bights were not international waters. ICONN, sited inside of the imaginary line between Cape May, New Jersey, and Long Island's Montauk Point, would lie in United States territorial seas. Taken with the harbor, the river, the pass through the mountains, the Cholera Bank, the Hudson Trench and the downwind location, "that's the *seventh* geographical blessing," Chattey said. "It's as if Mother Nature has dealt us *all* the aces."

That being just one example. There was, in fact, a great deal more to the ICONN-Erie thesis than Chattey was willing to tell anybody, including the people in the Commerce Department, until he saw the color of their money. And the amount.

The amount turned out to be far less than the $325,000 Dyson had promised. Late in 1977, he estimated that perhaps only $250,000 would remain in the Commerce budget at the end of the fiscal year. Reluctantly, Chattey agreed to the amount.

"Gov. Hugh L. Carey announced today the awarding of $250,000 toward the research and development of an 'energy island' in the Atlantic Ocean off the coast of New York and New Jersey," began an undated, tentative press release prepared in December. The four-page first draft explained ICONN-Erie in some detail. At six places in the document, the phrase "Chattey said" was scratched out and replaced by some variation on "According to Gov. Carey." Chattey did not like the changes, but he accepted them. Without energetic political leadership akin to De Witt Clinton's, he believed, the project would be hopeless.

When Mike Curley and Roy Sinclair at last put together the odds and ends of money remaining in the department's budget, however, they found Dyson had overestimated again. They wrote a contract anyway and mailed it to Chattey in February of 1978.

In hard cash, only $160,000 was involved — $30,000 for Chattey's future expenses, and $133,000 for his fee, and Eristoff's, and for the payment of "as many competent professional and non-professional personnel as may be required." In order to make good on the promise of a quarter of a million dollars, Sinclair said, "We were also going to give him some pro bono stuff out of the Job Development Authority — use of space in our offices on Park Avenue, a secretary, stationery, telephone, use of a telex and a conference room, services of a staff attorney and a staff accountant, all that sort of jazz." Under terms of the year-long compact, all work was to be the exclusive property of the State of New York.

Sinclair said he thought it was a pretty good offer. Chattey's personal lawyer, Louis Goodkind, thought the deal stank, and he advised Chattey not to sign. Eristoff advised likewise. "There's a hell of a difference between doing a piece of work *for* a state office and running a project *out of* a state office, especially when your aim is to create a coalition of state governments, the federal government, industries and the rest," he said. Chattey was simply furious. He had feared the state would try to steal the plan and saw it happening now. The $160,000 "didn't even represent what I'd already put into it," he said. "This was just another example of the insensitivity of the governing process to the contribution that an individual can, or should, make to society."

Only Bernard Lawson represented the state at the March 1978 ICONN-Erie meeting, and Chattey, with his lawyer in tow, came down on him like the Fifth Horseman. "They come in, and the first thing they start talking about is there's an agreement between us," Lawson recalled. "Next thing, they start accusing us of leading them down the rosey path. Third thing, they say Nigel has done all this work for us and he hasn't gotten paid. Then they say our offer is a sham. I sat there, and I said one thing to myself: keep cool. Both these guys were going at me, the lawyer from a lawyer's point of view, which I could deal with, because I'm a lawyer. But Chattey — you could see a volcano there.

"At the end of the meeting, he exploded. His characterizations were like 'you set me up,' 'you led me along the path,' you know, 'I've been yanked around' and 'I'll see you in court,' that kind of low-ball stuff."

Sinclair phoned Chattey the next day. "I said, 'All right, Nigel, if this isn't adequate to do what you propose to do, what is? Give us a full proposal.' Well. Chattey came back with what I regarded as an arrogant proposal, one that could only be construed as a challenge." The thirteen-page document (with eleven pages of technical appendices) outlined not only the study of an LNG terminal but *all* of the work required over a three-year period to allow a 1980 construction start on the energy island.

Listed were $360,000 each for technical and environmental studies; $250,000 each for socio-economic and financial studies; $200,000 for a legal study; $450,000 for technical support, such as the production of motion pictures; $1 million for an acre-sized working hydraulic model of the ocean region between Cape May and Montauk Point; $1.1 million for mathematical models to caulculate the height, period, frequency and direction of waves on the Cholera Bank, and to measure changes the island would make in tides, coastal and seabed morphology; and $3.5 million for the detailed engineering studies. Fifteen percent of the total — except for work contracted to Chattey or Eristoff — was to be paid to ICONN-Erie Inc., one of the promoters' non-profit corporations.

Then there were salaries. As project director and coordinator, Chattey and Eristoff were to receive $72,000 and $50,000 a year, respectively. Salaries for an executive assistant, a research assistant and a secretary came to $64,000. Office expenses were set at $64,000 more. Figured in as well was a charge of $300,000 for work done and expenses incurred by Chattey and Eristoff in 1976 and 1977. The bill for the proposed three-year study totaled $11.9 million.

When Commerce officials read the document, "We just kind of stood there with our mouths open," Curley said. "You could never get that much money out of anybody, but Nigel didn't see it that way. He saw it, you know, go around, infect a bunch of people with this fantastic idea, open the money coffers and let it all pour in, then sit down and get the work done." In fact, Chattey did see it that way, more or less. He felt an urgency about the project which apparently escaped Dyson and his people.

Moreover, such an approach terrified them. "All you need is a few 'industry now' right-wing nuts behind you, or some heavy-duty money from a bunch of weird politicos, and you might as well pack it in," Curley said. "To get the kind of support you'd need for a thing like this, you've got to convince people that not only is it an amazing idea, but that you've got a rational scheme for accomplishing it."

I later questioned Eristoff about the proposal, and he explained: "That big scope was sent in frustration, to be frank. We had been promised and promised, money for this, money for that, and never delivered. We first went to them in November of 1976. Now it was March '78 and we still had no funding, no endorsement." Eristoff said the proposal carried a cover letter "in which we said, in effect, this is what needs to be done overall, and what portion of it, if any, were they willing to fund? I think I recall that. But whether or not they read the letter, I don't know."

Apparently not. "Obviously, $11 million, that was half the Commerce Department's budget," Sinclair said. "Nigel knew that. It was difficult enough politically to pursue this thing with the governor and the legislature — and when your main man suddenly turns on you, and the numbers go up by a factor of ten, and he annoints himself king of the project, there is really no more deal to talk. I don't think he believed that we didn't have the money, but I can attest to you for sure that we didn't."

Everybody was mad then. Chattey and Eristoff

thought that Dyson was trying to buy the plan — at bargain rates — to make it a state project and use it for his own political aggrandizement. Dyson thought that Chattey and Eristoff "had stars in their eyes" and were "trying to make their collective family's fortunes for the rest of time." Chattey and Eristoff caught wind of Dyson's contention and were enraged. "It seems to me there's a tremendous difference — light years of difference — between $72,000 and a fortune," Chattey said. "That was less than I made in a year before I started the bloody project."

Eristoff thought he could patch things up, but neither Dyson nor Sinclair would return his phone calls. Dyson tried to phone Petty, "but John was so mad I think he was ducking Dyson's calls," Eristoff said. "He was disgusted with the state." Petty recently had written letters requesting follow-up contributions from the industries that put up the initial $50,000, and in the letters he had mentioned pending state funding and endorsement. "Now we had neither," Eristoff said. "So John had egg on his face," Chattey added. "He had egg *badly* on his face," Eristoff said. Thereafter, Petty kept a lower profile. "I think I could be criticized for not being more openly, wildly supportive of the project, publicly, than I have been," he told me in 1980.

As I spoke with all those involved in the debacle, it seemed to me that none of the parties was guilty of the crimes the others suspected. Chattey and Eristoff *were* anxious to recoup their investments, but they soon would come to abandon any entrepreneurial pose — the 15 percent payment to ICONN-Erie Inc., for example. "It is simply too vast an animus," Chattey said. "The best one can hope for is to be one of the technocrats involved." Where a steal of the project was concerned, "Nigel is forever at anyone's peril,"

Mike Curley said, "but for us, this was Nigel's baby. I think the proof of the pudding that we weren't trying to take it from him is that we never pursued it another foot when he left. Nobody ever lifted a glove to do it otherwise. When Nigel walked out, we just figured good luck and God bless you." It seemed to me that a little straight talk at the time would have put the project back on track, but the talks never happened and the misunderstanding was never resolved.

I later asked Mike Curley if failed relations with Dyson necessarily precluded a general endorsement by Governor Carey. "Carey loved the idea," Curley said, "but as any governor would be, he is a cautious man. I mean, if I were his chief political advisor, I don't think it would be prudent for him to do it. It seems to me that this is the kind of thing that a commissioner should do. He should get out on a limb and honcho something, and be the lightning rod, and draw the fire. And if the thing proves out, then the governor starts coming onboard, and he brings his whole administration."

So I asked around the Commerce Department to learn if there were commissioners other than Dyson in the State of New York with smarts enough to understand the plan and pluck enough to promote it. The bureaucrats were of a single opinion. "I hate to say this, and I hope you won't quote me by name because the legislature would kick my ass in," one of them said, "but the answer is no. Not a one."

I suspect Chattey never imagined such a possibility. He was more angry at the waste of a year and a half than he was worried about finding a buyer. There were a dozen departments more to approach in state government, and another 1,300-odd agencies in the metropolitan area. "This is extremely interesting," he told me in a moment of confidence, "like playing on ten chessboards at once." But if Chattey was a visionary, there was a blind spot. He had just walked out on the only offer of funding, adequate or not, that the ICONN-Erie Project would see for years.

Chattey was a man of principle, by the way, and he never regretted that decision. He believed that Dyson had done him wrong.

To get the project going again, he needed only to find the right people, the people who decided the future, he thought. So in March of 1978 he briefed the Association of Canal Consultants, the federal Maritime Administration, the Long Island Association, the New York Small Business Federation, and William Hennessy, New York's commissioner of transportation. Hennessy told him not to worry about the numerous negative studies of canal modernization done by the Army Corps over the course of decades. Corps studies "are meaningless," Hennessy said.

In April, Chattey outlined the plan for the Edison Electric Institute, the Westchester Association, the World Trade Association, and he did repeat briefings for Dome Petroleum officials and the staff of Senator Javits. In May, he explained the plan to the assistant chief of the Army Corps, aides to the secretary of the U.S. Department of Interior, the director of the U.S. Office of Ocean Management, the General Public Utilities Corporation, the Public Service Electric & Gas Corporation, the Civil Works Division of the Army Corps, and the National Wildlife Federation. Most liked the idea, and he came away with written endorsement to prove it. That he even got in to see all those people seemed to me an amazing accomplishment.

Next Chattey arranged a meeting with officials of the U.S. Department of Energy. George McIsaac, assistant secretary of the DOE, said any project recommended by John Petty must be worthwhile, so he and his staff suggested to Chattey the approach to take to receive a $1 million study grant from the department — more than enough to get the studies started, Chattey thought. But at the top of the DOE's list of requirements was a strong letter from Hugh Carey, which ought to say ICONN-Erie looked interesting, would benefit the country, and merited examination.

Such a document existed, but it had been lost to Chattey forever in the collapse of negotiations with John Dyson. In a letter to Dyson, part of the press release which was never released, Carey said he hoped the plan "would be looked at very, very closely."

However troubled the dealings with Dyson, at least he had recognized the potentials of the plan. Chattey was never sure whether McIsaac or others at the DOE grasped it or not. Few people knew anymore that primary industry and an efficient transportation infrastructure were the foundations of a healthy economy, a stable society, a secure place in the world community. Few truly knew what to make of America's energy problems. Not all that many people even knew that there *was* still an Erie Canal.

The canal was there, all right. It was a hell of a thing to overlook.

III

No love was lost between C. W. McKeen and his ducks. For one thing, the Muscovies were ugly, their beaks bewattled in flesh of red and black, creating faces more suggestive of Hindu demons than waterfowl. For another, they were ill-tempered. Daily, as McKeen approached with a ration of corn, the males attacked, hissing as they came, heads awag, beaks nipping at shins and fingers.

The birds nonetheless represented investment, so the farmer moved four of them from the freedom of his yard to a small corral near the creek out back, in hopes that forced proximity of drakes and hens would inspire procreation. Instead, confinement provoked a yen for adventure. So when McKeen slopped in knee-high galoshes through the mud of his yard one day soon after, the ducks, en masse, pitched themselves over the low fencing and scrambled toward the northern horizon, an ancient, overgrown levee only a few yards distant, which marked the back boundary of

McKeen's tiny farm. He dropped the corn and gave chase, but the ducks were faster.

"They went up the heel path, up through the bushes and brush and the weeds, and slid down into the canal, into the slime, two or three inches thick — and stink? You wouldn't believe it," he said. The ducks splashed out to one of the hundreds of collapsed swamp willows which lay shuffled across that stretch of the original Erie Canal. Stabilized by bark-piercing claws, they perched on the half-submerged tree, bowed their heads and began to dine. The slime turned out to be duckweed. By day's end, the birds had eaten a hole a yard wide.

McKeen kept track of the runaways. Each day, he fed the remaining yard ducks with corn, then checked on the birds in the ditch as he took his dog for a run along the old Erie's tow path, cleared anew each winter by snowmobilers and widened, too frequently, by nocturnal firewood poachers who got in from the highway with Jeeps and four-wheel-drive pick-ups, to cut trees.

The hole in the duckweed expanded, as did the ducks, and in a few months they outsized by far their corn-fed siblings in the yard. McKeen never tried to weigh the difference, though. The birds were still nasty, and he was outnumbered.

About a quarter of a mile east of the duck's canal pond, nature offered ample evidence that the waterway was nothing but history and had been so for quite a long time. In dense forest between Jordan and Weedsport, New York, lay a pristine limestone lock from the original Grand Canal. Rising from the dry earth in the center of the structure was an oak tree, six feet in girth, at least sixty in height.

If Americans late in the twentieth century thought of the Erie Canal at all, they tended to picture a scene like that — an abandoned fragment of what was once a wonder of the world, doing little more now than making fat ducks — or something equally quaint. Only in one sense were they right. Bits and pieces of the first Erie Canal were indeed to be found throughout the state — in hollows beyond thruway embankments, alongside the tracks of Conrail, lost from sight in the woods. In Waterford and De Witt and Macedon, picnic grounds surrounded the ruins. Hikers and joggers and cyclists took to the tow paths. There was no commercial utility, of course, except in Newark, where a mushroom farmer put a roof on a deserted lock half a century ago; Harold Rohlin still used the enduring structure as a garage for his construction company, fitting inside a dump-truck, a trailer, three bulldozers, two back-hoes and a pick-up truck, with room to spare.

But such remnants marked only the original Erie Canal. There had been two others.

New Yorkers in Clinton's time realized before the canal was ten years old that they had made a dreadful mistake in construction — they had made it too small. So in 1836, they began creation of the "enlarged" Erie Canal, rerouting it slightly here and there. In 1980, that system, too, was in ruin.

Not far to the north of C. W. McKeen's humble farm, however, ran the third old Erie, the "modernized" canal, it was called. Another expansion of the original, it was begun in 1902, a year before the United States started work on its canal in Panama. The work was finished in 1917; in 1980, the same physical plant remained in operation. "Rebuilding the Erie Canal would be nothing new," Chattey said.

Neither new nor likely. For most state officials, the waterway had been the target of focused neglect for years.

William Binder of Scranton, Pennsylvania, was unaware that the system survived until he read about a trip by canal boat advertised in one of John Dyson's "I ♥ NY" tourist brochures. I was unaware of it until an editor at the *New York Times*, who had read the same brochure, asked me, as the paper's stringer in central New York, to sign aboard.

Binder made tombstones for a living, and he was a practical man. He scheduled his canal trip, then looked at a map and saw that the waterway passed through Palmyra, New York, where two of his markers were bound, "so I called the boat captain and asked if he ever hauled freight," Binder said. "I had two parcels, I told him, 180 pounds apiece."

The freight proposition was appealing. In six years on the canal, the captain, Peter Wiles, had carried only passengers. Touring and recreation had been the system's principal trade for more than a decade, but operations were anachronistic. "The lock tenders were still pretending they were dealers in major commerce," Wiles told me later. "They'd want to know how much wheat or clay or potash we had onboard. 'None,' I'd tell them. 'You want to know how many people I've got?' and they'd say no. Their record books didn't have a column for passengers."

The *Emita II*, a converted Maine ferry Wiles used as a packet boat, lay moored under a light rain at Liverpool, New York, when Binder and his tombstones and I came aboard. Mike Connor, like me a full-time reporter for the *Post-Standard* in Syracuse, signed on for the ride. He and I stood wet on the open upper deck, sipping coffee and trying to wake up before the three-day trip to Lockport, near Buffalo, began. Wiles sidled into the pilot house and, for the hell of it, hit the packet's fog horn. The thing was mounted about a foot from our heads. Connor withstood the blast. I lurched into the rail. The coffee went over the side.

Wiles, with long hair like corn silk, his blue-grey
eyes gleaming, joined us in the rain. He wore slickers,
a Greek fisherman's cap, and a plastic bag snugged
over each boat shoe. He, like Chattey, was fifty-two
years old. "Just wanted to see if you'd jump," he said.

Wiles, as he judged it, had finally beaten the system and gotten away from it all. No more saloon
keeping for him, no more restaurant or golf-course
management. At about the same time that Nigel
Chattey decided to drag America into the century
ahead, Peter Wiles (despite either his refusal or inabil-
ity to swim. I was never sure which) returned to the
one left behind. "No McDonald's stores, no sir," he
said. Just blue herons overseeing, startled raccoons at
bankside, occasionally a grazing deer, now a banded
owl rolling out of a tree in search of prey, here the
fish jumping, there the fisherman, now and again a
kid skipping stones or cannonballing off a bridge —
the shape of life on hundreds of miles of beauteous
Erie Canal.

An hour west of Liverpool, Wiles and his mate,
Tom Beardsley, snubbed *Emita II* into Lock 25 at
May's Point, then worked in the steady drizzle to dis-
mantle the pilot house while the lock filled, lifting
the squat, sixty-four-foot packet six feet to the next
level of canal. The roof came off, then the doors, then
the topmost two feet of each wall. With the small
cabin intact, *Emita II* rose sixteen feet, six inches,
above the surface of the waterway. Clearance of the
lowest spans over the channel between there and
Buffalo was just under fifteen feet.

"You can duck for the bridges as you feel inclined," Wiles told those among his fifty passengers
who joined him on the upper deck. And then, with
purposeful nonchalance: "I'm inclined to duck for
most all of them." Most of us at once remembered
one old ditty or another, often something about some

mule named Sal. Other chanteys were less known. "When the bowsman he forgot to yell, 'Low bridge, duck 'er down,' the bullhead steerman went to hell, with a bridge-string for a crown."

"Low bridge!" Wiles called as the first causeway drew close. The more intrepid passengers played chicken with the structure, then turned chicken in a jiffy. The girderwork would have caught the shortest of us beneath the chin. Often on such trips, the mate Beardsley removed the forward section of bow rail to get the boat under bridges. Occasionally, when the water was especially high, Wiles flooded the bilges to sink the boat enough to win clearance. "The Coast Guard frowns on that," he said, "but what the hell. . . ."

No doubt the boat-and-bridge clearance on the canal Chattey envisioned would be similarly tight. It always had been. "On fine days it is pleasant enough sitting outside," a packet passenger wrote in 1825, "except for having to duck under bridges every quarter hour, under penalty of having one's head crushed to atoms." A notorious clod who once ran for election as public works commissioner in Syracuse promised to remedy the problem of the low canal bridge at Salina Street by digging the waterway deeper at that point. Politicians saw an advantage and seized it, given the custom of taking presidential straw votes on packet boats. "All those for John Quincy Adams, down on your knees!" a Federalist might call as an election, and a bridge, approached. "Let those for Andy Jackson stand up!"

Canal commissioners faced another problem. Farm and road bridges were forever in disrepair because passing boatmen made a habit of tearing them apart for firewood. Raising the bridges did not help. Canallers, who understood the economies of scale, responded to higher bridges by building taller boats.

Between bridges aboard *Emita II*, my friend Mike Connor leaned on a rail amidships and watched canal waters fall from the limestone rip-rap on the shoreline as the packet's prop sucked water from in front of the boat and churned it up astern. The speed was ten miles per hour, a limit set to forestall prop-wash erosion of the banks. "This is the pace that living should have," he said. "I wish my life had it."

He was not alone. Motorists on the infrequent roads that broke through deciduous tree lines to parallel the tow path slowed to run with the packet. Some parked to watch us, then drove ahead and parked again. They waved. We waved. "We've caused four or five accidents that I know of," Wiles said. "Once, cars were coming both ways on a bridge, and both drivers were watching us. They mated head-on." Wiles understood the distraction. "I've always felt the magic of the Erie Canal," he said.

The feeling was contagious. The mate, Tom Beardsley, had never seen *Emita II* until she pulled into the boatyard where he worked, for routine maintenance. When the work was done, he stowed away in her hold. As Wiles pulled her clear of the dock, Beardsley ran to the stern, shouted notice to the boatyard owner, then walked up to the pilot house and asked for a job.

Passengers certainly felt it. During a three-day trip from Albany to Syracuse in 1980, about an hour before passengers were to debark for the bus ride back to their cars, Wiles unhappily announced that several million-gallon Mobil Oil storage tanks at the Port of Albany had exploded and were burning out of control, right next to the lot where the passengers' cars were parked. The port was closed, roads into it were blocked, the vehicles would be at best inaccessible, at worst, incinerated. "In reaction to this," said passenger Kathryn Heavey, "we sat around and chatted as though the announcement had been that the galley had run out of cheese. I wonder whether the beauty and peace of the trip induced a euphoria that subdued panic and outward manifestations of distress."

"We don't stay satisfied with what's wonderful," wrote Walter Edmonds in *Rome Haul*, his novel of canal life. "We've always got to make perfection better. The railroads will give us more speed, but they'll make people forget how fine the world could go at four miles an hour."

In the beginning, that was plenty fast enough. "Commending my soul to God, and asking defense from danger," wrote a pioneer in the year the canal opened, "I stepped on board the boat and soon was flying to Utica!" Whatever the towing horses could manage — four miles an hour sometimes, more often one or two — was speed enough to reshape the settlement of a continent.

In 1820, five years before the canal was completed, Colonel William Stone, editor of New York's principal newspaper, visited the as yet unnamed community at Syracuse, naught then but "a few scattered and indifferent-looking wooden houses erected amid the stumps of the recently felled trees," he wrote. "You call this place a village?" he asked a local resident. "It would make an owl weep to fly over it." Five years after the canal opened end to end, Stone visited again. He stepped from a packet, "and as I glanced upward and around, upon splendid hotels, rows of massive buildings in all directions and the lofty spires of churches glittering in the sun, the change seemed like one of enchantment," he wrote.

"Anybody who looks at a map of the state and can't see what the canal did is an idiot," Wiles told me. "Move up the Hudson from New York and across the canal to Buffalo, then take all that out, and what's left? Binghamton, and that ain't much." The route he described cut through New York City, Albany, Utica, Syracuse, Rochester and Buffalo. Spaces between those places were filled with such unlikely sounding inland villages as Weedsport, Port Byron, Port Gibson, Fairport, Brockport, Lockport, Spencerport, Middleport and Newport. In fact, in 1980, more than eleven million New Yorkers, two-thirds of the state's population, lived within a dozen miles of the Erie Canal or its Hudson River connection. Moreover, one American in three lived within the same distance of the river, the canal, or the shoreline of the system's Great Lakes hinterland. Wiles, like Chattey, had been hyping the merits of the system for years. If lawmakers were content to leave the canal to rot, Wiles told me, it certainly was not because the Erie was poorly placed.

Lawmakers similarly resisted Clinton's efforts. The legislative delegation from New York City, for example, was convinced that the canal would rob them of business, not expand it. They voted to a man against that "damnfool dig." The canal would "bury the treasure of the state, to be watered by the tears of posterity," they charged. And later they sang, "Clinton, the Federalist son of a bitch, is taxing our dollars to dig him a ditch."

They had no imagination.

Commerce on the middle stretch between Utica and Montezuma, which began in 1820, changed their minds in a hurry, as it had Thomas Jefferson's. The eastern and western sections were finished in 1825, and the grand opening of the waterway — 363 miles of channel with eighty-three locks and half a dozen aqueducts — inspired the most elaborate celebration seen in America since the Revolution was won. When the first three boats left Buffalo, word was sent to New York through a sequential salute of cannonfire. Field pieces stationed within earshot of one another, across the state and down the Hudson, were discharged as preceding shots were heard. Overexuberant cannoneers at Weedsport overloaded their weapon and touched it off, blowing the cannon, and themselves, to bits. Despite the mishap, news of the opening reached New York in less than two hours. The boats arrived nine days later and were met in New York harbor by a fleet of twenty-nine steam boats, seven barges, the ship *Hamlet* and the revenue cutter *Alert,* all dressed out in flags and bunting; by a British man-of-war, her sailors cheering on the decks; by more than one hundred private sailboats; and by thousands of New Yorkers who lined miles of docks and coastline in ranks ten and twenty deep.

Imagination was suddenly everyone's forte. During the first year of the Erie's operation, hundreds of freighters and scows and packets and line boats made thousands of trips, and new businesses grew like dandelions. Boatmen who could not initially afford the expense of tow horses leaned into the lines themselves until momentum was achieved, then harnessed the lines to dogs, who managed the load just fine. A canal superintendent in the Schenectady region recorded 19,000 lockings through one village in 1826. The vessels carried shingles, staves, lumber and timber; wool, cotton and fur; limestone and sandstone; gypsum, flint, copper and lead; oil and tar; bituminous and anthracite coal; bar iron, pig iron and iron castings; horseshoes and nails; phosphates, pot and pearl ashes; furniture, glassware and crockery; whiskey and malt; beef, pork and fish; flaxseed, wheat, barley, bran, rye, oats, clover and corn; dried fruits and apples; peas, beans and potatoes; lard, butter and cheese; sugar, molasses, coffee, tobacco, ginseng and salt; and passengers — immigrants by the thousands.

The scope of the commerce surprised everyone, including De Witt Clinton. He had presumed that most trade would run eastbound, and it did, but westward activity was prodigious as well. "Most of Europe and all the East Coast was gushing into Buffalo," a landlord there reported. The same fate awaited Cleveland, then Detroit, then Chicago. New York officials would later boast that it was not the cavalry that won the West; it was the Erie Canal.

Business was so good on that simple scratch in the hide of the state, a cut only forty feet wide and four feet deep, that commerce outgrew it in only a decade. The first enlargement was begun immediately, though skeptics and critics and politics delayed completion until the time of the Civil War. Even before the enlargement was done — and despite the greater speed of railroads — the canal in 1860 carried four times the tonnages of the New York Central, the Pennsylvania Railroad and the B&O combined.

Tolls quickly repaid the costs of both construction and enlargement, and by the time trafficking by rail seriously challenged water transit, the canal fund held a surplus of $43 million. So the state legislature, hoping to preserve competitive advantage, "made it part of the constitution of the State of New York, by amendment in 1882, that the canal is owned by the people and shall operate toll free," Wiles told me. "People who tell you how bad the canal is because it doesn't make any money are illiterate. It's not *supposed* to make any money."

When turn-of-the-century New Yorkers decided to enlarge the system again, the canal was routed, where possible, into existing rivers — the Mohawk and the Seneca, principally — and elsewhere new channels were cut, 12 feet deep and 120 wide, for the most part bypassing city centers. Since then, the waterway had seen little work beyond routine maintenance, and lately very little of that. "Where in the world can you find anything that's this old, that's this big, that's seen this much use, and still works?" Wiles asked. "I think it's the cat's ass. It's super."

Men like Chattey and Dyson thought so too, believing a born-again canal would mean a born-again New York, but theirs was a minority opinion. The system had known a final moment of glory during World War II, when landing craft and patrol torpedo boats made in Great Lakes shipyards had followed its path to the coast. But tonnages shipped on the canal in the twentieth century had peaked soon afterwards, in the early 1950s, and had declined ever since. One reason was that railroads, competing for the business, had for a time charged less to carry freight than operating expenses demanded. This led to shaky railroads, which needed federal subsidies to survive, and eventually was a contributing factor in the largest business failure in American history, the collapse of the Penn-Central.

Other reasons included the opening of the St. Lawrence Seaway, major increases in the wages of bargemen, federal investment in the interstate highway system, and especially the antiquity of the Erie itself. The old locks could hold only one tug and one barge at a time. The same tug on the Mississippi River could handle a tow of thirty barges, with a relatively minor increase in operational costs.

So New Yorkers, knowing their state could not afford another modernization, voted in 1959 to give the canal to the federal government. At the time of the referendum, the Erie remained the only inland waterway in America to be owned and operated by a state. The public mandate was clear, but legislators balked. More than 40 percent of the state's fresh water resources, not to mention major systems for irrigation and flood control, tied into the Erie Canal, so lawmakers were reluctant to relinquish jursidiction.

Formal studies about what to do with the canal were done again and again and again between 1959 and 1980. A 1968 report by the Army Corps indicated that, economically, either a rehabilitation or a full modernization would be a dandy idea. The Corps volunteered to take over ownership, too. But Nelson Rockefeller, who was then governor, opted for the simple reparation and vowed to retain control. Then the Corps reworked the study, and the numbers changed dramatically. Costs more than doubled. No rehabilitation would pay, the study concluded. "What could have changed the expenses to such an extent?" asked a report done later by the New York State Senate Research Group. "Could it be that the Corps lost interest after the governor indicated no desire to modernize or turn it over" to federal control? Whatever the reason, nothing was subsequently done with, or for, the Erie Canal.

In 1980, only thirty or forty barges, some carrying heavy machinery, most carrying heavy oils or cement, still travelled Erie waters. The system was old, its structures in disrepair, and nobody seemed to care. Wiles attributed the lack of concern to ignorance, also to a linguistic atrocity committed during debate on the second modernization. Some lawmakers favored creation of a ship canal; some hoped to see only barges. The latter faction won, so the press took to calling the waterway the "Barge Canal," an appellation which excited no one's imagination. Then the state inadvertently encouraged use of the misnomer by naming the collection of New York's surviving canals — the Erie, Champlain, Oswego and Cayuga-Seneca — the state "Barge Canal System."

Appropriations for running the Erie Canal in 1980 totaled only $10 million (about as much as you would find in a highway department budget for construction of a single two-lane overpass), and the amount had remained constant, through all the inflation, since 1970. In 1978, officials of the state Department of Transportation said that unless they received more money for major repairs, the canal would last, at best, another ten years. But officials in the state budget department and others in Albany thought $10 million was already too much. "The canal doesn't get any votes," Wiles said. "Some relief to fix some potholes, to build the zoo — those are real vote-getters. But nobody gives a shit about a ditch running through Montezuma Swamp."

Wiles' packet boat service was the Erie's premier business in 1980, but, charming as it was, it mattered little to the economy of the state. The M/V *Emita II* carried her first and only cargo, Binder's tombstones, on a dying canal.

Ahead, off the starboard bow, an asphalt barge lay moored, befogged in rising steam from the blowers its workers used to warm the glop for unloading. "This could be the only commercial activity we'll see," Wiles told the passengers. He was right. Traffic in no way justified an increased allocation, let alone the $1 billion or more it would take to renovate the canal. "You know," Wiles said later, "there are abandoned works of man all over this state, and without more care, this will be one of them. The canal's a fragile thing now, and if it breaks bad enough, the Albany guys are going to say it's not worth fixing."

Those "Albany guys," of course, were in part responsible for the lack of commerce. For twenty years, the state's only stated policy concerning the future of the canal was that as yet there was no policy to state.

Shippers were not about to invest in barges and other equipment to operate on a waterway with so uncertain a destiny.

"It hurts my pride to say this," I was told later by Joe Stellato, who headed the Canal Maintenance and Operations Division of the New York State Department of Transportation, "but we're a low priority project. The canal was built so well it didn't need anything for quite a while, and now we're in an era of austere finance." Thus Stellato was left with the preposterous task of stretching $10 million to cover the operational and maintenance needs of 220 miles of canalized rivers, 128 miles of land-cut channels, 35 locks, 10 moveable dams, 2 taintor-gate dams, 24 guard gates, 2 guard locks, more than 100 fixed and lift bridges, and dozens of approach and retaining walls, breakwaters, bypasses, spillways, waste weirs, siphons, dikes, flumes, dive culverts and aqueducts. To make ends meet since his budget was frozen, Stellato had eliminated 10 percent of his full-time Erie workers, reducing their number to about 350. Several boats were dry-docked, tug crews were cut from seven men to four, and lock tenders on the night shift were assigned to serve more than one lock by roving between them in cars. Worse yet, the much needed dredging of the channel, which theoretically ranged in depth from eleven to fourteen feet, was hopelessly backlogged. Wiles had had trouble with the draft, and he had seen Ted Turner's *Courageous*, returning to the coast from a Great Lakes regatta, run aground on a bar near Rochester. The cutbacks in service combined to reduce the system's efficiency still more, which naturally drove more shippers off the waterway.

Nigel Chattey therefore reasoned that state transportation officials, on hearing his spectacular plan, would become fundamental supporters — would be the first to strap on packs, fix bayonets and go over the top at his side.

But if Chattey was a visionary, that was a blind spot.

"IF THEY WANT TO BUILD AN ISLAND IN THE SKY, that's up to them," I was told by William Hennessy, state transportation commissioner. "I just wish they'd leave the canal alone.

"They can look at it all they want. They can even plan to take fifteen feet out of it, I don't care. Just don't ask me for the million dollars, or the 5 million, or the 10 million, to pay for the study. Let those dreamers do their thing — I encourage it. But don't come to Bill Hennessy for a couple of million bucks. If I had 2 million, I'd rather fix Lock 5. Now, that's pretty narrow-backed thinking, and I acknowledge that it is, but unless I get some money to make modest improvements now, there isn't going to *be* any Erie Canal."

Although he had been briefed by Chattey more than once, it turned out that Hennessy was nursing some major misconceptions about the ICONN-Erie Project. For one thing, he believed Chattey wanted to re-dig the canal primarily to get rock and dirt with which to build the island. I explained that the synergy of construction worked in reverse: that the island provided an environmentally acceptable site to dispose of the spoil. "I didn't realize that," he said. Then I explained that much of the island — the first elements, certainly — would be built of materials dredged from the seabed. "I didn't know that, either." Sure, I explained. It would have to be done that way to get the island's power plants on line as quickly as possible. "I didn't know the project involved power plants," he said.

Chattey and Eristoff both thought that Hennessy had tuned out their presentations on purpose, that his lack of interest in ICONN-Erie stemmed from the fact that his Transportation Department had been advised of the plan only after the deal with the Commerce Department fell apart. "He got pretty bent out of shape," Eristoff said. "There we were, talking to Dyson about rebuilding Hennessy's canal."

As I spoke with Hennessy, however, his concerns seemed to me to run a lot deeper than that.

"Hell, I can't even put a new road together in five years," he said. "There's no way they would be able to put this project together in ten. There would be lawsuits upon lawsuits about water rights and everything else, up and down.

"Until these stupid studies stop and until all these flakey thoughts get off the table, we're not going to be able to obtain the dollars we need for repairs. Each time we think we're making some headway, an 'all-American' canal study comes up, or a deep-draft study comes up, or a new Corps study comes up, and [federal officials] say 'Wait 'til the studies are done, then we'll think about giving you some programs.'

"Now if you told me this project would do something to help fix up our highways, maybe I'd be more receptive. We've got 17,000 [highway] bridges in this state that are badly in need of repair."

(I was no expert so I made no suggestion. I did know, however, that the bulk of New York's freight traffic travelled by truck and that a single truck, according to a study by the General Accounting Office, did as much damage to a highway as 9,600 automobiles.)

Hennessy told me he hoped simply to preserve the Erie as a historical resource and as a system for recreation, irrigation and flood control. So I asked him about the possibility of renewed commercial activity in light of both the rising cost of fuel and the fact that a single barge on the existing canal could carry as much as one hundred tractor-trailer trucks. It seemed to me that savings on fuel, not to mention manpower, would be enormous.

"I don't think that's right," he said. "I wouldn't want you to use the wrong figure." He phoned Joe Stellato to check. "An over-the-road trailer will carry thirty tons," he said, repeating the statistics he had been given, "and a barge will carry 3,000. Okay, Joe. Thanks." And then to me: "You're right."

A barge-tow on the canal Chattey imagined would carry between four and ten times that tonnage. ("Don't get me wrong," Chattey told me once. "Hennessy is excellent as a *highway* commissioner — but he knows *nothing* about bulk cargo shipments by water.")

Another reason for his lack of interest in ICONN-Erie, Hennessy said, was that no full-blown reconstruction would be possible without federal financial involvement, which would as likely as not mean surrender of control to the feds. "I have people saying now, 'Hennessy, it's time to give it up.' I say never, not as long as this guy is commissioner. We've invested too much in this canal. Our people are buried in the tow path. I have a very paternal viewpoint about this. I would probably fight to resignation before I would give it up."

John Mladinov, Hennessy's deputy commissioner, later told me that in his judgment, Chattey's island might well prove to be feasible, but never a new canal. Preparation of the environmental impact statement alone would make the project unworkable, he said.

True enough, the Erie covered a lot of ground. The system was ten times the length of the waterway in

Panama. Had the levitation and transposition been possible, you could have placed upon the Erie Canal the whole of Oregon and then flooded that state from both sides.

"Why Chattey insists on tying a probable loser to a possible winner is beyond me," Mladinov said. "I hate to see him killing a good project by marrying it to a bad one."

ON THE OTHER HAND, once briefed, former U.S. Senator James Buckley found the canal project "a lot sexier" than the island. "That's the way it's been all along," Chattey told me. "We encounter four different reactions. People understand the whole project instantly, or they think one half of it, or the other — or the whole thing — is completely off the wall."

New York congressmen John Murphy and John LaFalce understood immediately, and they called for the studies. So did Francis Purcell and John Klein, the executives of Nassau and Suffolk counties on Long Island; Joel Jacobson, New Jersey's energy commissioner; and James Griffin, the mayor of Buffalo. Chattey believed their endorsements would help put pressure on Albany.

But his principal hope in the late spring of 1978 was to secure a study grant from the U.S. Department of Energy. He met several times more with George McIsaac and McIsaac's staff and finally drafted a "concept" study of ICONN-Erie. The DOE officials told Chattey the $1 million in funding was likely, and they promised a formal decision by August, two months away.

Twice in June of 1978 Chattey met again with officers of the Army Corps. Brigadier General Drake Wilson, who was deputy director of the Corps' Civil Works Division, said he was "flatly interested" in becoming involved in the project. The next month, however, Wilson was replaced by Brigadier General Hugh Robinson, who proved to be less of an ICONN-Erie fan.

Other Corps opinions of ICONN-Erie varied from man to man. One would be highly enthusiastic, if for no reason other than the fact that American rail rates were typically twice as high in regions where there was no competing water mode as they were in canal and river regions. Another, skeptical, would do fancy calculations and conclude that the project was impossible; transport of the dredge spoil alone, one guesstimated, would take forty-two years. In any event, Colonel Clark Benn, who commanded the New York District of the Corps, told me that the Army engineers had "no burning desire to operate the Erie Canal."

By the time the Department of Energy decision was due, Chattey had done full presentations of the plan more than one hundred times. With a suitcase in one hand, 46 pounds of bulky easel and story-board case in the other, and somehow still managing to cart behind himself up to 160 pounds of Blue Books, he made his way from airports to rented cars to briefings and back again throughout the United States. At night, in hotel rooms and motel rooms, after embracing a Bloody Mary or two, he studied maps, plotted strategy, detailed relationships between island industries, or watched television. War movies and westerns were acceptable. "The Rockford Files" was a favorite.

That summer he spoke twice more to the Army Corps, twice to Exxon officials (the avoidance strategy of a year earlier was abandoned), and twice to functionaries of the New York–New Jersey Port Authority.

Chattey next wrangled an invitation to address a convention of eight Northeastern natural gas companies. He found the response of gas managers particularly disappointing. One of them, in conversation with Eristoff, blamed the indifference on the selfishness of the times. "It is very difficult," said R.A. Morel of the Algonquin Gas Transmission Company, "to get senior people in the gas industry, who are thinking in terms of retiring in five years, to worry about long-range planning," Eristoff reported.

The same might have been said about leaders in the oil industry. The incomes of energy company executives (the average among the top guys was $740,000 a year in 1980; Mobil's chairman led the pack with $1,187,055) were typically tied directly to the companies' immediate profits. So instead of taking such risks as investing in the Chattey plan (or, in some cases, looking for crude), the oil giants were using much of their capital in "diversification," buying up shipping companies and copper companies and coal companies. Mobil went so far as to purchase a department-store chain, while Gulf negotiated for the sale of a circus.

"They can pass along the cost of any inefficiency to the public, to the consumer," Chattey said. "There is no market restraint in the normal sense, no market system working. If you can pass along whatever your inefficiency justifies through the price of oil or gas, why change?"

John Petty, who of course was no stranger to investment analysis, said he found the reluctance of energy companies to buy into the project "astonishing." The situation served only to encourage Chattey's conspiracy theory. ICONN-Erie seemed to him to be so patently logical that, if the project was not moving, there must have been somebody out there working to stop it.

In Washington, meanwhile, George McIsaac and others at the Department of Energy decided that the ICONN-Erie grant application required further study.

They failed to make their decision, as promised, in August. Also in September, October, November and December. A spokesman for the department later told me the reason for the delay: To pursue in the State of New York a project unapproved by the governor, he said, would be bad, bad politics.

So the shotgun approach to promotion continued. "If you were to plot some sort of diagram of the way this thing has gone," Eristoff said, "you'd find a line going off this way and then drying up and dying, then one off that way and drying up and dying, then something over there looking real, so we'd go after that."

Chattey went. "You must understand this," he said. "Once we are funded, we cannot afford to have people who matter complaining that they were never advised of the plan." So in New York, he briefed representatives of the Northeast Regional Energy Council, the U.S. Department of Commerce, the Empire State Energy Research Corporation, the Electric Power Research Institute, the City Planning Commission (an immediate endorsement), the state Division of Housing and Community Renewal (another), and the state Energy Research and Development Authority. In Bloomfield, he spoke to the New Jersey chapter of the American Society of Mechanical Engineers; in New Paltz, the Pattern for Progress; in Chicago, the Institute of Gas Technology; and in Trenton, New Jersey's commissioners of labor and industry, and transportation. Both men called for studies at once.

Chattey's letters of support were piling up. Otherwise, nothing was happening. A great many powerful people were saying perfectly lovely things about the project, then taking no action at all to pursue it.

Five editorial writers at the *New York Times* were briefed in December. One of them, Roger Starr, told Eristoff that ICONN-Erie was "the first exciting idea to come by since I've been here."

"But Chattey never said it *could* be built," one of Starr's colleagues argued.

"That's right," Starr said. "They need the money to find out if it's do-able." And afterwards, to Eristoff: "Can't you give me a good news story, since we can't write editorials until after news stories come out? I'm just dying to do an editorial in support of the project."

Eristoff tried, but a full year would pass before the *Times* got around to publishing a comprehensive report about ICONN-Erie.

"NIGEL IS MAD, DON'T YOU THINK?" Maria Chattey asked me with a laugh, one day several years after her husband gave up gainful employment. "Who else would run around like this, talking to all these people, with no promise of reward?" Her father was just as crazy, she said, but he never understood Nigel Chattey. He warned his daughter that the Englishman was a wanderer, an adventurer. Then he forbade their union. When they married anyway in 1954, he disowned her. Maria Chattey, a water-color artist, was wonderfully handsome, willful and smart and disarmingly direct. "Okay," she said when first we met, "What do you want?" I asked if her husband's new child, the one called ICONN-Erie, had wrecked the sense of normalcy in their day-to-day lives. She recalled their wedding: "Nigel told me then that his life was to have ideas and develop them," she said. "I have no complaints. I married this guy for what he is. I never question the harebrained concepts of that bloody English mind. I have always been Nigel's back-up." Of course family life was disrupted, she continued, but that was of little import, she said. "When you reach for the ultimate, anything goes. What you do every day doesn't matter."

Maria's father was Czech, her mother Austrian.

The family made and lost one fortune in eastern Europe, then emigrated to Uruguay to seek another. On a jungle hillside, the family built a three-room hotel, which they expanded over the course of years to create Tersopolis, a summer resort for the Montevideo rich. Maria visited America in 1951, decided to stay for a while, found work as a researcher at City Hospital, and later met Chattey, who was a resident alien at the time.

That Chattey had come to the United States at all was an accident of fate, more or less. His father was a soldier in the British foreign service, his mother a nurse in the ambulance corps, so he grew up alternately in England and India. At the age of three, on a tiny saddle marked with the regimental regalia, he rode astride a great dog — half mastiff, half Great Dane — alongside British cavalry units. His earliest memory, he told me, was "the sound of doves in the chinot trees on a small island, covered with iris, in the middle of Dahl Lake," near Srinagar in Kashmir. "We lived on a houseboat," he said. "Beyond the lake rose the Himalayas."

Chattey trained as a youthful Royal Commando during the final year of World War II — he was 18 — and afterwards studied geography, naval architecture, and marine engineering, receiving a bachelor's degree in the latter from Durham University. Then he returned to the East as a British horse-and-camel cavalryman in the newly formed nation of Pakistan. "The camel is probably the meanest beast of burden in the world," he told me. "He'll spit at you and kick at you and bite you, and any one of the three can kill you in the desert. But it gets bloody cold at night in the desert, so you have to sleep with him. Still, he wants to eat you or kick you or spit at you, so you rope his nose to a hind foot and curl up on the other side. Then he tries to roll over on you. The experience doesn't lend itself to restful sleep."

For a young man, those were exciting times. Chattey led patrols in pursuit of gold smugglers. He mapped mountainous regions only slightly more travelled than the surface of the moon. He served as formal escort to the offspring of visiting dignitaries, including, once, a daughter of the Shah of Iran. He trained vigorously, learning to shoot a .50-caliber Vickers machine gun from a platform strapped to a camel. "It made for quite an impressive deterrent, what with the sound of the gun and the beast, panicked, jumping all over the place. You had a remarkable field of fire up there. Of course, the chance of hitting anything was extremely slight. . . ."

In 1949, at the age of twenty-one, Chattey and two Hunsakoot guides made what he believed to be the final British excursion into the post-revolution People's Republic of China. His mission was to deliver a message packet — he never knew the contents — to an English operative in Urumchi, about a thousand miles from the Pakistani border.

They never made it. Chattey's party was spotted in central China by a patrol of sixteen communist cavalrymen, then chased by the horsemen, on and off for thirty days, all the way back to Pakistan. They at last lost the Chinese during a blizzard in the Hindu Kush, but the victory was small. Mintaka pass was blocked by an avalanche. Chattey was snow-mad by the time his group reached Killick pass, and none of them made it through.

After the snowfall stopped, a band of Turkomans, fleeing China, "ran into the Chinese patrol and shot the hell out of them," Chattey said. The Turkomans found Chattey's two yaks wandering free in the pass, so they searched for the owners and found three forms, near death, blanketed by snow. "My next memory, coming to, was of this Turkoman leaning over me," Chattey laughed on recollection. "I thought I must still be mad. His face would have put the fear of God into Genghis Khan himself."

In quieter times, Chattey was attached to the governor general's staff in Islamabad. There were only fifteen embassies in the capital at that time, so social life was limited. "But then a new American ambassador arrived, and he had what I thought was a very beautiful daughter," he said. "She had the longest legs of any woman I've ever known, and she wore these short tennis dresses. I was absolutely captivated. Well, she took one look at me and said I was very nice but awfully square — a word I did not know. I asked how you went about becoming unsquare, and she said there was nothing wrong with me that a good coeducational school in the States wouldn't cure. She said I behaved as though I'd never been to school with the opposite sex. And of course she was right."

Chattey decided to study business. He discussed possibilities with the American counsel, and they narrowed the options to Harvard, Stanford, Wharton and Dartmouth. Chattey's choice was unfortunate, but he would not know that for almost a year. Another blind spot.

He took one freighter to Singapore, another to Jakarta, then booked passage on a liberty ship bound for Manila. His quarters were bottom drawer — a converted gun turret at the stern of the ship. The day the vessel reached Manila, Chattey awoke only in time to see the thief slipping out of the room. He grabbed for the man, missed, then regained composure and surveyed his losses. Passport. Money. Everything. The American adventure might have ended then and there.

"So I ran mother naked up to the bridge and raised

absolute bloody cane and pulled rank and told them I
was from the Government House and jumped up and
down. You mention all these words — no one knows
what you're talking about, but it works anyway. I said
I was going to the British consulate, Buckingham
Palace, the whole works."

Officers onboard sealed the ship while Chattey
fetched the harbor patrol. "They came aboard with
their truncheons and said 'You go up and talk to the
captain and come back in ten minutes. Your things
will be on the bed, and you'll check them.' They were
a tough set of guys, that Manila Harbor Patrol. I came
back and sure enough, everything was there, laid out,
I mean *neatly*, two inches between each item."

In Manila, Chattey boarded the S.S. *Cleveland*, a
U.S. Lines cruiser bound for California. During the trip
he met a Stanford co-ed named Phyllis, was altogether
smitten, and spent the rest of the voyage regretting
his selection of another university. Phyllis later gave
him a tour of the Stanford campus. "I'd never seen
anything like it," he said. "All these beautiful crea-
tures all around." Ah, well, he figured, perhaps such
was the case at all American schools. So he flew on
to Boston, took a train to White River Junction, then
caught a bus up to Dartmouth.

Chattey had made the wrong choice, and the reasoning of Dartmouth officials was equally flawed. He
surveyed his classmates, sexually homogeneous, as it
were, then went straight to the registrar's office to ask
when the female students would arrive. "I remember
the person looking down. 'Name?' 'Chattey.' 'Where
from?' 'Pakistan.' After a while he looked up, and he
went grey. It seems that my name, spelled C-h-a-t-
t-i, is a Hindu name. The only reason I'd been accepted was to be Dartmouth's brown quotient from
Asia."

Soon after he arrived at the school, the English pound was devalued, its American exchange rate dropping from more than four dollars to less than three, so Chattey could no longer afford a second year of school. That was just as well, he admitted, because he spent most of the first chasing females at every girls' college in New England. One of his favorites was Yvonne. She, like Phyllis, was from California.

What then to do when the school year ended? Chattey and three of his Dartmouth mates drove to the coast. He arrived nearly broke but found lodging easily. Yvonne's father liked him, so he gave him use of the family's beach house, but did not trust him, so he shipped Yvonne off to Europe.

Chattey thought it would be fun to work with boats and boatmen, so he wandered the coast, stopping at docks and filling out applications. At Costa Del Mar, he was surprised to find an outfit called the Wing Sang Boatyard. "Wing Sang," as it happened, was the recognition code word used by two British gunboats which had once patrolled the Yangtsze River in China. Chattey's uncle had served on one of them. The owner of the boatyard, on the other.

Three of the vessels moored at the marina belonged to yet another old east Asia hand, one Carl Remberg. He asked if Chattey could handle a 45-footer. Sure thing, said Chattey, who badly needed a job; the fact was, however, that the largest vessel he had sailed was an 18-foot ketch, and he had sunk that one several years earlier during an equinoctial gale in the English Channel. In his life jacket, he floated unconscious for seven hours before another vessel found him. The story made the *Times* of London.

Remberg had held the Carnation Milk franchise for all of China before the revolution. He had more money than he knew what to do with, and he took an instant liking to Chattey. Remberg had already put six promising young men through college, and he offered to make it seven. "But before you thank me, let me tell you two things," Chattey recalled him saying. "First, you are a tax write-off. And second, if ever you can do this for someone else, do it."

Chattey chose Stanford. He and eleven classmates rented a house they all dearly loved, "but the neighbors complained that we were driving golf balls at baby carriages across the street — which was true, we were, but they weren't solid." They were Wiffle Balls. "Still, it scared the hell out of the mothers. A mattress came out of one of our windows on fire one night, so the community finally expelled us."

So much for rounding his edges. In the meantime, Chattey had earned a master's degree in business administration and begun a doctorate in geopolitics, a program he decided to leave, he said, "because I just couldn't imagine myself becoming a government worker."

To make money and see the country, Chattey went off on the lecture circuit. His program was billed: "The Last Man Out of China," and he was a hit. One of the presentations was attended by an executive of the Standard Oil Corporation of California, who was so impressed with Chattey that he offered him a job. Chattey took it.

In 1953, at age twenty-six, while working for the oil company as a project analyst in New York, he attended a coming-out "colonial" dance at the Park Lane Hotel. That was where he met John Petty, also where both men met the women they would later wed. "He walked in so full of energy, so full of life," the former Maria Smolka told me, "that before the evening was over I said to myself, 'This is the man you will marry.' "

Marry they did. The first priority, they agreed, was for Chattey to become a citizen by the quickest possible means, so he joined the U.S. Army. He rejected an offer to work in intelligence because of the four-year commitment for officers, and instead spent two years training Korean War combat photographers at Ft. Lewis in Washington State. He was so taken with the country that he considered homesteading in the Trinity Mountains.

Desire to earn a living overpowered that dream, however, so in 1955 Chattey returned to the oil corporation and, among other things, helped to site fifteen new refineries throughout the world. In 1957 he joined the Newport News Shipbuilding & Dry-dock Company as manager of marketing. A year later, he mentioned to Petty a plan he had devised for the firm to build a shipyard just south of Lisbon, Portugal. He had plotted the noontime position of every major commercial vessel afloat for six full months and concluded that Lisbon would be the best place in the world for a shipyard. Chattey's company did not buy the plan.

"Then, in the late sixties, I was sitting in the Treasury Department," Petty told me, "and I had all the loan papers there in front of me — and big as life, there was a project by the World Bank to foster construction of a shipyard just south of Lisbon. The rationale was identical with what Chattey had done eight or ten years before. That's characteristic of the way he thinks."

In 1959, Chattey went to work for the Continental Grain Company as assistant vice president for new products. In Haiti, he experimented with kenaf, a variety of hibiscus, as a substitute for jute in the manufacture of coffee-bean bags. In El Salvador, he mixed asphalt with bagasse, a waste fiber left after the crushing of sugar cane, to invent a new, inexpensive corrugated roofing material. In Guatemala he discovered that bagasse also might be mixed with resin to create inexpensive hardboard and particle board for housing construction. "We found we could make a 900-square-foot living space for about $1,000," he said. Guatemalan soldiers liked the demonstration house a lot, so they stole it. Chattey found it some miles away, on the perimeter of the grounds of the presidential palace. "There was one big old woman inside who was doing the cooking, and she said, 'This is a cool place,' and she flipped up her skirt and rubbed her ass against the wall as a way of demonstrating how cool it was. In a marketing sense, I knew we had a damned good product."

Three times a father by 1963, Chattey went independent — he never liked working for others — and set about selling his ideas. Between 1963 and 1975: for Columbia Sugar he sited a refinery on Staten Island; for Diamond Cement he reviewed a proposed limestone operation in Mindanao; for Esso Standard Oil he demonstrated the benefits of back-hauling coconut oil in tankers carrying lube oil to the Philippines and Malaysia.

He proposed transport of sugar in deep-draft barges between Hawaii and San Francisco for the AMFAC Corporation; the use of ice-strengthened tankers to move North Slope oil to market for ARCO (another oil company, which had invested heavily in the trans-Alaska pipeline, later paid Chattey to keep that idea to himself); and the barter of rice against crude oil in the Philippines for Shell. He studied European markets for U.S. Pipe & Foundry; pilferage of air cargo at Kennedy Airport for MPS International; the relationship between the values of gold and British Petroleum stock for the Wall Street firm of Gianis & Company;

and the transport of calcium carbonate from the Bahamas to Houston for Lone Star Industries.

Chattey advised Mobil against the construction of a submarine tanker terminal and advised Litton Industries against construction of a new Great Lakes shipyard.

For Continental Grain he evaluated a proposed deepwater port on the lower St. Lawrence River. He suggested that they build it. They did not. Years later, after construction costs had more than doubled, they decided they needed it after all.

For the Celanese Corporation he designed a marketing strategy for flame retardant building materials; for Helenic Shipping he sited a new Indonesian tanker terminal; for Williams Brothers Engineering he studied the feasibility of a new LNG facility at Corpus Christi; for Resource Sciences he negotiated oil prices in Saudi Arabia on behalf of a consortium of Midwestern oil companies; for Newport News Shipbuilding he helped to locate a new shipyard near Cape Charles; for Royal Dutch Shell he scouted locations for a new refinery in Indonesia (that was his last job before ICONN-Erie; he earned more than $100,000 in nine months of work); and for Mobil he went looking for a place on the east coast of North America to put a new generation of oil refineries and petrochemical plants.

Onshore, he found none.

ICONN-Erie was the first idea Chattey had tried to sell to government. I asked him to tell me the greatest number of presentations he had had to make to sell any of those other ideas to industry.

"Two," he said.

IV

ORDNANCE FOR OPPONENTS of the Chattey plan was delivered in January of 1979 — yet another study about what to do with the Erie Canal. William Hennessey's Department of Transportation had paid the private consulting firm of Roger Creighton Associates $175,000 to determine if modernization of the waterway would attract sufficient new traffic to pay for itself. The findings were strewn along the course of ICONN-Erie like underwater mines.

Chattey was hesitant to criticize the work of a fellow consultant in public, so he told interested newsmen simply that the body of the report, and the report's conclusions, seemed to him somewhat contradictory. Privately, he was enraged. "They're trying to hoist me with my own petard," he said.

The Creighton study accepted as a given the fact that "future business is more likely to come from the siting of new, large-scale, water-dependent industry than (from) the reconversion of existing industry back to water," which was precisely what Chattey was saying. But then Creighton's people based the report solely on interviews with operators of those very existing industries.

"How good are the interview results?" the study asked. "There is probably underreporting, as respondents are unlikely to express interest in something they know little about," that "something" being the Erie Canal. Respondents who *did* know of the waterway "have adopted a wait-and-see attitude" because of the state's failure to set policy for the system's future, the report said. Chattey was saying that, too.

And on and on:

• "Have all feasible waterborne movements been identified?" the study asked. "Probably not."

• "Significant traffic increases are unlikely unless the canal system is improved or modernized."

• "State expenditure policies toward the canal system are neither rational nor realistic. They seem to be predicated on the concept of non-spending, with the hope that the problem will simply fade over time."

• "Whether the benefits obtainable from improving portions of the canal would exceed the costs is unknown at this time," yet "any improvement will increase the state's attractiveness to commerce and industry."

All of which sounded to me like ammunition for Chattey, despite the fact that the study was limited to goods produced in or delivered to the State of New York. Thus the transport potential for such unlikely barge commodities as cameras and microscopes was considered, while potential for the export of hundreds of millions of tons of coal and grain was not.

The Creighton Study concluded, however, that "to pull (a modernization) off, a tremendous amount of leadership, vision and foresight is required on the part of public officials, operators and industry executives."

But "given the mood of the times," the study said, those commodities were apt to be hard to find.

Therefore: Roger Creighton Associates "does not recommend that the state become enmeshed in a major waterborne commerce-oriented economic development program," the study concluded.

Few reporters had time to read the whole study, of course, and only the conclusion was noted in the state's press release. It prompted news reports about the Chattey project like one which appeared in the *Rochester Times-Union:* "Deeper Canal Wouldn't Pay," the headline read.

As a reporter — like most reporters — I had always taken seriously the results of state studies. After reading the Creighton report I had doubts, however, so I sought an objective opinion. Ronald Hanson, assistant director of the government policy research center at the Rochester Institute of Technology, told me: "Unfortunately, the people doing a study usually have incentives to bias the results in one direction or another. It's a very slippery business."

Hanson continued: "I remember hearing of a rather apocryphal story of a canal being built in the South, which was primarily to please a certain senator down there, in which the benefits came from being able to move logs from one mountain top to another mountain top, where there was a sawmill. The Army Corps of Engineers managed to get the benefits so high by doing a variety of double-counting techniques that eventually the benefits (they reported) were greater than the total value of the sawmill's output." In the government study business, "There's a lot of room for getting funny answers," Hanson said.

Chattey was not laughing. Nor, for that matter, was anyone at the Department of Transportation. William Hennessy would later describe the Creighton study as "a soft attempt, not very meaningful," to determine the canal's potential. Events just around the corner would make the report an embarrassment for the state.

For the time being, though, the document served to make more difficult than ever Chattey's search for a leader with sufficient vision and guts enough to take on ICONN-Erie.

Late in 1978, Chattey and Eristoff briefed three ranking members of the federal Council on Environmental Quality. One of them, Ed Strohbehn, liked the idea but suggested that perhaps, in the long run, it would be better to allow the deterioration of Northeastern economies, sparking the gradual redistribution of people and businesses and industries around the rest of the country. A special Presidential commission would later recommend the same thing. Eristoff was appalled by such thinking; to abandon an existing infrastructure was to abandon all the money that had built it, an unconscionable waste of national resources. President Carter, appalled for the same reason, refused to accept his commission's report.

Early in 1979, Chattey did presentations for editors of the *Buffalo Courier-Express* (they used ICONN-Erie as a cover story in their Sunday magazine), the *Wall Street Journal* (they would be interested in a story only when the studies were finished), and the *Tarrytown Daily News;* also for members of the New York Citizens Development and Resources Corporation, the Tri-State Planning Commission and the North Atlantic Division of the Army Corps of Engineers.

Supportive commissioners in New Jersey, meanwhile, set up a briefing for Governor Brendan Byrne. Chattey was allotted one hour. Byrne listened for two, posed a good many questions and at last leaned back, impressed. "What do you want me to do?" he asked. "Should I dance on the table, or what?" Chattey said a letter of endorsement would be appreciated. Eristoff was delighted. "We appear to have accomplished in six months in New Jersey what we have been unable to do in two and one-half years in New York."

The failure in New York prolonged the consideration of George McIsaac and his staff at the U.S. Department of Energy. Chattey continued to meet with them, but not in January, February, March, April or May did they reach the funding decision they had promised within two months a year earlier. Chattey began to think they were leading him down the rosey path.

In June, Ernest Bower of the federal Office of Deepwater Ports, who was a fan of the project, arranged for a gang briefing of numerous agencies with an apparently mandated interest in ICONN-Erie. Chattey explained the plan to four officials of the U.S. Coast Guard; three each of the U.S. Geological Survey and the Department of Interior; two each of the federal departments of Commerce, Energy, Transportation, and Housing and Urban Development; and one from the Coastal Engineering Research Center.

For a while Chattey feared he would have to brief every bureaucrat in Washington. There were simply thousands of officials, any one of whom, if he had a mind to, could fly around the Chattey behemoth, encircling its legs with tiny wires, and topple it. To succeed, he would need everyone's cooperation, and so, to be safe, he sent transcripts of the June presentation to the offices of transportation, oil and natural gas supply, coal supply development, and resource applications, of the Department of Energy; to the office of Port and Intermodal Development in the Maritime Administration of the Department of Commerce; to the Ocean Programs Branch of the Environmental Protection Agency; to the Office of Coastal Zone Management; to the Office of the Outer Continental Shelf of the U.S. Geological Survey; to the Deepwater Ports Project staff of the U.S. Coast Guard; and to the Minerals Management Division of the Interior Department's Bureau of Land Management.

Once I asked Chattey what all those people in all those agencies were doing to ensure the health and prosperity of the people of the United States of America. He said he had no idea.

"But I do think I understand now what is meant by 'big government,'" he said. "This is democracy carried *far* beyond anything the founding fathers had in mind. We have so fragmented the power structure in this country that thousands of people can say no to an idea, and almost no one can say yes. It's democracy carried to ridiculous extremes." He found it particularly galling that so many of the officials he dealt with were by training lawyers and accountants, "disciples of *negative* disciplines," he said. "Paper pushers. Most of them have never actually *done* anything in their lives." He was fond of citing the statistics. In Japan, where the economy was relatively healthy, 400 people in every 10,000 were either engineers or scientists; in the United States, the number was 40. In that same group of 10,000 Japanese, only three were accountants, only one a lawyer; in a comparable American sample, 40 were accountants and 20, attorneys.

"You know," Chattey said, "The Nazi planners were totally awed by the sheer power of the U.S. to move things. But in the last twenty years the unbridled legislation and regulation of life that's occurred has destroyed any freedom of action. We've had one discipline working at full speed and all the others working backwards. All these damned lawyers have never *moved* anything other than their baby carriages, yet *they* are the people making public policy."

In control of the board rooms, they were making industrial policy, as well, which might have explained the corporate reluctance to join in ICONN-Erie. Robert Reich, director of the Office of Policy Planning at the Federal Trade Commission, said industry was no longer run by the risk-takers, the self-made men, but rather by "paper entrepreneurs, trained in law, finance and accountancy," who made profits "by using the system in novel ways: establishing joint ventures, consortiums, holding companies, mutual funds; finding companies to acquire, 'white knights' to be acquired by, commodity futures to invest in, tax shelters to hide in; engaging in proxy fights, tender splits, spin-offs, divestitures; by buying notes, bonds, convertible debentures, sinking-fund debentures; obtaining government subsidies, loan guarantees, tax breaks, licenses, quotas, price supports, bail-outs; going private, going public, going bankrupt; but *not* by working to improve products or make sales," he wrote.

"Unless it's someone crazy like me," Chattey said, "who in their right minds would fight all that? I get desperately tired at times."

Later in June, Chattey was invited to testify before the Merchant Marine and Fisheries Committee of the U.S. House of Representatives, and, after that, to address the Marine Fisheries Service of the U.S. Department of Commerce. He tried to tailor each presentation to the particular audience.

To the marine groups: "There are actually five dike systems that have to be built. Two break the surface. Three are what are called 'sleepers' and 'dreamers,' they lie under the water. If properly contoured, they'll become excellent fishing reefs, also useful disposal sites for every wrecked automobile in the greater New York area. Instead of shipping all the old automobiles to Japan so that they can come back as Toyotas, we shouldn't even crush them, we should lay them on the reefs we build around ICONN."

To the commercial groups: "Every one of the major river ports which has grown as it has by leaps and bounds since World War II has had a common denominator: they made damn sure that bulk commodities could be effectively handled, which means deep water and industrial real estate, to store and convert them."

To the technical group: "The cost of fertilizer has already shot out of sight, because ammonia, the key nitrogen element, comes from petroleum. But note that there is ammonia in the natural gas Tenneco has found in the Baltimore Canyon. That gas naturally should be stripped at ICONN. Now: the phosphate reserves in the United States are in Florida. So barge them up to ICONN, treat them with sulfuric acid, use the ammonia stream from the natural gas, and you make diammonium phosphate fertilizers. The only missing ingredient is potash, and potash, conveniently, is in abundent supply in southern Canada. Ship it down on the canal. We should build on ICONN the largest fertilizer plant in the world."

To the labor groups: "Buffalo was an asset worth billions and billions of dollars. If for some reason you care to destroy such an asset, you do what we did, you pay to build the St. Lawrence Seaway, running through another country. We are so back-to-front here. The Seaway was the biggest steal of American jobs in the history of the United States, and what has it done? It has enabled the Japanese to sell Datsuns in Chicago."

To the political groups: "You stand at the helm of a ship entering a twilight storm. You can either seize an advantage here and shorten sail and go into this in good order, or you can face the inevitable swamping and possible sinking of this region — and perhaps this nation."

To the investors: "If we do nothing, the exodus of real jobs in this region will become a cascade."

To the civic leaders: "Do any of us really know

what unemployment does, in real terms, to the human being — in terms of the suicide rate, alcoholism, and dead hope?"

To the planners: "You could build the bulk of ICONN either by draining the polders and filling them with earth, raising their level above that of the sea, or by building your industries on the seabed itself. We are tending toward the latter with the final island elements, first because it lowers the windage, second because then each dike revetment becomes a blast barrier in the event of explosion, and third because it would lower the line of sight. There are congressmen in New Jersey who live on the beach and don't want to see this thing out there."

And: "We think year-round navigation would be possible. By bubbling at the lock entrances, and traffic heat transfer from friction and engine heat, ice formation should not present a problem. In fact, by partial inclusion of power plant cooling water, as now occurs on two of the Finger Lakes, it may be possible to limit ice formation to brash ice, which would have little, if any, effect on traffic or canal banks."

To the industrialists: "The natural gas barge would be made of concrete, naturally. At minus 263 degrees Fahrenheit, the LNG would shatter steel."

And: "Mobil has major gas and oil finds in the Baltimore Canyon; there are significant Chevron finds at Hibernia; the U.S. Geological Survey studies indicate major reserves on Georges Bank and beneath the Great Jurassic Fossil Reef on the mid-Atlantic coast. Now where is the most logical place to strip and refine those fuels?"

To the thinkers: "Perhaps our biggest problem in this country is that we steam-rolled over our geopolitique. Someone with a big chunk of land needed money to build cannon to blast England out of the water, so they sold us the Louisiana Purchase. Then Russia sold us Alaska. Then we lost some people at the Alamo so we steam-rolled over the whole Southwest. This country became so vast so fast that geology, not geography, became the governing discipline; whatever it was we needed, it was here; all we had to do was find it. In Europe — and if there is a difference between the European mind and the American mind, it is this one — the problem was the exact reverse: They did not have what they needed, so they had to figure out how to get it. Geography prevailed. Now, for the first time, America has the same problem, but how do you communicate that to a people that's spent the last hundred years thinking the other way around?"

To the environmentalists: "Please do not worry. My discipline, the geographer's discipline, antedates yours by 2,000 years. I am not about to contaminate my own back yard."

And to me: "I'll tell you what—We will create such a ruckus in this region that the government will have to come to terms with us, and *our* terms."

Chattey's presentations were brilliant, to be sure. I never left one without hearing someone remarking to that effect. Perhaps they were too entertaining, allowing audiences to forget they were hearing a serious proposal. More than once I had the disturbing thought that had he charged admission, a couple of bucks a head, say, by 1979 he would have had the resources to fund the studies himself.

Toward the end of June in that year, Chattey met one last time with DOE officials. George McIsaac, citing budgetary cutbacks, rejected the ICONN-Erie grant application. Phillip Kennon, who worked with McIsaac at DOE, told me later that "even though Chattey was a prickly man to do business with, we'd have given him the million if we'd had it. We didn't."

(At the same time, of course, the Department of Energy had offered $5 billion to synthetic fuel researchers and ended up funding what looked to me to be redundant projects — six to remove oil from shale and six to turn coal into natural gas, for example.)

Other officials at the DOE thought Chattey had been given a raw deal, so they suggested that enough groundwork had been laid for him to go over McIsaac's head to Secretary James Schlesinger. But ten days later, along with most of President Carter's cabinet, Schlesinger resigned.

That summer, Chattey proposed ICONN-Erie to the Center for Environmental Studies at Princeton, the Scripps Oceanographic Institution in California and the Woods Hole Institute in Massachusetts (again). James Mavor of Woods Hole said the project was "most enthusiastically received" and that the institute looked forward to working on the detailed feasibility studies.

At the same time, John Petty spoke with Amtrak officials with an eye toward neutralizing the possible opposition of Amtrak's sister railroad, Conrail, the federally operated freight railroad in New York. Conrail was less than a viable alternative to ICONN-Erie; Conrail was a national joke. Just to keep trains running had cost $3.3 billion in taxpayers' money since the feds took over operations in 1976. That sounded like a zillion. It amounted to $1.8 million in loans and subsidies every day, about $1,200 a minute.

Then Chattey and Petty met with honchos at the St. Lawrence Seaway Development Corporation and, to the surprise of a lot of skeptics, came away with a solid endorsement. Chattey had maintained all along that ICONN-Erie would not hurt the Seaway's business and would undo the damage that waterway had caused — the near destruction of the second largest city in New York, the city of Buffalo. The city had been built because of its strategic location for the shipment of Western goods to the East, and vice versa. The Seaway bypassed it.

William Kennedy, president of the Seaway Corporation, agreed with Chattey on both counts; he agreed as well with the grain and coal forecasts. "By the time they could get this built," he told me, "there will be enough commerce generated in the Great Lakes region to satisfy ICONN-Erie and not hurt the Seaway whatsoever. And by the time they could get it built, we'll be operating at maximum capacity. Energy will become nothing but more expensive between now and then. People are just going to have to learn to take advantage of the most economic means of transportation, and that's water."

In August of 1979, Chattey conducted preliminary surveys of Western coal fields on the Wind River, Crow, Blackfoot, Flathead-Nez Perce and Yakima Indian reservations, then travelled further west to explain the plan to officials of the Electric Power Research Institute (EPRI) in Palo Alto and the Atlantic Richfield Corporation in Los Angeles. He flew on to discuss the accumulation of carbon dioxide in the planet's atmosphere with astronomers at the Mauna Loa Observatory in Hawaii. "We will be out of the fossil fuel business within fifty years," he said at subsequent presentations. "We will have to be, if anyone is going to go on living on Earth. The transition from Persian Gulf oil to coal will be twenty-five years, and the transition from coal to fusion — the hydrogen cycle — must be no more than another twenty-five." During the transitional half century, he said, ICONN-Erie would provide the United States with the necessary flexibility in energy use and supply.

He returned to the East to brief the National Industrial Research and Development Council, the New York Bar Association, the Rochester Grant-Makers

Forum and the Empire State Electric Energy Research Company (ESEERCO). He explained the plan to Dr. George Low, president of the Rensselaer Polytechnic Institute and former senior administrator of NASA's Apollo Project. The man who had sent other men to the moon said he would be happy to have RPI serve as the academic engineering center for the ICONN-Erie Project.

The two utility groups, EPRI and ESEERCO, offered to provide $200,000 and $100,000, respectively, should Chattey secure major funding elsewhere, but that appeared a bad bet late in 1979. Agencies of the federal government, Chattey had learned the hard way, were all established to deal with existing needs and existing problems. None was set up to face the future easily. Moreover, the Chattey project had something to do with everything; it cut across the limited purviews of departments of commerce, economic development, labor, industry, transportation, energy, environmental protection, urban development and dozens more, giving each a handy excuse to refer the project elsewhere. No mechanism, save the Presidency and the Congress, existed between the bureaucracies to allow for a simple joining of forces, and no agency, in part because of the volumes of work a serious pursuit of ICONN-Erie would require, was eager to take it on alone.

"I don't mean to seem arrogant," Chattey told me, "but do you see what we're driving at? We're driving at forcing the political structure to come to terms with the twenty-first century, and they don't like it. Political institutions do not change of their own free will. You have to create a politically attractive reason to change. I think we've done that. The problem is that so many of these people have never thought around a corner in their lives."

John Petty put it differently. "There just aren't as

many risk-takers out there as is commonly believed,"
he said.

At least they had been warned. When Chattey first
discussed the idea with officers of the Army Corps,
"They told me there were no technical reasons that
both projects could not be built, but they said they
doubted that the Northeast had the political will, or
the political capacity, to execute.

"And God help us," he said, "they may have been
right."

ELSEWHERE, THINGS WERE DIFFERENT. Great projects
were not gone from the world.

The Dutch, for example, in 1980 began the final
studies of a plan to produce 20 percent of the nation's
electricity with a new generation of windmills. Some
five thousand turbines in parks of a hundred or so each
were proposed, many designed to float offshore, calm-
ing the fears of environmentalists that the units would
ruin bird habitats, create unacceptable levels of noise,
or mar the tourist-seductive lowland vistas.

Israelis that year studied a proposal to cut an 85-
mile canal between Katif on the Mediterranean and
Masada on the Dead Sea, so that hydro stations might
convert the 1,300-foot difference in sea levels into between 100 and 150 megawatts of electricity, enough
to power a city the size of Tel-Aviv.

In England, an audacious idea first suggested by
Napoleon Bonaparte in 1802 was approved for study
in 1980. A consortium of railroad interests began the
design of a thirty-mile tunnel under the English
Channel.

The Germans, meanwhile, were working to finish the Ludwig Canal, a waterway linking the already
canalized Rhine-Main and Danube river systems.
Chattey was fond of citing the example. The project,

scheduled for completion in 1985, would allow barge traffic to load at Rotterdam and deliver goods, without transshipment, anywhere from Antwerp to Munich to Budapest to Istanbul to Moscow. The canal crossed a spur of the Bavarian Alps on a route with a vertical lift requirement of 1,500 feet, almost three times that of the Erie Canal.

"If the Earth were flat," Chattey said, "and your eyesight were sufficient, and you stood atop a forty-story building in New York City, you would be looking *down* on Buffalo, the canal's western terminus."

In Egypt in 1980, engineers completed a five-year dredging program which increased the draft of the Suez Canal from thirty-eight to fifty-three feet, and they began the project's second stage, aimed at producing a 67-foot channel.

The Chinese in 1980 announced plans to deep-dredge the mouth of the Yangtze River and to build a massive coal port at Lien Yung Kang, north of Shanghai.

In Canada, construction started on a pilot power station designed to harness the legendary tides of the Bay of Fundy.

And the Japanese had glamorous schemes in the works all over the world. They announced plans to move Alaskan oil to their homeland in ice-strengthened tankers (the plan was identical to the one Chattey had tried to sell to ARCO years earlier). They sealed a deal with the Trujillo regime to study a reconstruction of the Panama Canal. They proposed a cloning of the Suez Canal, in anticipation of the shipping volumes forecast for the year 2000.

Nippon engineers were also pace-setting the design and fabrication of stupendous barge-mounted industries. In 1980, Ishikawajima-Harima Heavy Industries of Tokyo agreed to build for the Union Carbide

Corporation a waterborne polyethylene plant, which the corporation planned to tow 14,000 miles for operation at Bahía Blanca on the Argentinian coast. The same Japanese firm, two years earlier, had completed construction of a pulp mill and a power plant, each mounted on a barge as long as three New York City blocks, for American entrepreneur Daniel Ludwig. Tugs nursed the barges on a three-month, 15,000-mile voyage through Indonesia, around the Cape of Good Hope, across the South Atlantic to Brazil and up the Amazon River for delivery to Ludwig's pulpwood plantation at Jari, 200 miles inland.

And for their own crowded island homeland, where a population half that of the United States lived on a land mass barely bigger than Montana, the Japanese were making more islands. Machine shops and other noisy industries already operated on land reclaimed in Tokyo Bay, freeing their former inner-city sites for development as parks, playgrounds and green belts. Off Kaizuka City in South Osaka Bay, work continued in 1980 on a square mile of island designed to hold Osaka's main sewage treatment plant and 170 of the city's most environmentally obnoxious factories. For the bay north of that site, the Japanese planned to build a floating international jetport.

Nearby, off the city of Kobe, work neared completion on the first of a pair of artificial islands. Port Island, 1,100 acres of commercial and residential space, was scheduled to be finished in 1981 (the schedule was met), and the Japanese planned to celebrate with an international exposition, "Portopia '81" (which they did). Rokko Island, another 1,400 acres of land, was expected to be fit for occupancy by 1985. Between them, the new islands would hold 40,000 new homes and provide two and one-half square miles of space for port expansion. In terms of total tonnages handled,

Kobe, in 1980, was the second-ranked port in the world.

The artificial island adjoining the first-ranked port, Rotterdam, was already a decade old in 1980. That was Chattey's other favorite example. The deep-draft harbor and 5,000-acre land mass of "Europort," as the Dutch called the plateau they had built from the mouth of the Rhine River out into the North Sea, allowed Rotterdam to handle 300 million tons of cargo a year, more than twice that of the Port of New York.

"How is it possible," Chattey asked, "that the Republic of West Germany and The Netherlands, each with a gross national product smaller than that of the State of New York, can afford such improvements, and we cannot?"

That would be a good question to ask the governor, I thought. New York's port was ranked third in 1980. So early in the year I phoned Bill Snyder, press aide to Hugh Carey, to request an interview. He asked what my questions would be. I told him I wanted to know Carey's opinion about the implications of ICONN-Erie for the Port of New York — and for that matter, for the state and the nation. "Oh. That flake Chattey . . ." Snyder said. "Is *he* still running around?"

Elsewhere in America, work of varying merit continued. In the ocean about twenty miles south of Grand Isle, Louisiana, construction neared completion of an oil-receiving terminal set on a triad of platforms, which rested on the seabed. In Virginia, state officials mustered support for a $1 billion floating oil terminal proposed to lie about seventy-five miles offshore, east-northeast of Norfolk. Recent river canalizations had made port cities of such unlikely places as Lewiston, Idaho, and Tulsa, Oklahoma. And construction continued on the "Ten-Tom" canal, a waterway being built across a corner of Mississippi to join the Tennessee River to the Black Warrior and Tombigbee rivers, north of Mobile. (That canal was first proposed, by the way, by Jesse Hawley, the jailed, indebted flour merchant who suggested an Erie Canal in 1806).

Sad to say, a lot of those projects had been approved less on their value than on the political strength of their promoters. The late Senator Robert Kerr of Oklahoma was personally responsible for the $1.3 billion canal to Tulsa, for example. He told friends that he never voted for *anything* in the U.S. Senate unless there was something in it for Oklahoma. You want his vote for aid to mass transit in New York? Fine. Then vote for his waterway. Real world stuff.

Not much was happening in the Northeast. In 1980, work was almost finished on a $160 million Long Island Railroad tunnel under the East River, which would have been exciting but for the fact that in 1975 the railroad had publicly abandoned plans ever to use it. Construction continued solely to support a subway tunnel that ran overhead. City Council President Carol Bellamy, incredulous at the waste of money, called the tunnel "a dead-end to nowhere."

Governor Hugh Carey, meanwhile, had nothing to say about ICONN-Erie, nor was he inclined to speak with me, either. Despite repeated offers over a four-year period, he had never so much as sat down for an hour to hear Chattey explain the plan. The *Daily News*, which once or twice a year ran reports on the project, nevertheless took to calling ICONN "Carey's Energy Isle." Strange world, I thought.

My first chance to speak with the governor came by accident. When Carey visited Syracuse, the *New York Times* regularly asked me to dog him, just in case he were to announce a major new policy or be run down by a bus or something. At a formal press conference at the airport, not far from where I had met Nigel Chattey, the collected Syracuse media could think of nothing to ask Mr. Carey. So I piped in with, "Governor, I'd like to know what you think of the ICONN-Erie Project and what, if anything, the state is doing about it."

He answered: "Well, we're looking into everything, and fortunately we have Jim LaRocca, who has been heading our energy office, and John Dyson, [then] chairing the Power Authority, and widely divergent groups of people who are in labor and management, and I'm at the point of appointing a blue ribbon panel to look at every possible alternative for energy. And those are the kinds of things that, very frankly, New York has got to do to survive." Otherwise, he said, "The Northeast could well become an abandoned area."

I asked if he might be a little less frank and a little more specific. Then his press secretary announced that there was no more time for questions.

His answer was flapdoodle, of course. Dyson was out of the project. I had already spoken with LaRocca, too. He was at the Hennessy briefings, and Chattey and Eristoff believed that he, too, had intentionally tuned them out. The problems of energy cost and supply, pollution, unemployment and the rest aside — "I've never heard the proposal defined in terms of a current need," LaRocca told me.

Elsewhere in New York's government there was strong, impotent support for ICONN-Erie. Following a project presentation to the state Urban Development Corporation, corporation president Richard Kahan told Eristoff he would be happy to make UDC the lead agency for canal studies. Robert Morgado, secretary to Governor Carey, later told Eristoff, "Nobody else has any ideas. We can't afford *not* to study ICONN-Erie." But Kahan said he could act only at Morgado's request, and Morgado, only at the governor's.

Chattey next explained the plan to Basil Paterson, New York's secretary of state. "There is no question that a project like this warrants study," Paterson told me, "but it is important that none of us misunderstand what our roles are. It's up to the governor to decide."

The governor never set up a "blue ribbon panel," by the way.

"I'm starting to feel like Alice in Wonderland," Chattey said soon afterwards. "These people in government, they *agree* with me. And they do nothing. They say, 'Oh, Mr. Chattey, this is very logical, this is the right way to do things,' and nothing happens. Nobody is accountable for anything, or hardly anything, unless it's sanitation or something like that. It's all a shadow play. These shapes appear and promise, and give you a glib talk, and then they change sizes, or disappear, and nothing happens. I feel just like Alice."

Not long after that, I met with John Dyson, who had nearly funded the Chattey project three years earlier. In 1980, he served as chairman of the New York State Power Authority, and he was facing profound public opposition to his proposal to build a coal-fired power plant on Staten Island. (Chattey had no sympathy. "Surely to God, a blind man could have seen what the opposition would be," he said. Earlier, Staten Islanders, who desired to be neither blown up nor fried, had blocked utilization of two $100 million storage tanks, built to hold liquefied natural gas. In 1980 they stood there, empty, a monument to someone's stupidity.)

Dyson agreed that Staten Island was no ideal site for the new power plant, but the region needed it, and two more besides, he said, adding that of course the most logical place for all three would be on an off-shore island.

"Then why aren't you out pounding on doors in promotion of ICONN-Erie?" I asked.

"Talking to you, I've been asking myself the same thing," he said, but he went on to explain that just then, what with the Staten Island problem and all, he was simply too busy.

I believed him, largely because, without my asking, he phoned the other principals in the early ICONN-Erie negotiations — Mike Curley, Roy Sinclair and Bernard Lawson — to ask that they speak openly with me about the affair.

Two things surprised me enormously. First, Dyson and two of the others freely admitted that Chattey's impatience and anger had offended them, and if they had not reapproached him, it was because their feelings were deeply hurt. And second, each of the four, independently, said he hoped that whatever I wrote would get the project back on track in the State of New York. "Well, hell," I said once or twice, "you're the government. Why don't *you* get it back on the track?" Government just did not work that way, I was told.

Of the four, only Dyson's former legal advisor, Mike Curley, was gone from government service in 1980. He was in private practice.

"I've been kicking Dyson in the ass for years to get him back in on it," Curley said. "I told him, look, if you don't like dealing with Nigel, *I'll* deal with him. Shit, I'm a lawyer, I deal with entrepreneurs all day long. They're a little crazy, you've got to cover their ass, but I love people like that.

"I'll tell you," he continued, "I'm certain that, one way or another, we could have raised the eleven million, and I'm certain that Nigel could have been kept onboard. You know damn good and well that when you've got a Number One who's ego-sensitive, what you do is you stroke him. You pay him well, you stroke him and you put him out front. You say lovely things about him all the time in front of large audiences — which are true. I find that very easy to say about Nigel. He *is* a genius.

"And in terms of a project, um, boy, that's one super project."

With more strength and stamina than I had, though I was twenty years his junior, Chattey scampered, in business suit and with 8-mm Cannon movie camera in hand, up a steep embankment alongside Route 131 in northern New York on a brisk day in the spring of 1980. "Come on, Chattey-bird, think!" he said to himself, setting the exposure and rehearsing the reverse zoom in his mind. "Get it right, Chattey!" He aimed the camera at an empty upslope horizon and began shooting seconds before the radio mast of the *Stolt Viking*, a Liberian freighter loaded to her marks with dry chemicals bound for Rotterdam, rose over the grassy slope, into his viewfinder.

From our vantage halfway up the embankment, more and more of the ship appeared as she slid into Eisenhower Lock at the western end of the ten-mile Wiley-Dondero Ship Canal, a cut thirty feet deep, north of Massena, New York, on the St. Lawrence Seaway. When *Stolt Viking* all but filled the frame, Chattey zoomed back, widening and deepening the image to include the highway tunnel dug directly under the lock. As luck would have it, a station wagon appeared just then from the tunnel's darkness, adding both scale and comparative motion to the shot. "Jeremy Cricket, I got it!" Chattey said, and he bounced on his toes — whether in excitement or for warmth, I could not tell.

Chattey was making a film he hoped to show to member groups within the AFL-CIO. "They tell me pictures matter more than words to those guys," he said. During the preceding fall, on a trip to discuss ICONN-Erie with Dutch engineers, he had shot some excellent footage of the man-made island Europort, and of the river system leading inland from Rotterdam's harbor to most of the rest of Europe. Where he would get the money to piece all the clips into a finished print, he did not know. He filmed anyway. "I'm a born optimist, I suppose," he said.

We watched crewmen snug *Stolt Viking* to the lock wall before the 49-foot lift began. "This is what an optimally modernized canal might look like," he said, "but with barges, not ships." Chattey was not sure which would be most cost-effective: a small island served by a small canal, a medium by a medium, or a large by a large. The studies would determine that. For the canal, 14 feet was obviously too shallow; 29 feet, the depth of the Great Lakes' lanes, was maximal. He hoped to study incremental depths between the two to determine the best. "My hunch is between 20 and 24 feet," he said. So too with the locks. He planned a width of 105 feet, a length of between 660 (for tows of four barges) and 1,000 (for 35,000-dead-weight-ton jumbos). The existing Erie locks were 45 feet wide, 300 long.

East of us, the *Montcliffe Hall,* a Canadian laker carrying 25,000 tons of iron ore to Gary, Indiana, crabbed into an approach wall, awaiting a turn in the lock. "I'm glad you've seen this," he told me. "ICONN-Erie involves not a single technology that's not at least twenty years old."

Later that day, Chattey addressed a knife-and-fork club of Massena businessmen at the request of John Adams, who was chief engineer of the Seaway Corporation and a proponent of ICONN-Erie. Before Chattey's turn to speak, one member read a request that the group purchase a booth at a charity fair to be held a week hence. The men voted unanimously to table action on the request for three weeks. Next up, another member delivered a ten-minute installment of his original comic epic, a tale having something to do with the history of the club's gavel. "Few people are aware of the role the gavel played in the exploration of oil," one of the anecdotes began. "The first discovery of oil in the Middle East occurred when a Spanish explorer stopped in the desert to rest, took out a stake, and drove it into the ground with his gavel, and tied his camel to it. He soon noticed the black substance oozing up from the ground, and, being Spanish and highly emotional, he kept shouting, 'Ole! Ole!' Little did he realize that he had discovered Oil of Olay."

"This is going to be a hard act to follow," I whispered to Chattey. He ignored me. He had been putting up with such nonsense, from coffee klatches masquerading as professional groups, for years.

At last he was introduced. The host mis-accented the first name, however making "Nigel" sound, to my ear at least, like a soporific for people with excess stomach acid.

The presentation was not one of Chattey's best.

In the spring of 1980, Chattey gave a lot of thought to the design of other projects, work which could earn him an income. He was, he said, "within a walk around the block of heaving to, dropping anchor and battening the hatches" of ICONN-Erie. The lack of formal support from government after four years of work "is threatening not only my own finances but the integrity of the project itself," he said. By his own estimates, *operations* at ICONN should have begun in 1980. Yet by 1980 the studies still lay ahead, to say nothing of construction.

Chattey, I thought, was mildly manic. Sometimes he spoke as though he expected to see ICONN rising from the sea like the Kraken a week from next Tuesday. At other times he thought he had no chance at all. Conspiracy theories and other fears occasionally got the best of him.

"I probably shouldn't be telling you this," he said, "but I don't know that Connie really wants this thing built. He is a politician. He gets a great deal of exposure out of the project as it is. It allows him to meet people.

"And it gives the bank the image of The Pioneer — but if they get a little closer to the digging, maybe they're going to antagonize some clients.

"Sometimes I think I'm the only one who wants to see it built. I have to fight all the time to advance it, even in the inner circle."

I wrote those speculations off to the pressure Chattey was under; later, he would regret them openly. (Eristoff, after all, had a law firm to keep him busy, and Petty had a bank to run, while Chattey's whole life had become ICONN-Erie.) Yet the fact that he was capable of such mistrust, even fleetingly, both embarrassed and worried him terribly. He was in grave danger, as he put it, of "cratering out."

The year had begun well enough. Judy Flynn, a Marine Midland vice-president and one of the first ICONN-Erie Irregulars, noticed my story about Peter Wiles and the Erie Canal in the *New York Times*. She phoned me in Syracuse and told me the first I had ever heard of the project. Chattey flew in forty-eight hours later and gave me a personal, day-long briefing. I asked hundreds of questions and had trouble believing that the answers were *all* satisfactory. So I phoned my editor at the *New York Times.*

Deputy Metropolitan Editor Jon Friendly had the memory of an elephant. Yes, of course, absolutely, such an idea deserved coverage, he said, but he was certain that the *Times* had run such a story years earlier. I acquiesced. But the more I looked over my notes, the more energized I became, so I pestered him. A gentleman to the end, Friendly offered me a deal: if he could find an ICONN-Erie story in the newspaper's morgue, I would shut up; if not, he would run with my story.

I later discovered that Friendly was correct. On April 24, 1978, the *Times* had run a three-inch story, an Associated Press dispatch, about a meeting of the World Trade Association. The story was buried on the slop-class page between a book review and the bridge column. The piece contained five sentences about ICONN-Erie, and none of them mentioned the Erie Canal.

Fortunately for me, Friendly was better at recollection than discovery. He could not find the story, so my ICONN-Erie report appeared — on January 6, 1980. The copy desk turned the story inside out, but no matter; Roger Starr had an excuse for his editorial, wholly supportive. It ran on the ninth.

The difficulty I had had in writing the piece convinced me of one of the problems ICONN-Erie faced: the thing was too huge to make sense within the confines of a news report. A magazine story would be needed just to explain it. To deal with the truth of the story, something more would be needed. So in mid-January, I quit my job at the *Post-Standard* in Syracuse and took to chasing Nigel Chattey.

I was frankly relieved to find that in all things he was not the perfect planner. I saw him lose his wallet at least half a dozen times. I once waited while he searched for his car on one level of a parking garage, while the car sat two levels away. Chattey once drove me at thirty miles an hour straight toward the concrete wall of an underground parking lot as he glanced absently from side to side, looking for the exit. He would pay no more than one dollar for a pen, having recognized his habit of leaving writing utensils on conference tables and restaurant tables all over the world. His wrist watches disappeared, too, so he abandoned their use and carried instead, in his jacket pocket, a tiny Staiger quartz alarm clock.

Soon after my *Times* story appeared, Chattey won an audience with Ed Koch, the mayor of New York City. Aides warned him to limit the presentation to eight minutes, as the mayor's attention span was only ten, they said.

Koch liked the idea. So did Francis McArdle, the city's commissioner of environmental protection. McArdle told Eristoff that the need for new sites for unpleasant and dangerous industries was so paramount that no matter how many potential uses they envisioned for ICONN, others would surely appear in due course. Chattey stressed the need for letters of endorsement from Koch and McArdle, but two months later, the letters had yet to arrive.

There was no conspiracy there, I found. There was no hidden agenda. The mayor just had not gotten around to it.

That failure undercut the project elsewhere. Personal friends in Washington — cousins-in-law or something — had put Chattey in touch with yet another official at the Department of Energy — Ruth Davis, the deputy secretary for resource applications. She agreed that during his last dealings with the DOE, Chattey had been given, as he put it, "the hind end of the goddamned elephant," and she promised to review his grant application.

"That's the only way this project has moved from the start," he said. "I went to people I knew, people I knew I could trust." Chattey had done more than two hundred ICONN-Erie presentations by the time I met him, and all but a handful had been arranged by Rube Goldberg connections of one kind or another. He or Petty or Eristoff knew somebody who was related to somebody else whose best friend or next-door neighbor was owed a favor by the guy they needed to see. "It doesn't matter how good an idea is," Chattey told me. "If you don't know somebody, you're dead."

Other friends put him in touch with Peter Brennan, one-time U.S. secretary of labor, who in 1980 was president of the Building & Construction Trades Council of the AFL-CIO, and with Patrick Sullivan, secretary-treasurer of the Great Lakes District of the International Longshoreman's Assocation. He had no idea what to expect from either of them, but Brennan, at least, owed him a favor. During an early work session between the two men, a group of a dozen very angry black construction workers burst in on them at the AFL's executive offices in New York City. They demanded to see Peter Brennan. "He's not here," Brennan casually lied. The group believed him, decided to wait, then tore phones from the wall so no help would be summoned.

Chattey's smile was warm and disarming. "What's the problem?" he asked the group's leader with authentic concern. She said they were there to protest the lack of employment opportunities available to minority workers. "Well, listen to this," he began, going on to tell of all the wonderful jobs ICONN-Erie would create. The group listened, then calmed, then left. One AFL official I spoke with credited Chattey with defusing a minor riot.

Defusing riots earned no one any money, however, and funding for Chattey's promotion grew less and less certain early in 1980. Each month, John Petty reevaluated the bank's involvement.

Without ICONN-Erie, "New York City won't disappear," Petty said. "It will have missed a good bet. It's growth will be moderated, it will become a location where paperwork and desk work are the activities that are performed. Baltimore and Washington will benefit. But as a practical businessman, I've got to examine how long I can let our stockholders be the sole support of the project," he said.

At the same time, new studies which attacked the theoretical foundations of ICONN-Erie appeared. Gunner Hall, a transportation analyst for the New York State Department of Transportation, told me that projections by the Faculty Consultants of the state university at Buffalo and by the Frederick Harris consulting firm shared the conclusion reached in the 1979 Creighton study, "that there appeared to be no potential for the large-scale movement of western coal to the East."

(Calls from the media concerning the Chattey project usually wound up on Hall's phone. "There will come a day," Chattey said, "when the weight of ICONN-Erie will descend on Gunner Hall. Nothing will remain but a greasy spot on the carpet.")

Then, in March, the Army Corps published the preliminary findings of its study of water routes between the Great Lakes and the East. The news was not good. The Corps concluded that only modest modifications of the Erie Canal — a rehabilitation of the system as it was, with a lock capacity of one barge, between Albany and Buffalo, or an expansion to a capacity of two barges, between Albany and Oswego — would pay for themselves in the long run. The Army study, like the others, found no potential for the movement of Western coal. Of course, like the others, it considered neither coal and grain export possibilities nor the cost-effectiveness of a canal-and-island combination.

A few weeks later, in April, I found Chattey in Irvington, at work in his garden. He wore a knit cap, an old Army jacket, corduroy slacks and French canvas-topped swamp boots. He sat by a low retaining wall, grafting a branch of a copper feather-leafed Japanese cut-leaf maple onto the stalk and root system of a green, and hardier, Japanese cut-leaf maple. The activity was therapy, and more. He had been raised Episcopalian, Maria as a Catholic, together they attended Presbyterian services, "but this garden is my church," he said. "I find more religion in the circle of life here than I do almost anywhere else."

He gave me a tour of the grounds, extolling the wonders to come. "We have seventy-five feet of vertical difference in an acre," he said, "so everything must be arranged by height. It becomes almost a composition."

Later, resting on the great rock by the waterfall, we got down to business. "You know, I want to tell you something which may sound terribly arrogant," he said. "ICONN is only the tip of the iceberg of solutions to the energy problems of the U.S. I've probably shown more of the iceberg to Petty and Connie than to anybody else, but I haven't shown the whole iceberg to anybody, nor will I. If I were to say now that I know what the energy policy of the United States should be, who in bloody hell would listen? I'd be considered a crazy man, and you'll notice I'm on the edge of that always. But it just so happens that I *do* know.

"What I am asking is that people will appreciate sufficiently the logic sequence which led to ICONN that they will give me an opportunity to think at higher and higher levels. But nobody should be given a shot at that until they've proven themselves with something of order-of-magnitude size, something like ICONN-Erie."

(That may have been the way things should have been, but, what with politics and all, it was not the way they were. Just then, the secretary of energy of the United States of America was a man who, before coming to Washington, had been an executive in the Coca-Cola Company. After the 1980 Presidential election, he would be replaced by a man who, before coming to Washington, had been a dentist.)

Chattey no longer knew how to proceed; he felt ham-strung. For one thing, the endorsements from New York City's mayor and commissioner of environmental protection had still not arrived, and their absence was jeopardizing Chattey's talks with Ruth Davis at the Department of Energy. "The failure to get those letters on time bugs the hell out of me," he said. "Connie can live with it. He always sides with bureaucracy, the governmental process. We have been constantly aborted from achieving target on schedule — I've been waiting *eight weeks* for the mayor's letter. That doesn't sound like much, but *every time* it is eight weeks. Every single time. Just string out the number of things that can't be done until you do the first, and you've got something that's going on until you're Methuselah. I am really appalled."

For another, Chattey imagined that his future efforts, like so many past, would be stymied by the lack of support for the project by Governor Carey. As we strolled over the grounds, he considered asking the unions to put the screws to Carey, or ambushing him with a reporter's investigation (there was that business about the governor's brother owning a small oil company, after all), or embarrassing him into commitment, somehow, "or even *convincing* him, for God's sake."

Chattey felt a bit better two days later when letters from Mayor Koch and Commissioner McArdle finally arrived. Getting them had been no big deal for Eristoff. During negotiations on New York's transit strike, he had simply taken one of the mayor's aides aside and asked for them *now*, please.

Chattey felt a bit worse two weeks after that when John Petty told him that, unless a major breakthrough toward project funding were reached by summer's end, the bank would have no choice but to end its financial support. By then, Marine Midland had put more than $300,000 into the ICONN-Erie Project.

Then Ruth Davis of the federal Department of Energy phoned to tell Chattey that she had sent the ICONN-Erie grant proposal off to the Army Corps of Engineers for further review, which meant she was abandoning it. "We were back-burnering it for a while," one of her aides told me. "I mean, it's so goddamned *big*."

That turned out to be only part of the reason — not the primary part — but I did not learn that until later.

Toward the end of April, at a repeat presentation for the New York Chamber of Commerce and Industry, Chattey noticed in attendance Charles Fox, the civilian engineer who had directed the Army Corps' recent study of water routes between the Great Lakes and the East. Chattey aimed the briefing at Fox directly, and checked off the study's failings:

• The Corps had not considered the respending effect of investment dollars.

• The Corps had not considered the job benefits.

• The Corps had not considered "the synergistic

benefits that accrue when improvement of the port terminus of a canal system is undertaken at the same time as the canal improvement itself," Chattey said. And on and on.

Under the law (incredibly, I thought), the Corps was not *allowed* to consider such things. Only such benefits as might be derived by diverting existing traffic from other modes of transportation went into the formula. That sounded to me like robbing Peter to pay Paul.

Chattey was fully aware of all that, but he felt nonetheless compelled to go after the Corps' engineer, partly in challenge, partly in plea for concession. "Nothing about this project is speculative, Mr. Fox," he said. "We could sit here and discuss it until midnight, but the Europeans have *done it,* and it works. To service the canalized Rhine River system into Western Europe, the Dutch have built Europort, built it right out into the full-face slot of the North Sea gales.

"But don't take *my* word for it," Chattey said. *"Go to Rotterdam, Mr. Fox. See for yourself."*

Chattey went on in April and May of 1980 to explain his plan to the Lake Carriers' Association and the Dominion Marine Association, both in Florida; the staff of New York Senator Warren Anderson in Albany; and the Marine Square Club, the Transportation Research Forum of New York's Chamber of Commerce, the Northeast Industrial Development Research Council, and the Council of Master Mariners, all in New York City.

I went to Rotterdam.

THE ONLY WORK OF MAN VISIBLE FROM SPACE, according to popular wisdom, was the Great Wall of China. Not so.

Also plainly visible in Landsat imagery, within the boundaries of one of the smallest countries in the world, were the world-wonders of Dutch engineering: the Great Barrier Dike, built to hold back the North Sea, a dam so long that to stand at one end was to see the other disappear over the curve of the earth; the North-East, East Flevoland and South Flevoland polders, more than five hundred square miles of new agricultural and residential land, all reclaimed from the former Zuider Zee; the three colossal storm surge barriers built, and being built, across estuaries in the Rhine River Delta; and the enormous curving hook of Europort, the man-made island extension of the Port of Rotterdam, reaching more than two miles out into one of the least hospitable bodies of water in the world, the North Sea.

From a vantage far closer to the surface of the

planet, I surveyed that port city on a clear day in May of 1980. The westward view from the fifteenth floor of Rotterdam's World Trade Center held fully 20 miles — an image, again, cut short by the horizon — of quays and jetties and dock basins, cold storage sheds and storage tanks and warehouses and bulk storage yards, silos and loading bridges and dry docks, floating docks and elevators, conveyors and slipways, floating cranes and luffing cranes and slewing cranes, roll-on/roll-off terminals, LASH terminals, container terminals, power plants, oil refineries, petrochemical plants, granaries, shipyards and myriad industries more whose functions I could only guess at. In the channels between whole forests of cranes were amphidredgers and omnibarges, floating fire-fighting fortresses and tour boats, tugs and lighters by the score, ships by the hundred, river barges by the thousand. No where else on Earth did such a sight exist. The Dutch thought of Rotterdam — the Gateway to Europe — as a port with a city attached, not vice-versa. On the average, ocean-worthy vessels called at a rate of eighty-two a day, more than twice New York's average. The barge rate per diem was 685 — several hundred times, every day, the annual traffic of the Erie Canal. Rotterdam had eclipsed New York as the world's premier port back in 1963.

Marco van der Sande LaCoste, managing director of the Rotterdam Port Promotion Council, commandeered a harbor launch that day to give me a sea-level view of the port, a tour necessarily incomplete. In area, it was the size of one and one-half Manhattans; at five miles per hour in a launch, it would take a full day to travel from one end to the other and back.

We bounced in the wakes of dozens of freighters and tankers and bulk carriers many times too large ever to visit the Port of New York. We yielded to the tiny, awninged bumboats, one-man catamarans which ferried cases of Heinecken Beer to thousands of shipboard sailors. We passed so many barges that I quit counting. Like those of the old Erie, many were privately owned and carried living quarters astern for the boatman and his family. Most had flowers in the windows. Some had clothes drying on lines strung stem to stern. Many, atop the cabins, carried a Fiat or a VW or a Simca or a Toyota to be craned ashore for the family's use before the barge unloading began. Atop the loaded hold of one barge, I saw a child playing with Tonka Trucks in a pile of wheat fifteen feet deep and two hundred long. Other children were tethered to the cabins so as not to go over the side.

LaCoste told me that Rhine barges accounted for about 250,000 loadings and unloadings in Rotterdam each year; that fully 63 percent of the port's annual 300 million tons of cargo entered or left the city by barge. (For the sake of comparison: the barge share of New York commerce was an insignificant fraction of 1 percent.)

Relatively speaking, the entire port complex was new. Following the German blitz of the city and port during World War II, Rotterdam's burghermeisters chose first to rebuild not the ruined commercial district, nor the devastated residential sections, but the port facility itself. The 1946 reconstruction accommodated ships of 46,000 deadweight tons, then the largest vessels in use in world trade. Business justified that capacity almost at once, so improvements continued. Land reclaimed for terminals alongside the new channel, dredged to handle ships of 80,000 tons, was in use by 1950. "The whole world was laughing at us then," LaCoste said, "because ships of that size did not then exist." They did, though, before long.

Port expansion westward along the Rhine, always

in anticipation of trends in world shipping, culminated in the late 1960s with the completion of Europort, new land where a power plant, a steel mill, a coal company and twelve oil firms — Mobil, Shell, Exxon, Gulf and British Petroleum among them — established operations. Ships drawing ninety feet of water found moorings in the facility, helping to make Rotterdam the spot oil capital of the world. "Right now, we can take tankers of 240,000 deadweight tons," LaCoste said, "and when our dredging is done we will manage ships of 500,000. The only limit for us will be the depth of the North Sea itself." At Europort there was also a factory making bricks out of harbor silt — the same sort of spoil New York was dumping into the sea — and a hostel for sailors; the commute into town was too long.

The artificial Europort, in construction at least, was the model for Chattey's island. While LaCoste and I spoke, I wondered how many of the people whose opinions meant life or death to the ICONN-Erie Project had ever heard of Europort, or had even seen it, or knew anything about it, or even know what country it was in.

I mentioned to LaCoste Chattey's contention that, while Rotterdam, Shanghai, New Orleans, Buenos Aires and others of the world's great river ports had tried to keep pace with growth in world shipping, New York officials, somehow content with a harbor only forty feet deep, had "let the rest of the world sail by." LaCoste perfunctorily praised the container terminals of Port Newark and Port Elizabeth, then agreed.

One of the principal engineering firms involved in the design of Europort was Hydronamic, the hydraulic engineering arm of Royal Bos Kalis Westminster, the company to which Chattey had sold the option on ICONN's design. Jene Langevoord, a canal and lock engineer with the firm, was between assignments when I visited The Netherlands. With exceptional patience and grace, he gave me the tour.

Through Langevoord I learned that notions like Chattey's ICONN, sheer fantasy to so many Americans, were the cherished foundations of Dutch national heritage. They were used to doing things big in The Netherlands. Langevoord and I stopped at some distance from the great storm barrier built across a Rhine estuary at Haringvliet so that we might see it all at once. I could see that it was big, but my eyes failed to tell me quite how big until I watched a group of tourists wander off in its direction. The people got smaller and smaller as they approached the thing, finally disappearing completely from sight long before they reached the first of the seventeen sluices built into the dike.

Such feats of civil engineering were all that made Holland possible. One-fifth of the country's land mass had once been ocean bottom, and half of the 14 million Dutch people now lived and worked below sea level. In Amsterdam and Rotterdam and Utrecht and The Hague, tourists eagerly photographed little wavy blue lines, typically painted on walls or on lobby pillars, sometimes six feet above the floor, sometimes twelve. They indicated where, but for Dutch ingenuity, the surface of the sea would lie. In one way or another — first with terps; then with weed dikes and stake dikes and pile dikes; later with earthen dikes and pumping engines powered by oxen and men; later still with their windmills — the Dutch had been capturing land from the sea since the year 400 B.C. or thereabouts.

On my second day with Langevoord, he drove me out to a work island, a couple miles long and half a mile wide, shaped something, I thought, like a grasshopper, which lay in the middle of the Oosterschelde, the last of the Rhine estuaries to be sealed by storm barriers. In what I took to be gigantic sand pits, workers on the island were assembling the cassion components of the barrier, sixty-six of them in all, each of them huge, the largest as tall as a twelve-story building and weighing 18,000 tons, I was told. The monoliths were to be placed, in line, across the mouth of the estuary. Gates in each cassion would allow saltwater tidal passage, preserving the shellfish industry on the barrier's inland side, to be closed only when storm surges threatened.

Part neophyte and part moron, I commended nature's wisdom in placing such an island, solid against the force of the North Sea, precisely where it was needed. It would eventually become the bridgehead of the barrier. "No, no," said Langevoord, laughing, amused by my mistake. "The Dutch built this island. It took two years."

The work areas I had taken for sand pits in fact were polders, opened and drained. The workers were driving their trucks and running their cranes on what two years before had been seabed. The far walls of each pit were not walls at all but rather dikes against the Oosterschelde. When construction was finished, the dikes would be broken to flood the polders. Then great cradle ships would enter, lift the barrier elements and carry them out for placement in the estuary. "I'm impressed," I told Langevoord. "I don't blame you," he said.

Later that day, we arrived in Willemstad, a tiny, ancient hamlet snugged against the dikes which protected it from the Greveligen estuary and the River Maas. For centuries, craftsmen there wove enormous mattresses, with fascines of brushwood, and these underlay most of the dikes in the country, protecting both dike base and sea bed from the scouring action of currents and tides. Only in this century had synthetic materials, like nylon, been used in such revetments. Most recently, asphalt was used, and a special ship was built to lay the gummy strip.

In offshore dike construction, Langevoord said, first a compacting barge tamped the seabed solid. Then the foundation mattress was laid. Then sea-going barges dumped mountains of sand and fine gravel upon the mattress, and upon that layers of increasingly coarser gravel, forming the body of the dike as a shallow pyramid, roughly six feet wide at the base for every foot of vertical rise. Fine stone, then quarry stone in pieces weighing up to a ton, formed the next strata. Asphalt and concrete poured atop that completed the inner dike face. On the seaward side, chunks of quarry stone weighing up to twenty-five tons apiece were layered onto the dike, and these were armored against the force of hostile seas by several levels of concrete cubes, cubes longer on a side than a man is tall, simply thousands of them tumbled together every which way, resting against each other at all angles to dissipate the energy in an onslaught of waves. Such were the dikes protecting the outer wall of Europort.

The same technique could build Chattey's island. Americans were adept at making concrete. Quarry stone was abundant in northern New Jersey. And vast deposits of sand and gravel lay on the Cholera Bank, there for the dredging. Bos Kalis Westminster wanted that job. The group's fleet included 54 hopper barges, 31 transport barges, 21 suction hopper dredgers, 40 suction and cutter-suction dredgers, 10 bucket dredgers, 14 barge-unloading dredgers, 2 dipper dredgers, 62 elevator barges, 5 drilling barges, 5 pipe-laying barges, 25 floating grab cranes, 39 tugs, an assortment of split hydro-dump barges, sea-going split-hoppers and amphibian transports, and 121 launches and service craft.

One of the men with access to that Navy was Cornelius Stigter, who was recognized internationally as a dike-and-island genius. When only ten years old — while other children built castles of sand — Stigter made dikes of it, barriers forty or fifty yards long, which blocked the retreat of high tides from beaches at Hook of Holland. The police frowned. No tourists were likely to sunbathe or picnic on blankets spread in Stigter's personal tidal pools.

Stigter was Langevoord's boss, the president of Hydronamic, the man who had purchased from Chattey the option on ICONN's design.

I met him one day in Utrecht. "We can talk while we drive," he said. "There are things I want to show you." We drove out onto the South Flevoland polder, an area one-fifth the size of Rhode Island entirely covered with grasses, holding wave patterns in winds which once stirred waves in the Zuider Zee. "I once sailed where we now drive," Stigter said. That polder, still too new for use by farmers, was reclaimed in 1969. After the dikes went up, but before the polder was fully drained, aircraft flew over and seeded the region with starwort and glasswort and bastard mudgrass. The roots helped to consolidate the seabed. When the water was gone, reeds sown in the mud served the same function, and were later burned off to make way for the planting of grasses.

The huge grassland ended abruptly as we crossed a small ridge, which Stigter recognized as the dike containing the southern edge of the East Flevoland polder, about two hundred square miles, dry since 1957. It supported hundreds of dairy farms laid with an almost disturbing order in the greenery on either side of roads straight as lasers, save where designers deliberately kinked them to help keep drivers awake. We crossed that polder — for all I could tell, it might have been Nebraska — and reached the oldest of the Yssel Lake polders, the North-East, completed in 1942.

There the ecosystem of reclamation had reached young adulthood. A second generation of natives lived in the towns and villages. Squirrels and rabbits prospered in places nature had intended only for fishes. The canopies of deciduous and fir forests formed thirty or forty feet above the ground.

"Just look around," Stifter said with an obvious pride but with an undertone of anger as well, one he would later explain, as we drove through the countryside. "Do we have to be sorry we developed Holland like this? Nobody could be offended by a landscape like this. If you didn't know where you were, you might think this was rural New Yersey."

Prettier than that, I thought. Marveling at the man-made country, I was troubled by an aphorism I had read in a tourist brochure on my arrival in Holland. The German poet Heinrich Heine was quoted as saying that, if the world were coming to an end, he would go to The Netherlands, where everything happened fifty years later.

Just the opposite, it seemed to me. "Our expression 'Yankee ingenuity' ought to be changed to 'Dutch ingenuity' " I said to Stigter. "No need," he answered, explaining that the expression in fact was 'Janke ingenuity' — Janke being a variation of Jan, the Dutch form of John — and that the word "Yankee" was drawn from it. Hmm, I thought. Next I asked how it happened that so many grand civil works were to be found in a place so tiny as Holland.

"Disasters," Stigter said flatly, quickly.

Work on the Great Barrier Dike, which made Yssel Lake from the old Zuider Zee, was begun, he said, only after a storm in 1916 whipped the Zuider to violence, causing extensive flooding and widespread destruction. The idea was first suggested in the late 1660s. During the last half of the nineteenth century alone, there were ten separate plans for the damming. Rotterdam's port expansion began only after the German bombing. And the storm surge barriers at Haringvliet and in the Oosterschelde were approved only after a once-in-ten-thousand-years storm came ashore in 1953, demolishing three hundred miles of ancient dikes and leaving much of southern Holland under water. The plan which would have prevented that horror was first proposed in 1929. Failure to implement, on one day of disaster two decades later, cost 1,800 Dutch lives.

Stigter's had nearly been one of them, he said. His village abutted one of the Rhine dikes in danger of failing, but the skipper of a small inland freighter spotted the weak spot. He purposefully grounded his vessel, broadside against the dike, and scuttled her there, blocking the seepage. Stigter was thirteen years old at the time. From that day on, he told me, the thought that he would grow up to be anything other than a hydraulic engineer never occurred.

The story beat that business about a thumb in a dike all to hell, I thought.

In mid-afternoon, still on the North-East polder, we arrived at the hydraulic testing station at De Voorst, one of two such research facilities operated by the Dutch government. The testing sheds nestled in thick woods, so I had trouble gauging their size. Stigter led me into one large enough, I saw from the inside, to allow fabrication of an aircraft carrier. Stretching more than one hundred yards along the floor was a model, water and all, of the storm surge works in the Oosterschelde. Near the mouth of the estuary was an island, ten feet long, a facsimile of the work island I had visited with Langevoord.

Here, and at the sister facility in Delft, Dutch engineers conducted wind-flume and wave attack tests, to measure the effects of storm energy on works of man, and tidal motion tests so that island and dike designs accounted for erosion and littoral drift. The horizontal scale was 1-to-400; the vertical scale, 1-to-200. A 24-hour tidal cycle was scaled down to about fifteen minutes, which required a slowing of current velocity, as well, so ground styrofoam was used instead of sand to study erosive effects. Spotted throughout the tidal models were dozens of little machines which looked to me like egg beaters powering tiny augers. They were gyroscopes, simulating the Corelis force of the earth's rotation on the motion of tides.

"Of course Mr. Chattey's project is possible," Stigter told me later, as we drove across the Great Barrier Dike. He thought a moment, drumming his fingers on the dashboard. "The only conceivable obstacle will be politics."

He spoke from first-hand experience.

STIGTER WAS STILL ANGRY, five years after politics had undone his own industrial offshore island. Between 1970 and 1975, Hydronamic had been part of a consortium of twenty-seven Dutch firms and one each from France, Great Britain, Sweden and the United States — oil and petrochemical companies, steel companies and shipyards, even an airline and a television industry — which had designed multiple feasibility studies on an island fifteen miles square, proposed for siting thirty miles offshore, northeast of Europort, in a North Sea depth of between eighty and one hundred feet.

Hydronamic had conducted the studies and produced a 200,000-word technical report which considered possible users, optimal location, relevant law of the sea, design and construction, cost, labor, transportation, environmental impact and international economic consequences. Island industries were arranged in synergistic clusters so that the wastes of one became raw materials of another, to the economic benefit of all. For example: intense cold, a by-product of LNG regasification, would be used in an air separation plant, to isolate pure oxygen; liquid nitrogen, a by-product of oxygen production, would be used in a scrapping plant, to separate metals for recycling. Ethane, another LNG byproduct, would be converted to ethylene; chlorine, a by-product of ethylene production, would be used by bauxite processors. And on and on. The possibilities seemed limitless. The details differed, but the synergy was a lot like what Chattey imagined for ICONN.

Stigter's group designed the North Sea island to hold refineries, ferrous and non-ferrous industrial clusters, petrochemical plants, transshipment yards for bulk commodities, an emergency harbor and a tanker cleaning facility. Their planning included roads, shops, post offices, apartments, restaurants, infirmaries, hotels, radio and television stations, even police administration. Workers, as many as 12,000 of them, would spend five days on the island, five days off. Twelve mass-capacity helicopters would accomplish the commute. Hydronamic had planned the thing right down to trees and shrubbery. "It would not be an ugly place," Stigter said. The study concluded that the island was entirely feasible, and a dandy idea besides.

"It can be done," Stigter wrote in the report. "The advantages amply outweigh the disadvantages. The question is whether we dare to engage in it, whether we can think on a larger scale and dare to accept the consequences."

Stigter turned the study over to the Dutch government, which had the final say. Politics swallowed the work, and the government reached no conclusion. Pollution would blow to the mainland, critics charged. The island would cost too much. Were workers to spend such lengths of time at work, the Dutch family structure would collapse. "And then there were many people who said that welfare takes priority over prosperity," Stigter said.

Chattey agreed. "Their island did not happen because the Dutch have even a worse case of socialist indigestion than we do," he said. Others recognized the same malady; the *Economist* of London called it "the Dutch disease," defined as the transfer of national wealth from productive to unproductive segments of society by spending resources on social welfare, not economic growth — by investing in people who consume more things than they make.

If such a disease indeed existed, it was compounded only months after Stigter's report was released by the near-simultaneous arrival in The Netherlands of some 400,000 immigrants. The Dutch had decided to end their colonial history by making independence possible for Dutch Guiana, now the nation of Surinam. No hard feelings, the Dutch said, and to prove it, they welcomed emigration by any soon-to-be Surinamese who wanted to move. Roughly half the population relocated in The Netherlands. There were few jobs for them.

The politics were hard for Stigter to take. He had worked on Europort — which was built, by the way, with local, not national funding. He had designed port and river modernization projects in Africa and South America and throughout the Middle East. His firm had built fourteen islands for oil exploration in arctic seas. Even as we spoke, Hydronamic was completing a feasibility study of an artificial island Exxon of Canada hoped to build in the Gulf of Labrador, in a depth of six hundred feet. As an engineering intern, Stigter had helped to reclaim Long Island marshland for the creation of Kennedy Airport. And now, in his own country, he was stymied.

"A people that lives, builds for its future," he told me, quoting the inscription of a monument we later visited, erected at the point where the Great Barrier Dike was sealed, near the center, more than ten miles from either shore. "People today who cannot decide must learn to give someone with courage the opportunity to live out his courage. They should step aside to let the few who *can* decide, decide.

"Consider Europoort," he said. "We did not wait until our clients were here. We could not prove they would come. We built for the future, then waited." He leaned back, accelerated a little, drew a large breath. "They came," he said. "*This* is courage."

FOR THE SAKE OF COMPARISON, I hoped to tour the Port of New York, so on my return to the States I phoned Leon Katz, supervising information officer of public affairs for the Port Authority. It would be useful, I thought, to go out in a harbor launch, as I had with LaCoste in Rotterdam.

"First of all, you're asking the wrong question," Katz said. We don't give tours like that. And second, even if we did, why should we give one to you?" I later visited Katz in his office at the New York World Trade Center, a Port Authority project which had cost $1 billion (in 1980, it was up for sale). He showed me an informative film, gave me many interesting materials, and refused to compare on any level the virtues of the Port of New York with those of other port cities in the world. He had never heard of ICONN-Erie.

I eventually got a partial tour of the port aboard the *Newtown Creek*, one of the bottom-dumping tankers which daily made repeat trips to waste zones in Lower New York Bay. I boarded the ship at the Bowery Bay sewage treatment plant in Astoria, Queens. During the seven-mile trip through Hell's Gate, past Roosevelt Island and down the East River to the southern tip of Manhattan, I counted only ten working freighters and two working tankers. One of the latter was another sludge-dumper.

Most of Manhattan's waterfront, and much of Brooklyn's, was in ruin, testament to, among other things, the port's loss of twenty shipping lines and 10,000 jobs for longshoremen since 1965. The city in fact was then soliciting federal aid to raze rotting piers before they fell into the East River, fouling navigation. The healthiest section of waterfront was the old South Street Seaport. It was there New Yorkers had seen their first "skyscrapers" — the topsails of clipper ships come to take on the cargo of boats from the Erie Canal. In 1980, the South Street docks were neatly maintained as part of a museum.

Port officials knew they had problems. A year earlier, their "Congress on Regional Recovery" had concluded that "the economic decline of the last decade was more severe than originally understood." Peter Goldmark, the port's director, said, "We've taken a beating since 1973, but nothing will compare to the beating we will take over the next ten years if we do nothing." He then called for the rebuilding of the regional infrastructure. I later asked him if that might include ICONN-Erie. No comment, he said. The Chattey project would lie outside his jurisdiction.

The Congress on Regional Recovery also stressed the need for a coordinated system of freight movement. "The consensus was that too much studying and planning has been going on without substantive results," the report said. Members of the group then scheduled more meetings for study and planning and established "the Committee on the Future." A year later, the substantive results included:

• A proposal to decorate an eight-block stretch of East River waterfront with floating restaurants, hotels, shops, apartments and an ice skating rink.

• A proposal to build in the abandoned Brooklyn Navy Yard — where the likes of the ironclad *Monitor* and the battleship USS *Missouri* had been launched — a small industrial park, designed for two job-printing companies which, together, would employ about fifty people.

• A $20 million plan to further refurbish the South Street Seaport Museum.

• And a $36 million plan to create three more small industrial parks, one each for the Bronx, Staten Island and Elizabeth, New Jersey. The latter plan was "typical of Port Authority ventures into other areas," complained Edward Regan, state comptroller. "It diverts the authority away from its function, which is the promotion of world trade through port development."

The true activity of the Port of New York and New Jersey was to be found at the container terminals in Newark and Elizabeth, and at the air cargo terminals of Kennedy Airport, where the value of each ton of cargo was perhaps the greatest in the world. The commodities were such things as shoes, scientific equipment, motors, sporting goods, books and so on. The port offered virtually no facilities for handling bulk commodities, however. Bits of litter and rubbish blew like tumbleweed over the great deserted rail yards that once served bulk carriers in the upper bay, north of Jersey City.

There was little activity to witness from the decks of the *Newtown Creek*. "I remember, not so many years ago, the harbor was dotted with car-floats and ferries crossing back and forth all day long," said skipper George Gantz. "I miss it now. I really do." Gantz, by coincidence, had once piloted tow boats on the Erie Canal. He liked that job better, he said. The new one "bores me to tears." The one operation we did see was that of "lightering" — the unloading of cargo from small tankers and modern container ships into even smaller vessels for the shallow-draft trip through Kill Van Kull to ports Newark and Elizabeth on Newark Bay, and down the Arthur Kill to the Jersey oil refineries. The double-handling of course increased the cost of everything.

An hour southeast of the Verrazano Narrows Bridge, *Newtown Creek* reached the "mud dump," her cargo's destination, in open sea about two-thirds of the way to the acid dump, which was the proposed site of ICONN. From the sludge dump, little of Manhattan could be seen save the upper stories of the World Trade Center. This place was the proper home of tautog and pollock, Atlantic cod, skipjack and bluefin tuna, Atlantic and chub mackerel, Atlantic bonito, bluefish and striped bass, silver hake and squirrel hake and sea trout, but the fish no longer felt welcome. A dozen doors in the hull of the vessel opened and began the release of twenty-five hundred tons of sewage sludge, industrial waste chemicals and other bad news.

"That's hot stuff," an able-bodied seaman told me as we stood astern, watching the waters behind us boil black. "You get any of that on your skin, you get rashes you never heard of. Best thing, if you touch it, is jump over the side. Seawater washes it off." The dumping lasted fifteen minutes and left the ship's route plainly visible, a mile-long sickle of filth across the dump zone. "This wouldn't bother me much, if we did it once or twice a month, " the AB said, "but we do it every day, lots of times a day." As he spoke, another sludge tanker entered the dump.

Officials of the National Oceanic and Atmospheric Administration said the sludge gunk, and the contaminated dredge spoil which was dumped nearby, were laden with nickel, chromium and lead, among other things, and they blamed it for fin rot, genetic deformities in crabs and lobsters and the death of starfish. Others blamed it for "swimmers' itch" and the black mayonnaise of tar and raw sewage which periodically washed up on regional beaches.

Three lawsuits to stop the dumping, filed by the National Wildlife Federation, were pending in 1980. And the U.S. Congress, under pressure from environmental groups, had ordered a ban to dumping by the end of 1981. But waivers were already in hand to allow the practice to continue past the deadline. Port officials argued that the ban would mean an end to the dredging of the harbor, thus less and less shipping, thus another staggering blow to the regional economy: the loss of $4.5 billion in business, $400 million in taxes and 60,000 jobs; and an increase of at least half a billion in the cost of imported oil.

Port officials were studying the problem, they promised, but as yet had found no alternative.

DOUBLE STANDARDS are always of interest. The day after my ride on the sludge tanker I was back in central New York, visiting with Peter Wiles aboard the *Emita II*. Coast Guard officials the day before had read him the riot act. No longer would heads aboard the packet be allowed to flush directly over the side, into the Erie Canal. He was therefore in the process of torching a hole in the deck to admit a containing tank to the hold. The work irked him considerably. An earlier Coast Guard inspiration had cost him $1,400 in a failed experiment with macerates-chlorinator heads. The containing tank cost another $1,900.

"I mean, what the fuck," he said. "I'm the *only* passenger vessel on 350 *miles* of canal. Now, the lock at Little Falls, by itself, holds six million gallons of water, so who knows how much is in the whole system? The deal is, how much could you piss? They allow four or five parts per million of sewage in drinking water. That means everybody I have onboard would have to shit six tons and piss 200 million gallons a day to make a problem. The great blue herons we all love so dearly put in more than we ever could."

Wiles and I stood alone in the pilot house of *Emita II* during a trip to Albany in July of 1980. Two passengers who had been with us had just been called to lunch. One had come in with a question. "Is there a current in the canal?" "Sure," Wiles said. "Which way does it run?" "Downhill." The other had come for stories and had gone out laughing after Wiles told of his great aunt, Roxalanna Druse, the only woman ever hanged in the history of the State of New York. The "pig lady," as the press took to calling her, was strung up from a hook at the rear of the Herkimer court house in 1887. "Seems she got mad at Uncle Charlie one day, so she chopped him up with a cleaver," Wiles said. "Couldn't think of what to do with the body, though, so she tried to feed him to the pigs."

When we were alone again, I asked: "You ever get to thinking you *own* this canal?" The question struck him as stupid. "Oh, yeah. Of course," he said unabashedly. "This is a real ego trip for you, isn't it?" "Sure it is," he said. "No question.

"You know, years ago, we'd tie up in Albany, and

we used to feel kind of embarrassed. We'd tie up under these large ships come up the Hudson to unload Volkswagens or bananas, and you couldn't even see us. But it turns out that the masters of those vessels are so intrigued with a canaller that they get off and come over and ask if they could please come aboard, so the cocktails are usually on our boat."

A crowd of picnickers in the lock park at Whitesboro felt the same tug, smiling and waving at us while *Emita II* descended sixteen feet to the next level of canal. Wiles loved the attention. He returned the greetings.

Not far east of there, a bend in the canal near Sprakers, New York, opened to give us a vision of mountains and woodland. The waterway in that section was cut into the bed of the Mohawk River. We were flanked on the north by Adirondacks, on the south by Catskills. Henry Hudson was right, I mused, though he never knew it; his river *did* lead to the Northwest Passage. "It's such a fucking shame," Wiles said — we could see a mile downstream, and *Emita II* was alone on the water — "anywhere else in the world, a canal like this would be considered a national treasure."

Only the working men on the canal saw it as such. Lock tenders throughout the system, in the face of a limited budget, spent their own money to spruce up their parks and to paint their offices and gear stations and ballards. Brass gleamed everywhere. Some of the men were the fourth family generation to oversee lock passages — some of the very few men in the world, I thought, who in 1980 were doing a job exactly as their great-grandfathers had done it, and with the same equipment, at that. They made most of their replacement parts — they had to. In sixty years, the canal had survived a lot of companies. Those still in business had trouble remembering. Dale Hatch, one chief lock operator, told me he once tried to order a switching circuit from General Electric and had spent hours arguing with an executive, who maintained the company had never produced such a part, despite the fact that it was clearly stamped: "GE."

William Hennessy, transporation commissioner, credited the workers with the fact that the system still worked at all. He called them "perhaps the most dedicated group of civil servants in the world."

One of them, a division superintendent named Dave Conroy, maintained a steam boat — again at personal expense — to survey his domain. He had little hope the canal would see an increased allocation, despite all his lobbying. "Albany thinks we don't know anything out here," he told another reporter. "They think if we knew anything, we'd be in Albany." Conroy said he had almost been relieved, several years earlier, when a section of canal at Bushnell's Basin, near Rochester, had ruptured. "At least it got us some publicity," he said.

In that section, the canal was cut in a ridge, high above the surrounding countryside. Wiles recalled: "They were digging a tunnel under the canal, through the embankment, for cables I think, and the state engineers were there, and everybody's watching," but the engineers' calculation that the tunnel was running level was wrong. "Actually it was going up. It got close to the bottom of the canal and the water started coming in. They saw it was getting bad, so they left, they got out.

"Well, in a thrice, the fucking canal let go. I mean, it dug a hole that was probably 40 feet deep, the whole width of the canal and 150 feet long. It took three houses completely away and damaged maybe another twenty-five. No boats went through, nobody got hurt. There was this one lady in the cellar of her house, and the water came in and broke the wall in. She went right out through the sliding glass doors and wound up in a tree. I was working right on top of the break, eight or nine days before. I'd have been in the lady's living room."

The canal did not drain, of course. Guard gates on either side of the rupture were lowered to isolate that section of Erie. Still, "It got a lot of extra publicity then because there was a question about whether the state was going to fix it. It took maybe a year," he said, for Albany officials to decide.

Even so, Wiles was doubtful that anything would improve were the system turned over to federal operation. Two locks — where Hudson tidewaters met the canal near Albany, and at Black Rock, near Buffalo — were already federal affairs. "Their equipment is newer than anything they've got on the New York canal — large buildings, four or five people at desks, flashing lights, push buttons, special relays. It's a Corps operation. They've got guys with walkie-talkies — it's ludicrous — there's a tower with parapets, then three acres of open ground, then barracks, then the lock. They've got the best fencework in the state there, biggest fence you ever saw with a sign that says "Keep Out!" and "Danger!" — like they're doing something unbelievable in there.

"And the deal is, it doesn't work. When it goes down, they don't know how to fix it. You complain and the guy says, "Do you realize this lock is twenty-five years old?' So I say, 'Do you realize the one up the line is sixty, and it works just lovely?' The one guy chews tobacco, the other can't read or write, and they keep it just fine. The switching is so simple in the New York locks, so perfect, and the care they took is fantastic. I don't like this stuff because it's old; I like it because it works.

"At a New York lock, if there's a problem, I've

seen a guy come out and take a huge electric drill with a wrench-fitting and run the whole lock with the drill. It works just fine." (I later related that story to Transportation Commissioner Hennessy. He was not surprised. "I bet the buy built the drill himself," he said. I checked. He was right.)

Wiles, for some years, had thought of himself as something of a one-man special forces in defense of the Erie Canal. He went to the public hearings. He presumed to represent the historian, the fishermen, the kids, all the people who did not know there *were* any hearings. "You've gotten rid of trains and trolley cars and a lot of stuff you need now and wish you still had. Don't do it again. A single stroke of the axe can end a century of growth," he testified.

When I told Wiles about Nigel Chattey and the project, he considered it only a moment before becoming an unequivocal ICONN-Erie Irregular, even though modernization of the Erie might ruin Mid-Lakes Navigation Ltd., Wiles' packet-boat business.

"Look," he told me, "I'm taking something that's in existence and making a buck on it, and doing it in a neat way. But I'm no dummy. You've got to put everything into perspective. What I do with the canal is what they used to do. What Chattey wants to do is what they *ought* to do."

Besides, Wiles told me, recreational possibilities on the waterway just might be enhanced, were ICONN-Erie properly managed. Chattey certainly hoped so. He proposed, to accompany the modernization, the creation of an unbroken strip of parkland, on both sides of the canal, running from one end of the state to the other.

When *Emitta II* reached Albany that July, Wiles found moored in the harbor a small Brazilian freighter, unloading a cargo of mahogany into a waiting line of

The text on the model reads:

THE ICONN PROJECT
ISLAND COMPLEX OFFSHORE NEW YORK/NEW JERSEY
FIRST STAGE IN DEVELOPMENT OF LNG POLDER COMPLEX
CONCEPT DEVELOPED BY NIGEL CHATTEY ASSOCIATES INC · ICONN DIVISION
COPYRIGHT MARCH 1977, ALL RIGHTS RESERVED

Nigel Chattey with model of ICONN's first polder

The proposed Island Complex Offshore New York & New Jersey

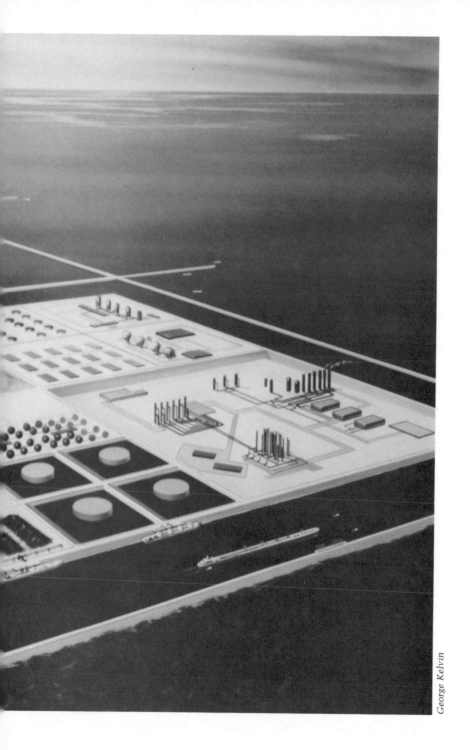

The proposed lock size on a modernized Erie Canal

Nigel Chattey

John Petty

Constantine Sidamon-Eristoff

Francis Coleman

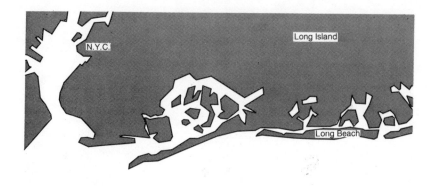

Lower New York Bay

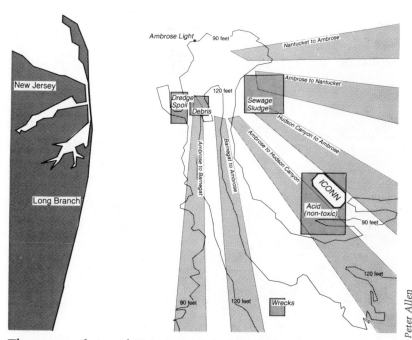

The proposed site of ICONN in relation to shipping lanes, waste
dumps, and depth contours of the Hudson Canyon

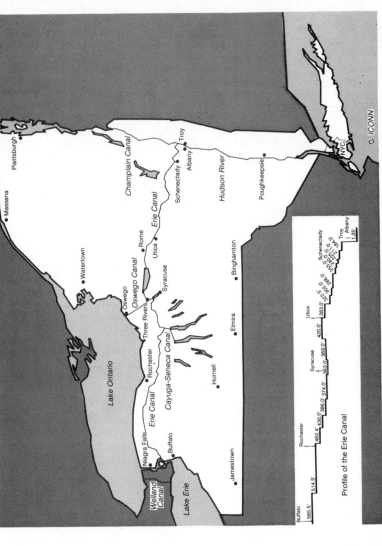

Peter Allen

The State of New York

Profile of the Erie Canal

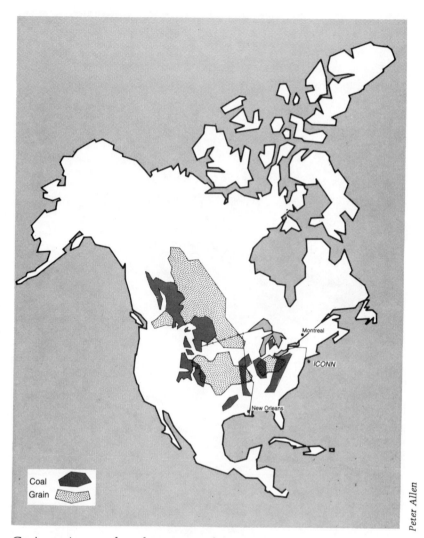

Peter Allen

Grain regions and coal reserves of North America

Chattey at a presentation in Rochester

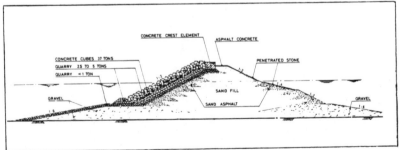

Cross section of sea defense for a dry polder
Cross section of sea defense for a wet polder

Europoort in 1975, before full industrialization

The proposed North Sea Island

"Process of Excavation, Lockport," from Colden's *Memoir*, 1825

"Grain Boat on the Erie Canal," from *America Illustrated*, 1874

"Queer Floating Village in the City of New York," from *Leslie's Weekly*, June 12, 1902

Peter Wiles

James Ehmann

The M/V *Emita II*

James Ehmann

Emita II on an under-utilized, and unnoticed, Erie Canal

An oil barge locking through in 1981

"Anywhere else in the world, a national treasure"

Tom Beardsley

tractor-trailers, all bound for Toronto. He asked around and learned that the stevedoring costs alone came to $23,000. Delivery costs to Toronto would be $500 for each of the fifty or sixty trucks. "So I asked them why they didn't use the canal. They could cut the stevedoring in half and put the whole load on one barge, making the run for maybe $10,000." He did some quick figuring. "They could have saved, what, about $25,000. *Then* they tell me they didn't *know* there was any canal. Jesus."

Wiles went straight to the offices of the New York State Department of Commerce and asked if anybody there kept an eye out for canal-suitable cargoes as vessels approached the Port of Albany. He learned that officials logged goods as they arrived and recorded the means of departure. "Well, that's not *commerce*," he thundered. "By the time it's departed, it's *history*." The functionary with whom he spoke listened politely and fidgeted a little, as if that idea had never before occurred.

"How can they be surprised when tonnages keep going down," he asked me later, "if nobody is out there promoting the goddamned thing?"

"EVEN THOUGH THEY CALLED IT CLINTON'S FOLLIES, I don't think people did it in a sarcastic way," said an imaginative Peter Brennan to the Building and Construction Trades Council of the New York AFL-CIO. "They did it as a way of expressing the good times and prosperous times that the building of the canal meant to the people of the State of New York. When it was being built we had full employment, and not only that, we had happy people. The people had jobs and they weren't jumping out windows, they weren't looking for a quick exit, they weren't on drugs. They had jobs and they could have a good time."

Brennan's fanciful interpretation of history served its purpose. He was president of that labor group in 1980. At its July convention, he introduced Nigel Chattey.

"Now back then, Governor Clinton and those guys didn't have to go to any idiots to ask for approval. That's why the country is so loused up — because we've left so much to idiots who couldn't get out of a phone booth with no door on it. Now, those people have been giving this man a really hard time. I want you to listen to him closely," Brennan said.

And just like that, the two-hundred-member council — a group generally disinclined to sit still for speech-making and occasionally downright rude to speakers — gave Chattey an hour of careful attention as he outlined ICONN-Erie.

With one exception: early in the presentation, while Chattey spoke of the coal fields in the West, one man in the second row began to laugh. Chattey stopped cold. His knuckles went white around the microphone. He strode quickly toward the man, and I half expected him to leap over the table and throttle the fellow. "You, sir! Have you ever worked in a strip mine? No? Well, this might just interest you," he said, sliding neatly back into the presentation. "Production in Eastern mines is 15 tons a man-shift and going down. Production in Western mines is 150 tons. . . ." Everyone's attention was his again, you bet.

("I'm not at all sure that guy was laughing at you," I said later. "I think his friend told him a joke."

"Doesn't matter what he was laughing at," Chattey said. "The others didn't know it wasn't at me. You've got to nip that sort of thing in the bud.")

Brennan returned to the podium when Chattey concluded. "Any questions?" he asked.

"Yeah," someone said. "I live in Tonawanda, and

I got the canal running about three hundred feet in front of my house, and I'm just curious: How much wider would you have to make it?"

"About three hundred feet," someone else in the crowd answered.

Everyone laughed then, Chattey included. The group was his.

"Now gentlemen," Brennan said, "I know by your silence and your applause afterwards that you have the same response to this project that I do. As this was going on I could hear the heartbeats of our operating engineers, and the laborers, when they saw this job going, and Jimmy Bishop imagining all those pipes and things, and then the pneumatic tubing and the steam-fitters start to get excited, and the carpenters are already planning to put in all the protection walls and the forms and so forth — you see, this is something for everybody. Even our friends in the Glaziers would be putting in some glass, and we'd be helping to break it so they could keep working.

"It *is* exciting. We hope this is the start, that we take the lead here, because you are the people that must build this. I would like to say to Nigel now, and let's see if you agree with me: Nigel, we're going to build this damn thing with you, and we're going to do it as quick as we can." And then, to the members: "Am I right?" If I was any judge of applause, he was.

"Brothers," said Brennan's vice president, Ed Boyle, "this man is offering us the biggest job we'll see in our lifetimes. If we don't get behind him and show full support, then shame on us." Before the day was out, the council endorsed the ICONN-Erie studies, and a month later Brennan and Boyle won the endorsement and, presumably, the lobbying strength of the entire New York AFL-CIO.

Other labor leaders were already in formation.

Two weeks before the Brennan convention in Albany, Patrick Sullivan, the longshoreman, returned from the convention of his union's Maritime Division with formal and enthusiastic approbation of the Chattey project. Sullivan and the Reverend James Healy, a dockfront priest and the chairman of the state's Labor Mediation Board, had been lobbying on their own for a new American canal from Lake Erie to the East ever since 1959, when completion of the St. Lawrence Seaway rerouted Great Lakes traffic and economically all but ruined their hometown, the city of Buffalo. They had been mad at the Albany leadership for a very long time.

"We've spent more money on the Love Canal in the last two years than on the barge canal in the last fifteen," Sullivan said.

"Nothing happens," Healy joined in. "We've had commitments from Carey, when he's running for office. We've had Senator Moynihan on the record over and over again. Nothing ever happens."

Frustrated in their own efforts, when these two heard of the Chattey plan they became project patriots. In the summer of 1980 they designed a demonstration project for barging grain from Buffalo to New York, hoping to show, by 1981 or 1982, that even the old canal could compete effectively with the only alternative, Conrail. Few New Yorkers would be surprised if they succeeded. Conrail was the most labor-intensive railroad in America, its rates were the highest, and it certainly ranked among the least efficient. Flour dealers there told me it took thirty days for a hopper car to get to New York City and back. Sullivan figured a barge could make the round trip in ten.

"I'm an agitator," Healy said. "I move across the state in my work on the board, and I talk to a lot of people, and I push this thing. And everybody always thinks it's great. I was talking to this one guy in Albany, and the guy comes up with, 'Yeah, but if you widen the canal, what happens to the deer? How are they going to get across?' That's really the *only* negative reaction I've heard.

"But how do you motivate people? How do you overcome inertia? The problem is it is much easier *not* to do something. You go around and you don't find people who are opposed to ICONN, they just don't know about it. How do you get them to the boiling point?"

Sullivan interrupted with an idea. A lot of his longshoremen were unemployed, a lot more were angry about the dearth of opportunities. The Seaway had cost Buffalo 50 percent of all waterfront jobs "and 80 percent of the good ones," Sullivan said. "There's an awful lot of energy they have to expend. If we had the proper project, the proper goal, we could muster a tremendous amount of support. Our members could vent their pent-up energy on something positive.

"Take a look at history," he continued. "Revolutions always begin on the waterfront. We could make this a crusade."

While I was in Buffalo with Sullivan and Healy, an attorney named Francis Coleman was with Nigel Chattey in Washington, in executive offices at the Department of Housing and Urban Development. Coleman, who worked for the City of Rochester, had learned of ICONN-Erie in a newspaper story and immediately volunteered his services. He arranged for Chattey to brief an old acquaintance, Robert Embry, assistant secretary of HUD. Embry loved the plan and said $1 million in HUD monies might be granted to study the project's economic impact on cities.

John Petty recognized that Chattey's efforts to-

ward building support were working, and he soon
thereafter decided that 1980 was no time to abandon
the bank's involvement.

"You get things like this primarily by working at
them," Petty told me. "If you read history and biographies, you find that things get done through persistence. That's probably the most distinguishing characteristic, more than brilliance. If you know where you
want to go, and you're determined to get there, and
you stick at it — and you get bounced down, you get
trod upon, you get kicked in the nuts, but you go back
at it and you keep at it — then you will prevail."

Petty then increased the bank's contribution to
ICONN-Erie by 50 percent, to $15,000 a month.

All of that was splendid news for Chattey and the
project, of course, but I was suddenly troubled. James
Healy, the dock-front priest, had voiced a concern
which I had considered dimly for some time but
which, after speaking with him, came solidly to the
fore. By then I had spoken formally with more than a
hundred people, most of them people who mattered,
and I had discussed the plan informally with hundreds
more. I outlined it in barest terms one night for a cop
who spent his off-hours running a sandwich shop, and
for an hour afterwards *he* explained the potentials to
me.

Sure, there were opponents to the idea. Some were
reporters, who were cynics by training. Others were
lower-level government workers I had to talk with to
earn interviews with their bosses. But among the people whose support was crucial, I found very few
ICONN-Erie adversaries. Those I did find were more
or less ignorant of the details of the plan; and none
of them seemed to be in active opposition — out
there actually fighting to stop the advance of ICONN-
Erie.

So where was the problem? Why, after five years of promotion, did the studies go unfunded? It occurred to me coldly one night that I had yet to speak to a single informed individual who thought Chattey's plan, viewed on the merits, was in fact a *bad* idea. That began to bother me a lot.

VI

No ordinary intelligence would concoct such a plan. No typical energy nor everyday faith would pursue it. It therefore seemed to me only reasonable to expect that a man possessing such characteristics would be uncommon in other ways as well — not the least of them being sheer force of personality. As Eristoff once suggested, that may have been part of the problem. If Chattey was a team player at all, his skills were unrefined.

"Nigel would antagonize people," said Bernard Lawson, Dyson's admiralty lawyer. "I don't mean to take anything from him. The guy busted his ass. But it was like, you know, if you weren't on his side, you were *the enemy*. I went to one of his presentations after our deal folded, and if you ever wanted to see icicles, boy, I'm telling you, you saw them then. He didn't even come up to me. He wanted nothing to do with me at all. Now, if you're the kind of guy who comes up with an idea like this, then maybe that's the kind of guy you're going to be. But I'll tell you:

I've always maintained that the beast wasn't the people we were going to with the idea, it was the guy who was advocating it."

Some other opinions:

"His deportment, which was naturally dignified, was considered by many to proceed from arrogance and a sense of superiority."

"He was perhaps too pleased to hear his own praises."

"He was too reckless in his remarks about gentlemen who differed with him in opinion." (Soon after I recorded that remark, Chattey blasted the leadership of the state during a televised press conference in Albany, proclaiming them "a bunch of nervous Nellies.")

"It was against his character to be subordinate to any man."

"His objects were always magnificent, his ends were always such as evidenced an elevated and lofty mind, but he did not seem to be aware of the necessity of providing ways and means to accomplish those ends."

Any number of people told me such things about Chattey — but none of the sentiments quoted above referred to him. They were observations about De Witt Clinton, made by Senator J.D. Hammond and Dr. David Hosak, two of Clinton's life-long friends.

Clinton antagonized people. Members of the opposing Federalist Party, as was their lot, opposed him. Members of his own Republican Party did not trust him; they believed he was in secret league with the Federalists. Clinton was not a team player.

His appearance intimidated many: He was slender, his brown hair was brushed back from a high forehead, he was well over six feet tall — an extraordinary stature for those days. And his conversation, drawing from wide-ranging expertise, overawed many others. By avocation, Clinton was well versed in zoology, botany, mineralogy, ornithology, icthyology, herpetology and so on; by profession he was a lawyer, a soldier, a philosopher, a polite scholar, a criminal judge, a university regent, a statesman. People who could deal with all that while keeping their own egos intact were nonetheless apt to find him "overbearing, outspoken, impatient and brilliant," Hosak wrote. All in all, he was an easy man to dislike.

Publicly, Clinton proclaimed opponents of his plan to be "obscure pettifoggers," "miserable drivellers," "men stupid to a degree approaching idiocy." At one rally he called Colonel John Swartwout, who was an Aaron Burr cohort, "a liar, a scoundrel and a villain, a dishonest man wholly incompetent to judge between right and wrong, a knave and a fool." (Swartwout demanded satisfaction, and in the subsequent duel five shots were fired. Clinton was not wounded. Swartwout, who was hit twice, pleaded that the contest continue, but Clinton allowed as how he had grown tired of shooting his adversary, so he declined.)

To varying degrees and for various reasons, Clinton's plan for an Erie Canal was challenged by Federalists, Burrites, Livingstonians, Martling Men, Madisonites, Lewisites, Coodies, Jacobinites, Bucktails and the boys from Tammany Hall. Personality and politics clearly played a role. None other than Martin Van Buren himself was solely responsible for delaying the start of construction for more than a year — not because he opposed the canal, but because he opposed De Witt Clinton.

That Clinton was able eventually to overpower such an army of opponents was due largely to his ability to muster the support of the public at large, and he did that by two means: the power of his position as governor of New York; and the power of the press.

His position as governor gave him access to masses of people at assemblies across the state: "This canal, as to the extent of its route, as to the countries which it connects, and as to the consequences which it will produce, is without parallel in the history of mankind. The commerce of the immense extent of country [will be] yours forever, and to such an incalculable amount as would baffle all conjecture to conceive."

The press gave him the chance to appear to be a far larger force than he was. Among other things, Clinton was a sneak. He regularly wrote essays to newspapers under fictitious names to extoll the wonders of the plan. Twice he wrote great series of them, under the pen name "Atticus" in 1816, while legislators debated whether or not to build the thing; and as "Hibernicus" in 1820, while some lawmakers conspired to abort the plan and others engaged in outright sabotage of the works already in place.

Atticus told New Yorkers that the canal was an object "of such magnitude that even the blind may see it," and that "New York City will stand when the canal is finished unrivaled by any city on the face of the earth."

Hibernicus got a lot more specific. "The moment coal is discovered, what sources of wealth will immediately be developed!" he wrote. (Chattey would love this, I thought.) "I am so anxious for the discovery of coal, in order to promote the prosperity of this growing country, that I can hardly turn my eyes to any other subject. If America will not stand on its own legs and rely on its own exertions, what can it expect but supercilious arrogance and contemptuous assumption by foreign countries."

(Love it? Hell, he should *use* it, I thought. The

same week I read that, Saudi Arabians impudently asked the U.S. State Department to block a Public Service Broadcasting presentation of "Death of a Princess," a film they found offensive. PBS ran the show anyway. Two days later, the price of Saudi oil went up again.)

As Hibernicus, Clinton alleged himself to be a European canal engineer on tour in the United States, lending both objective and technical credibility to his remarks. He then made his case at length.

There was economy: "Suppose that 100,000 farmers should each save twenty dollars a year in gypsum, and ten dollars in salt, by means of a canal. Here would be an annual savings of three millions of dollars, a sum more than sufficient in two years to make the whole canal."

There was efficiency: "One horse on a canal can draw as much as sixty on a road. When the great six-horse teams are banished from use, [imagine how] the roads will improve."

There was national self-sufficiency: "Why should Americans seek for the materials of manufactures in foreign countries? It is as absurd as for a man to look for happiness in taverns, bagnios and gambling houses, when he has a lovely wife, promising children, and every comfort at home." The canal would "check the consumption of foreign merchandise," which in those days included immense quantities of iron and coal, "thus enriching the treasury. America already suffers by foreign capitalists drawing from her resources large sums."

And morality: On the frontier — Ohio and beyond — the settlers, "all being agriculturists, producing the same thing, there is no incentive for them to produce more." To decide on the canal was to decide "whether the population of the Great Lakes will be civilized or savage," he wrote, because only "the opening of a market for grain will prevent its conversion into ardent spirits — the curse of morals, and the bane of domestic felicity. Whiskey now sells [in Ohio] for 18 cents a gallon. What a temptation to inebriety! A man may keep constantly drunk for three or four shillings a week."

And wealth: "Our natural advantages are so transcendent that it is in our power to put competition at defiance. As all other communications are impeded by mountains, the only formidable rivals of New York are New Orleans and Montreal, the former relying on the Mississippi, the latter on the St. Lawrence."

And politics: "Nature has poured down her benefits on this favored land, and the mighty genius of enterprise has brought them to perfection. But alas! Faction is at work to undermine the boon of heaven. Is it not extraordinary that wretches should be encouraged to instill poison into the public mind against it, and to destroy its embankments? By the bye, can you tell me why accidents in the bursting of embankments and mill dams occur more frequently in the night time than in the day? Are they owing to a greater pressure of the atmosphere?"

And geopolitics: "However serious the fears which have been entertained of a dismemberment of the Union by collisions between North and South, it is to be apprehended that the most imminent danger lies in another direction, and that a line of separation may be eventually drawn between the Atlantic and the western states, unless they are cemented by a common, an ever-acting and a powerful interest." The canal "will form an imperishable cement of connection, an indissoluble bond of union."

(Some prophesy, there. But for the Erie Canal, settlers in such states as Ohio, Michigan, Indiana and

Illinois would have relied on commercial connections via the Mississippi River, and historians have suggested that their political leanings would have tended in the same direction. Had the Midwest thus allied with the South, the Union might not have survived the war between its states.)

And even romance: "Sometimes I think I am in the region of enchantment, and that the magical operations of eastern fiction are acted over again in this country," he wrote.

All of which combined to do the trick. Clinton's talent for using the media inspired so much popular support that his political opponents, if they hoped to keep their jobs through reelection, could no longer reject the plan out-of-hand.

Two things bear mention here: First, I do not think Nigel Chattey ever fully realized how similar his arguments were to those of De Witt Clinton. That they were similar was not surprising, though. Their plans were the same. The only real difference was that Clinton envisioned prosperity born of the development of new lands in the West; Chattey hoped to exploit Western lands, too, but the "new land" he was counting on would lie to the east.

And a second: While the media served Clinton's efforts to a significant degree, Nigel Chattey had no such luck.

THE PRESS changed considerably between Clinton's time and Chattey's. The press had learned ethics, or tried to, and one of the primary tenets of those media which tried the hardest was that the appearance of championing any cause, by paying too much attention to it in news columns, was to be avoided at all costs, avoided like rat bite. Newspapers were terrified of accusations of advocacy — or, as working journalists called it, "puffery."

There were several ways to head off such accusations. The most common was to attribute absolutely everything in a story to a "credible" source, or failing that, to an official one.

Spokesmen for government would do, as anything done by politicians was journalistic fair game. So would spokesmen for industry, where any activity was reportable as "business news." Had a thing like ICONN-Erie come out of any stray bureaucracy or industrial mediocrity, and had the public relations department in whichever played its cards right, reporters would have flocked to the story. By 1980, ICONN-Erie would have been a household word. But editors hesitated giving major coverage to such a plan when a lone, more or less unconnected individual was the source of credibility. They all found themselves asking the same prerequisite question: Who the hell is Nigel Chattey? The answer posed the first problem. In the scheme of things — certainly where the power structure was concerned — Nigel Chattey was nobody.

(Consider this: the *New York Times* gave the story about Governor Carey dying his hair from white to chestnut brown about as much space as was allotted to ICONN-Erie. Editors there gave the story about Carey's new marriage at least twice as much space.)

Many of the best newspapers, like the *Wall Street Journal*, refused to touch the ICONN-Erie tale until there was some objective proof, beyond Chattey's assertions, that the project was possible. .

Others, where editors believed the idea important enough to print, did their best to soften controversy by presenting pieces written at the base level of skepticism, or pieces grossly underplayed, or both. The former was evidenced in the *Rochester Times-Union's* ICONN-Erie story, which led with Transportation Commissioner William Hennessy's opinion that the plan would not work. At the *New York Times*, meanwhile, my ICONN-Erie story was run with neither maps nor artist's conceptions. Of the fifteen hundred words I filed, five hundred were cut, all of them explaining the plan, while the findings of the soon-to-be-described-as "not very meaningful" Roger Creighton Erie Canal study remained intact. I had thought the piece would make a perfect page one Sunday feature; it ran toward the middle of a Sunday second section.

All of which posed a second problem, the problem of chickens and eggs. To win funding for his studies, Chattey needed governmental support. To win governmental support he needed to generate public support. To win public support, he needed to educate the public by means of ongoing media coverage. But to win ongoing coverage, he needed some greater credibility than his own. That of any of the governmental leaders he was trying to sway would have done nicely. But any bureaucrat would have risked a great deal — his whole career, perhaps — had he gone out on a limb and drawn the fire and honchoed ICONN-Erie. Most suffered what the networks' Kalb brothers called "CYA Syndrome." Your first priority as a public servant was to Cover Your Ass.

A third problem, and a fourth. The project was technical, and reporters, some of them, were ignorant. In my old paper, the *Post-Standard,* one writer noted that ICONN was proposed "to lie downwind of the prevailing winds." It seemed to me the same could be said of every location on Earth.

Moreover, the plan was simply too involved to be explained within the confines of a standard news story. The Buffalo *Courier-Express,* the Rochester *Democrat & Chronicle* and the Gannett Westchester Group all realized that and used ICONN-Erie as a cover story in the Sunday magazines. Chattey and Eristoff realized it, too. Charlotte Curtis, editor of the Op-Ed page of the *New York Times*, had long since offered to run an essay about ICONN-Erie, but she limited the piece to 750 words, about three double-spaced typewritten pages. Impossible, both men agreed. They decided no description was preferable to partial description.

And if the story would not fit in a printed report, there was no way it could be done in a two-minute news burst on TV. Several public broadcasting stations, including WCNY in Syracuse, therefore featured Chattey now and again on "Issues and Answers"-style programing. WCNY even hoped to make a documentary about ICONN-Erie and had shot much of the necessary footage but, like most public stations, was in fiscal trouble and could not find funding for a finished production.

The fifth problem was probably the worst. Beyond the simple existence of the idea, what in all of this was news? News was what *had* happened, not what *might* happen. I once suggested to Chattey that he could get all the coverage he wanted by involving himself in a series of spectacular car crashes and telling reporters of ICONN-Erie while firemen worked to cut him out of the wreckage.

Where less sensational stories were concerned, it seemed clear that problems were demonstrable, hence newsworthy; solutions were theoretical, hence not. To test that hypothesis, I scanned the *New York Times* for fourteen months. I chose the *Times* for two reasons: first, it was perhaps the most staid of the major newspapers in America and was therefore among the most credible; and second, it just happened to be the paper I typically read. During the monitoring period:

• The paper published 292 stories about problems directly addressed by the ICONN-Erie thesis. For example, there were 93 reports concerning oil price and supply. They told me things like this: OPEC price up by one-third; Iranian price up by 6 percent; Kuwait, Algeria, Libya and Venezuela reduce production; Saudi production increases; price at the pump drops; domestic production declines; Indonesia and Malaysia raise prices. And on and on and on. I claim no expertise in these matters, but it seemed to me that all this mass of reportage was saying was this: when prices go up, consumption goes down; when consumption decreases, production increases to create an oversupply; the oversupply lowers prices a little, which inspires increased consumption; with consumption back up, production decreases to create a shortage which — following the laws of supply and demand — drives the price a lot higher. Then the process repeats itself. No surprises in that, I thought.

• The paper published 74 reports about matters tangentially related to all the problems — for example, a discussion about whether or not the 1980 Census was accurate; the opinions of several congressmen who thought Washington was biased against the Northeast; the success of Tenneco in locating natural gas in the Baltimore Canyon. Things like that.

• And the paper published 31 stories about solutions of one kind or another. The sources cited in all but two were spokesmen for government or industry.

Three or four of the stories described major efforts to meet specific needs. The best example was the report about the completion of the Louisiana Offshore Oil Terminal. Several delved into the trials and tribulations of President Carter's Synthetic Fuels Program. Most of the rest explained plans which were modest in the extreme — a proposal to build new tourist attractions over rotting sections of Manhattan waterfront, for example.

The final tally: Of the 31 "solution" stories — and of the 397 in all with some bearing on the Chattey plan — only 2 dealt with ideas vast enough in scope to solve multiple problems at once. Both were about ICONN-Erie.

The second story was 800 words long when I filed it. Editors cut it to 250 and placed it so inconspicu- ously that, though we both knew it was scheduled to appear, Chattey and I missed it independently on our first scannings of that day's edition.

The third piece the paper published about ICONN-Erie supported my contentions. In a letter to the editor, William Boyd of Poughkeepsie com- plained: "While an occasional newspaper article on this project has appeared, the news media of the Northeast (unlike their more astute rivals in the Sun Belt) have not been publicizing the potential of a ma- jor public work that could totally revitalize this re- gion."

The *Times*, of course, was not alone in that lack of publicity. If anything, by mentioning the idea at all in its columns, the paper had done more to educate the public than had most media, and Roger Starr's ed- itorial was arguably the finest accolade the plan had yet received from the fourth estate. Nevertheless I sensed a certain irony. At the time I was monitoring its pages, the *Times* began publication of cute little cartooned advertisements designed to increase circu- lation. One of them read: "These times demand more solutions. These times demand *The Times*."

TANTALIZING PROSPECTS for the project — the lack of substantial media coverage notwithstanding — ap- peared in quick succession in July of 1980. Two days after the state AFL-CIO endorsed the studies, Chattey received a call from aides to New York's secretary of state. They asked him to come to Albany the next day to apply for a $150,000 economic development grant, which would go toward the ICONN-Erie feasibility test. "They're just trying to cover their ass," Chattey told me. He agreed to go, though.

An hour after that call, an aide to Robert Embry, the deputy secretary at the Department of Housing and Urban Development with whom Chattey had discussed a study grant of $1 million, phoned to ask that a dozen copies of the project prospectus be sent at once, by air freight, to the Carter White House. (To maintain the project's non-partisan pose, Chattey then prepared a duplicate package and sent it, through a well-placed supporter, to candidate Reagan's camp.)

That same day, a column by Michael McManus appeared in dozens of newspapers around the nation. Embry had given the story to McManus and was quoted as saying: "Solutions of this magnitude are needed to turn around the basic trends facing the North. This may not be the answer, but it deserves serious study." Embry had also met with the editorial board of the *New York Times* to lobby for another editorial, when the grant was announced.

If Chattey was a visionary, he had called those developments closely enough, two weeks before. Each Thursday, when their schedules would allow it, Chattey and Petty and Eristoff met to discuss the project's progress. Following the July 3 session, Chattey and Eristoff hung around the Marine Midland tower to chat.

"You know, I am at last convinced that we will be funded," Chattey told his partner, "not necessarily for reasons I expected we would be, nor even for reasons that we should. Looking back on it," he said to Eristoff, "you were dead right to structure it this way. I was always impatient with this process, but you were dead right."

By then, the formal endorsements for ICONN-Erie had come not only from several dozen industrial and commercial groups, and a dozen more agencies of government — Ernest Bower's Office of Deepwater Ports, for example — but from a whole slew of New York State senators and assemblymen. One of each, of different parties, had gone so far as to prepare legislation authorizing legislative grants of $100,000 or so to the ICONN-Erie studies. They were waiting for Chattey to sense that the time was right to introduce the bills.

"Connie has moved us up on both sides of the aisle in both chambers," Chattey said to me. "I was impatient as hell at the process, I'm the first to admit it — I lean more toward shock tactic — but I have to say now, having watched, that Connie was right. Now we're in a position to dive out of the sun if we have to."

Eristoff was equally fond of metaphors. "A good chess player uses his knights as well," he said.

"I'll tell you," Chattey replied, "we may well now be in for a Nantucket sleigh ride."

"A Nantucket sleigh ride?" Eristoff asked.

"Do you mean that this Asiatic cavalryman has to tell you, an Easterner, what *that* is?"

I could not resist. "It has to do with having all the line that's attached to your harpoon play out," I said, "so that nothing is left between you and the whale but the tension."

"And you will notice," Chattey said, "that the whale has turned out to be an order-of-magnitude larger than the one we at first thought we'd hit."

So two weeks later, with the union endorsements in hand, with the bank promising continued support, with the project under consideration in the White House, with $1 million from HUD looking quite likely, with fresh stories appearing in the press, and with even the State of New York offering funds, Chattey at last believed that the huge rock he had been rolling had reached the crest. "It's so refreshing," he told me. "For years all anyone said was that I should be pushing it faster. Now I've got all these little Sisyphuses pushing all these little rocks, and all I have to do is to tell them which way." The metaphor was catchy, but not quite correct, as things turned out.

At the time, though, he thought he deserved a break, so an hour after the call from Embry's people, he went out to play in his garden. Tension and overexertion overcame him there. While pulling weeds in a flower bed, muscles in his back let go. The pain was awful.

Maria Chattey was beside herself with anger when she learned he nonetheless intended to attend the Albany meeting, only half a day hence. No one else could do an effective presentation, he told her. "How long," she demanded of me, "can one man be expected to carry this weight all alone?" I had no answer. Chattey was still the big Sisyphus.

The next morning, he was effectively crippled, unable to bend at the waist, only barely able to walk. He somehow got himself dressed, though, and we loaded him into a nest of pillows in the back deck of his Nova, then headed for Albany. En route, he filled out the preliminary grant request while lying on his back, writing on the roof of the car.

Representatives of the departments of State, Commerce, Environmental Conservation and Energy, the Power Authority and the offices of the governor and the lieutenant governor allotted fifteen minutes for the session. They questioned Chattey for twelve times that long, and he answered reflexively, concentrating on keeping a straight face against his pain. I milled around outside the room, eavesdropping. Many of the questions seemed to me less requests for en-

lightenment than probes for excuses for this department, or that one, to stay clear of the project.

"Good God," Chattey said, exiting the session.
"Oh my Good God Father . . . this *infernal* war with
lawyers. I must say it was amusing to watch twelve
top hands of government mull for three hours over a
$150,000 grant," which, where the ICONN-Erie stud-
ies were concerned, was peanuts. Chattey thought only
one of the people in attendance had known what he
was talking about. The grant, he said, was apt to be a
lot more trouble than it was worth.

Chattey found the prospect of crawling back into
the cluster of pillows, in the middle of downtown Albany, quite embarrassing, so he said his back was better — he was lying — and insisted on taking the wheel.
Still one hundred miles from Irvington, he recalled
having left the gas-cap key at home, so he reckoned
from the gauge and his car's typical mileage per gallon
that we might make it to the Harriman exit of the
New York State Thruway. From a rest area, he phoned
his wife and asked that she meet us there with gasoline, and the key.

"And it is always good to have a contingency
plan," he said when we were back on the road, "so if
we don't make it, we'll pull over, walk to the nearest
pub and get blind drunk."

The gas-gauge needle lay motionless on dead
empty for ten minutes before we finally made it. Maria
Chattey was astonished to find her man driving despite his indisposition. "You know," she said to me,
both annoyed at and proud of the tenacity, "you just
can't kill a weed."

By the time we reached Irvington, the wild opti-
mism Chattey had felt the day before was gone.
Whatever energy had been left to him before the state
session was sapped. I had seen him first crest, then

crater, in the space of twenty-four hours. Suddenly he believed none of the pending initiatives would succeed. (And as it happened, whether through self-fulfilling prophesy or not, he was right.)

"But I don't regret having jumped around like a madman, having run around like a three-ringed dingbat all these years," Chattey said as we each sipped a drink in his living room, washing the miles away. "Sometimes I walk around my ten-by-ten downstairs and I just want to cry. I hope we don't have to have a bloody disaster before the inevitability of this logic sequence becomes obvious to people."

Chattey imagined plenty of disastrous possibilities. Many were purely economic; many were matters of life and death. As we spoke, unemployment — inarguably worst in the Midwest and Northeast — stood at its highest levels since the post-World War II recession. Along with the coal miners, steelworkers, auto workers and the rest, the number included 40,000 people laid off by the shipbuilding industry, people who were not making industrial barges for Chattey's island nor transport barges for Clinton's Ditch. At the same time, the New York Metropolitan Area was suffering business failures at four times the rate of any other metropolitan region in America. At the same time, productivity in the United States declined by the second largest percentage in the nation's history. And inflation showed no sign of slackening; at the current rate, a 1980 dollar would be worth nine cents by the year 2000. The very day we spoke, the National Bureau of Economic Research, after an extensive study, declared that the nation was in a recession. That made all the front pages, but I doubt it was news to anyone.

Taken together, most of the thirty-one major stories about such things, published in the *New York*

Times during my fourteen-month monitoring period said simply this: bad inflation meant investors had no money to invest; therefore there was no rise in productivity; that made for worse inflation, which made for a weaker dollar; therefore OPEC prices rose, because they were based on the value of American currency; and higher OPEC prices generated higher inflation. Then the cycle repeated itself. No surprises.

Almost everyone agreed that one way to throw ourselves clear of the spiral was to vigorously exploit American coal reserves, both to reduce oil imports and to achieve, through exports, a favorable balance of trade with the rest of the world community. The MIT World Coal Study, which laid to rest forever the short-sighted studies of coal movement potential that had so plagued the Chattey project, reached a conclusion "devastating in its simplicity," Chattey said. This was it:

"A massive effort to expand facilities for the production, transport and use of coal is urgently required to provide for even moderate economic growth in the world between now and the year 2000. Without such increases, the outlook is bleak.

"The public and private enterprises concerned must act cooperatively and promptly, if this is to be achieved. Governments can help in particular by providing the confidence and stability required for investment decisions, by eliminating delays in licensing, by establishing clear and stable environmental standards, and by facilitating the growth of free and competitive international trade."

Increasing the use of Western coal had been the rhetorical answer to the threat of another oil boycott through the Nixon, Ford and Carter administrations, but the MIT study demonstrated the dollar-and-cents possibility: coal could become America's single largest source of foreign exchange. Even with the cost of scrubbers included, $60 worth of coal produced as much energy as $165 worth of oil. America held the Btu equivalent of at least *two* Persian Gulf oil regions, and the U.S. Geological Survey estimated that for every ton of coal already mapped, another lay awaiting discovery. Lots of people got very excited there for a while. The *New York Times* began running editorials with headlines like "Americans as Saudis." One *Times* reporter noted, however, that whenever people in the know spoke of the wealth to be earned from coal exports, the word "potential" was always used as a modifier.

"You haven't sold it until you can get it out of the country," a buyer from France told the President's Interagency Coal Export Task Force. France planned to increase its coal use five times over by 1990; the Japanese planned a fifty-fold increase. "But we cannot be tied to you by long-term contracts if you do not have the port facilities to move the coal," said the Frenchman, Philippe Julienne, "and your railroads are saying that they will not build the piers without the contracts." Another chicken, another egg.

(Chattey had another theory. Much of the Western coal resource was owned by Indians and the federal government. But coal companies, which had the most to gain were the supplies to move, owned only 12 percent — less than was owned by railroads. Those concerns with perhaps the most to lose were the resource developed — oil and natural gas companies — held fully 45 percent of the coal lands, and these owners were doing quite nicely, thank you, without selling coal. During the five years before the first Arab oil embargo, oil company profits never exceeded 10 percent; in the year of the embargo, they averaged 70 percent.)

In fact, as of July, 1980, not a single U.S. coal producer had a long-term export agreement. The export facility itself was lacking. Hopper cars of the Norfolk & Western Railroad and the Chessie System, thousands upon thousands of them, awaited unloading for weeks on end because of port congestion at Hampton Roads. Chattey had flown over that port during his last trip to Washington. Colliers waiting their turns to load at the piers "look from the air like a World War II invasion fleet," he said.

Senator John Warner of Virginia then told the President's task force, "If nothing is done about this apparent breakdown in our coal transportation network, America will forfeit a multi-billion-dollar business." The forfeit had already begun. South Africa's exports had risen from two million tons in 1973 to twenty-nine million tons in 1980, while America's had not even doubled.

Carl Bagge, executive director of the National Coal Association, said, "It's going to take us another ten years, and maybe another war, to get serious about this."

Improvements were under way. The Consolidation Coal Company planned a new terminal at Baltimore. At Newport News, the Chessie System reopened an inactive pier. Seaboard Coast Line Railroads planned to build a new $50 million export facility at Savannah, Georgia. And the Army Corps proposed dredging the channels at Hampton Roads and New Orleans to depths of fifty or fifty-five feet. All those improvements, however, stood simply to meet the demands of the present efficiently. The future was another question altogether.

Consider this: the President's Interagency Coal Export Task Force estimated that by 1985, 8 percent of the coal ships in the world would exceed 150,000 deadweight tons; by 1995, 22 percent. They would be the most cost-effective. Yet such ships would draw between sixty and seventy feet of water, too much to enter even modernized ports of Hampton Roads and New Orleans. Still, the Corps lobbied for those improvements. Many Northeastern and Midwestern congressmen charged that the Corps' preferences stemmed essentially from regional bias, and their arguments included this interesting fact: In 1980, the Army Corps of Engineers spent more money in each of the states of Louisiana, Alabama, Texas and California than it did in the eighteen Northwestern and Midwestern states combined.

In New York, meanwhile, the Port Authority completed a study which indicated that perhaps a new coal terminal on the waterfront would be a good idea. Another study would be needed to figure out where to put it, of course, and another to figure out how to move coal to it. Just then, antiquated railroad infrastructure prevented unit train deliveries anywhere in the metropolitan area. Just then, New York's piddling share of the coal export market survived on deliveries by truck to Port Newark.

So: Were there alternatives to ICONN-Erie for moving coal to market? The St. Lawrence Seaway was not an option; it already neared capacity traffic, and it was fed by the Welland Canal between lakes Erie and Ontario, which would reach capacity sooner. Nor was the Mississippi River an option to any great extent; like the St. Lawrence, it would overload soon without major modernization. (The Army Corps of Engineers loved the Mississippi River. Earlier, the Corps had tried to slip past congressional eyes a $6 billion allocation to build new locks on the river, which Army officials justified under a 1909 law designed only to pay for maintenance.)

And Conrail, the Northeastern freight railroad, was certainly no option. When the federal government created Conrail in 1976 from the wreckage of the Penn Central and a number of other failed railroads, some curious deals were made. One was to guarantee lifetime jobs to the system's 45,000 workers. Thus, in 1980, Conrail operated with 4,600 excess firemen and brakemen; another 1,700 workers, who were laid off because they were either no good or in the way, continued to draw salaries averaging $29,000 a year. In 1980, this earned for Conrail the distinction of paying $1.15 in expenses for every $1 of revenue.

The option most widely discussed in 1980 was to build a pipeline from somewhere in the Midwest all the way to the East Coast, through which to pump coal slurry, a syrupy black goo, half water, half pulverized carbon. But there were two small problems with the plan. One was that railroads simply refused to yield rights-of-way to pipeline companies. The other was that there was not sufficient water out there for use in making slurry. Already, the water table in several states was dropping at a faster rate than it was being refilled, and even as Chattey and I spoke, a seven-month drought had left the Mississippi River running at its lowest levels in history. Trains of grain and coal barges were bottoming out and breaking up near Memphis in a channel depth of seven feet.

"I can't even watch the news anymore," Chattey said, "without seeing *something* the project could cure."

Plans for domestic coal use were faring about as well as those for exports. Back in March of 1980, President Carter had introduced legislation to convert 107 Northeastern utilities from oil- to coal-firing. The bill contained the offer of $4 billion in federal funds to pay half the costs of conversion. But the utilities, hoping to spend as little of their own money as possible, successfully lobbied a reduction in the number of targeted plants to eighty, and an increased subsidy, $4.2 billion, to boot. Then lawmakers from the Sun Belt states refused to vote for the plan unless there was something in it for their utilities, too, so they demanded that they be freed from a federal order to ban by 1990 the use of precious natural gas as a boiler fuel. Such was the nature of American politics. The net effect of the compromise plan was to increase coal use by 33 million tons a year in the Northeast, which was good, and to decrease it by 40 million tons a year in the South, more than cancelling the benefit. The bill fell dead of its own weight. The coal association's Carl Bagge called it "the most complicated monstrosity of any bill I've ever prayed over." The *New York Times*, editorializing on the defeat, concluded that "Sheik Yamani remains the most influential voice in American Energy Policy."

If there *was* such a thing as an American Energy Policy, it was promising to do for the United States what the potato famine did for Ireland. In a single week, one utility operating on Tampa Bay was ordered by the U.S. Department of Energy to switch from oil to coal, and the other utility operating on Tampa Bay was ordered by the U.S. Environmental Protection Agency to switch from coal to oil. Another utility, New England Electric, fought with the EPA for five years to win permission to convert a single plant from oil to coal. Then the EPA turned around and used the New England Electric conversion as a stellar example of enlightened administration energy policy at work.

Yet another federal program, designed to inspire increased coal production by small companies, made $750 million available to modernize facilities. But the guidelines for eligibility were so unrealistic (one was that a company needed a ten-year sales contract in order to qualify) that of the thirty-two outfits which had applied for aid, none was accepted. (Examples of other curiosities at the local level abounded. In fighting for his Staten Island coal plant, for example, John Dyson came up with the novel idea of paying several million dollars a year to New Jersey to purchase pollution rights. Clean Air legislation set limits on overall regional smog. Dyson's plan proposed that Jersey operations promise to quit pumping x amount of crap into the air so that the coal plant could do so without worsening air quality. When Staten Islanders still complained, fearing they would be breathing the worst of it, Dyson told them not to worry; prevailing winds at the site would carry the smog over Manhattan instead, he said.

Another New York example: the best idea anyone had yet devised to ease New York's reliance on OPEC was to pay Canadians $6 billion in exchange for hydro power generated in Quebec. "How on earth can such an expenditure in a foreign country be justified," Chattey asked, "with all the unemployment we have down here?")

Then there was the Synthetic Fuels Program. The President and the Congress agreed to set aside $20 billion immediately and up to $68 billion more by 1992 (the total sounded like a zillion because it was) to encourage research into and development of alternative energy sources. Of the 1980 allocation, $1.7 billion was reserved exclusively for people who wanted to study how to make gasohol out of wheat, corn, garbage, chickenshit and bullshit. This, despite the fact that all known gasohol processes consumed more energy than their products contained.

For the rest of the Synfuel allocation, a gold rush

ensued. Suddenly, everybody was in the energy business. In a single week, 550 industry executives lobbied for a piece of the action at the Synthetic Fuels Corporation. In all, more than a thousand companies applied. The SFC would eventually accept sixty-one proposals, many of which seemed to me to be redundant: fourteen for extracting oil from shale, seventeen for making natural gas out of coal, eight for removing oil from tar sands, nineteen for making oil from coal, and so on.

Like the DOE, the Synthetic Fuels Corporation was administered by a group of men who admitted they had little background in energy technology but claimed good records of public service. The organization looked to me a bit like Conrail. One top executive engineered a contract in which he would receive $150,000 a year for a minimum of two years and would get a severance check of $281,000 in the event that he were fired. He would need all of it, I thought; another job like that would be hard to find.

The entire $88 billion program was designed to reduce imports by 500,000 barrels a day by 1992, less than half the amount ICONN-Erie was designed to save. This, despite the facts that no one in the energy industry expected synfuels ever to be cheaper than OPEC oil or to be produced on commercial scales much before the turn of the century. The money budgeted to that program would have not only studied ICONN-Erie but *built* it, with tens of billions of dollars to spare.

Economists everywhere blasted the program. One of them, Robert Solo, a professor at Michigan State University, said: "So far as I can tell . . . this type of research and development operation — administered by minor and subservient bureaucrats without responsibility for the program's outcome, dominated by advisory committees with representatives drawn from industry, and scattering grants among flocks of incoming proposals . . . has never produced a significant technological advance or innovation.

(President Reagan would later consider the program ridiculous and threaten to scrap the whole thing. Later still, he would propose abolition of the Energy Department itself.)

While Chattey and I discussed such things, his middle daughter, Bonnie, turned on the news.

And there it was:

The lead story was about the discovery that seepage from solid waste landfills had at last penetrated not only the Glacial Aquefer, which began 150 feet down, and the Magothy Aquefer, down 450 feet more, but the Lloyd Aquefer as well, the deepest and last chance for pure drinking water on Long Island. Contaminants included iron, zinc, copper, chloroform, benzene, lead, mercury, trichloroethylene, vinyl chloride and several other substances with names too long for me to copy.

Chattey listened grimly.

The story carried a sidebar of interviews with people who lived near the landfills. The seagulls and rats and methane leakage were bad enough, they said, and now they were suffering from diarrhea, stomach aches, rashes and persistent coughs besides, all of which they blamed on the drinking water.

The national newscast an hour later carried two more relevant items. One said that the Petroleum Industry Research Foundation had revised its forecast that oil would cost $60 a barrel by 1990. A new study indicated that oil would cost $60 a barrel by 1985.

The other story reported the findings of a study by the Aspen Institute of Humanistic Studies; the report concluded that a sudden cut-off of oil imports "would lead to a thirties-style depression, endanger the Western alliance and provoke confrontation with the Soviet Union." Senator Bill Bradley of New Jersey was interviewed. He said that the relationship between oil imports and national security had somehow made *no* impact on the American public.

Chattey was on his second drink by then. He sat in his chair, shaking his head.

The relationship had made substantial impact on the Pentagon, however. The Soviets had troops in Afghanistan, and both air and port facilities in Ethiopia and South Yemen. They were more than capable of mining the Strait of Hormuz. Thus the American armed forces requested and received increased allocations to set up an entirely new military command, its sole mission being to protect the flow of oil from the Persian Gulf.

The command included:

• Fifteen airfields in Kenya, Oman, Somalia, Egypt and Djibouti.

• Seven chartered freighters and tankers on station near Diego Garcia with armor and provisions for 12,000 Marines.

• Eight commercial vessels for use in sealifts.

• A dozen new Navy ships, outfitted to support a Marine division (the price tag: $5 billion).

• And 130 new cargo jets (the price tag: $7 billion).

That was to say nothing of the basic ingredients: four Army and Marine divisions, each with naval and air support, and, as back-up, almost one-fifth of the Army, one-third of the Marine Corps, half of the Navy's carrier battle groups and a variety of Air Force wings.

And the kicker: Congress had reinstituted registration for a military draft, just in case the United States needed to defend its "vital interests" overseas.

"And people tell me ICONN-Erie would cost too much," Chattey said.

Perhaps none of that would be needed. The fact was, however, that despite all the official hoopla about moving toward energy self-sufficiency, the United States in 1980 was importing more Arab oil than it had before the first boycott in 1973. The price was up 1,500 percent since then, in fact had tripled since Americans tried to appease Saudi Arabians through the sale of military aircraft. Congress, finally recognizing there was a problem, authorized the expenditure of $4.1 billion to create a strategic reserve of one billion barrels of oil in Louisiana salt caves; but in 1980 the reserve held only 100 million barrels, the equivalent of about two weeks of imports. At the rate it was being filled, it would not hold two months' worth until 1989 and would not be full until 2005. President Carter had made a deal with Sheik Yamani: if the United States would hold off on filling the reserve, the Saudis would maintain high production. Such was the state of American foreign policy.

Even those officials who most ardently praised Americans for conserving fuel admitted that such savings were more functions of layoffs, plant closings and the fact that the price was so high, than of any outright "conservation."

"I can't say what will happen," Chattey told me. "I don't know what will move government to action. We have been disappointed so many times — from the initial euphoric reaction of bureaucrats to the eventual disclaimer that they ever intended to do anything. Maybe what we've got to do is to get this thing into place, clearly defined as a solution, and then wait for a disaster."

WAR IN FACT WAS THE REASON the project was finally begun. Not a new war. An old war. The War of 1812.

By 1812, after four years of promotion, De Witt

Clinton at last had won sufficient votes in the legislature to pass a bill authorizing the borrowing of $6 million for construction of the Erie Canal. Soon thereafter, however, the war broke out and, as the money was needed elsewhere, the bill was rescinded.

(President James Madison, by then, had refused federal aid to the project. Later, President James Monroe did likewise. They both thought the plan was insane.)

The war itself helped to demonstrate the desirability of a canal. Cannon, forged in Washington and selling there for $400, cost $2,000 upon delivery to Commodore Perry on the shores of Lake Erie. The additional expense was naught but the cost of overland shipment. Clinton used that argument, among others, when he resumed his dog-and-pony shows in 1815, the year the war ended. But by then there was a new state senate, a new assembly to convince. So he began again. As before, the lawmakers argued and studied and argued and studied some more.

This is what Clinton thought of them:

"If you place an ass at an equal distance between two bundles of hay, will he not remain there for all eternity?" That was the sort of question, Clinton said, "which was solemnly propounded and gravely debated" by legislators. "The motive to eat both, some contended, being equal, it was impossible for the animal to come to a conclusion. But this problem, so puzzling to scholastic philosophy, would be at once decided by the ass."

By 1817, Clinton had lined up as many lawmakers as he believed he could get. To carry the measure, he would need the support of Martin Van Buren and Van Buren's hangers-on, as well. Only a year earlier, Van Buren and his power sphere in the state senate had blocked appropriations for construction. Van

Buren had always and in all things opposed De Witt Clinton, and he knew this canal would make him a hero forever.

No history I read said for sure why Van Buren switched sides in 1817 and used his votes to pass the legislation. Some historians believed he put the welfare of his constituents ahead of his partisan interests. Others thought he had a hidden agenda and hoped to draw to his Bucktails some of the project's inevitable glory. As a matter of fact, in 1836, when he campaigned for the Presidency against William Henry Harrison, he proclaimed himself one of the visionaries responsible for the Erie Canal. He defeated Harrison handily.

Peter Wiles, the packet boat skipper, had another theory, and it made as much sense as the others.

"I don't know whether this is true — I lie a lot when I don't know the answer, the stories keep coming out anyways — but I imagine it happened like this:

"Clinton had a hard time with Van Buren, he was a stodgy son of a bitch, you know, very conservative, and he wouldn't vote for this thing. So I surmise that two or three days before the final vote, De Witt went out with Martin for lunch, and he said, 'Martin, let's think of it this way: We're going to have to cut a canal to Lake Ontario, too, and maybe we'll do it through Rochester, but we could do it through Oswego. And it occurs to me that your brother has got a farm on the Oswego River. And if there was a lock by that farm, it would make one hell of a good place for a hotel.'

"Now, you can interpret that however you want," Wiles told me, "but a canal *was* built through Oswego, a lock *was* built on the brother's farm, the hotel *did* go up there, right in the middle of what's now the Town of Van Buren."

Even with Van Buren's support, however, canal construction was not ensured. The bill had passed both houses of the legislature, but approval was still required from the Council of Revision, a small group of senators and assemblymen that oversaw both bodies and had the last say on all legislation. Of the five men on the panel, two were known supporters of the canal. Two were intractably opposed. The fifth, Chancellor James Kent, tended toward opposition. He had given the project little thought, he said, though it appeared to him a gigantic undertaking, "which might require all the wealth of the Union to accomplish." The Erie Canal proposal seemed doomed.

But in the nick of time, the cavalry showed up — riding backwards, it turned out. Into the council session walked Daniel Tompkins, then the U.S. vice-president, earlier the New York governor who had slowed Clinton's efforts by keeping his opinion of the plan to himself, for fear of political consequences. Tompkins had come in hopes of swaying Kent's vote.

Jonas Platt, one counselor favored the bill, reported that Tompkins "stated that the late peace with Great Britain was a mere truce; that instead of wasting the credit and resources of the state in this chimerical project, we ought immediately to employ all the revenue and credit of the state in providing arsenals, arming the militia, erecting fortifications and preparing for war.

" 'Do you think so, sir?' asked Chancellor Kent. Then the Chancellor, rising from his seat, with great animation declared, 'If we must have war, or have a canal, then I am in favor of the canal, and I vote for this bill!' His vote gave us the majority, so the bill became law," Platt wrote.

New Yorkers took it from there. No European canal engineer would stake his reputation on the scheme, so the locals winged it, learning as they dug and inventing what they needed along the way. Limestone discovered near Medina made a tolerable waterproof cement. An endless mounted screw, connected to a roller, cable and crank, applied the principles of both lever and screw and was used for toppling trees. A pair of wheels sixteen feet high, connected by a thirty-foot axle, became a giant stump grubber. New wheelbarrows were conceived, and new variations of the plow and scraper. At any one time, as many as 3,000 men and 1,700 horses worked on the canal. Laborers earned fifty cents a day. Some whistled. Some sang:

> We're digging the Ditch through the mire
> Through the mud and the slime and the mire, by heck!
> And the mud is our principal hire.
> Up our pants, in our shirts, down our necks, by heck!
> We're digging the Ditch through the gravel
> So that people and freight can travel.

Many of my contemporaries believed that Irish laborers by the hundreds fell dead of malaria spawned in the miasma of Montezuma Swamp, but Richard Wright, secretary of the New York Canal Society and without question the world's best authority on the old Erie Canal, told me there was no evidence at all to support the contention. The belief was mythology, he said.

Another popular misbelief held that no Americans would invest in the scheme, that the $6 million was borrowed in Europe. Much of it was. But the fact is — and this is particularly interesting in light of Marine Midland's lone, courageous support of ICONN-Erie — that the largest single investor in Clinton's Ditch was the Bank for Savings of New York City, which held as much as 30 percent of the canal stock at any one time. Hundreds of Americans of limited means invested in the plan, and a few of not so limited means, one of whom was John Jacob Astor. Foreigners did not outweigh Americans in their holdings until 1829. The canal bonds paid returns ranging from 9 to 19 percent.

Clinton, of course, was tickled to death as he watched the construction. When the middle section was finished in 1820, he said: "New York is now destined to become the brightest star in the American galaxy." It did, and remained as such for more than a century. Clinton was fifty-two years old when he made that forecast.

The canal opened end-to-end five years later, and a new American subculture was born. The rhino-fat skipper of a boat mud-larked in slack water might tell his hoggee first to stable the long-eared robins, then to flip the jigger-boss a fip so that the crew could relax in earnest, awaiting high water, as trippers leading boats flying light and hoodledashers — carrying only a foo-foo or two — passed them by. Bottoming out was not necessarily a big deal. The skipper needed six trips a season to pay expenses. The seventh was profit. And the eighth.

After travelling the finished work in 1825, Clinton wrote: "A free state has thus set an illustrious example to the world and [has] demonstrated that the people of this country have had the heads to conceive, the hearts to undertake and the hands to execute the most useful and stupendous work of the age."

A full century after the canal was dug, one historian, Dr. John Finley, who was Chancellor of the State University of New York at the time, concluded that Clinton's pronouncement had been excessively modest. De Witt Clinton, Finley wrote, "not only changed the face of the earth, but in so doing affected the whole course of civilization, and gave New York the opportunity to become the capitol of a re-created world."

VII

GOVERNOR CAREY AT LAST WENT PUBLIC, very much to Chattey's surprise, on September 28, 1980. It may have been a coincidence that John Petty was in Carey's audience that day, to remind him of the project. And it may have been a coincidence that by then Edward Kennedy was out of the running for the Democratic Presidential nomination and Carey's chances of being appointed to a job outside of Albany were ruined.

The governor had called a press conference in Buffalo to announce the state's request for federal aid to build two synthetic fuel plants in the Erie County region. There were twenty-five reporters in attendance. Each had a copy of Carey's prepared remarks. In the middle of his talk, however, the governor departed from the text.

"There is another project that I *dare* mention," he began, "and that's ICONN." He called the plan "a very worthy project" and said, "What has been referred to as a wild idea has suddenly become well-worthy of study, and perhaps implementation down-range."

For a magic moment or two, Nigel Chattey thought that all his troubles were over. Another blind spot.

Many of the reporters at the conference did not look up from the prepared statement. Some did not listen. Of those who did, none knew what Carey was talking about, and nobody reported it.

No formal letter of support from Carey ensued, either.

I was not at the session, so my stories — one for my old employer, the *Post-Standard,* the other for the *New York Times* — appeared three days late. It was the governor's remarks that justified the *Times'* second mention of ICONN-Erie. But, as I said earlier, editors cut the piece to ribbons.

Throughout the year, I had sought an interview with the governor. William Snyder, the press aide who had called Chattey a "flake," succeeded in putting me off at least twenty-five times. He would try to set something up and get back to me, he said over and over, then he failed to set anything up and did not get back to me. So I complained. He explained that the governor was a busy man. Carey's verbal endorsement of the studies gave me added leverage, I thought, so I pressed harder. "That was not an endorsement," Snyder told me. "It was a positive maybe." Then he said he would try to set something up and get back to me.

While I waited, two interesting things happened to Nigel Chattey. One was minor, the other of stunning import. First: Chattey was not invited to address one of the most natural of all possible forums for discussion of ICONN-Erie, a three-day seminar sponsored by the New York Upstate Chapter of the American Planning Association entitled "Upstate N.Y. in the '80s — The Challenge Ahead for its Economic, Environmental and Energy Resources." It may have been a coincidence that one of the leaders of the Association was Roger Creighton, the consultant whose firm had prepared for the state DOT the 1979 study advising against modernization of the Erie Canal.

In retrospect, Chattey found the slight amusing. The planning group had planned the confabulation badly, failing to send out invitations until two weeks before the session. Responses were insufficient, so the meeting was cancelled.

The other thing that happened to Chattey was disastrous. This, I learned months after the fact, was the sequence:

Robert Embry at the Department of Housing and Urban Development was so excited about ICONN-Erie that he assigned a subordinate, Donald Dodge, to work with Chattey and Francis Coleman, the supportive attorney from Rochester, in preparation of the grant application. Dodge explained precisely how to describe the project so it would qualify as one of the sorts of things HUD was empowered to study. Then Chattey and Coleman were invited to Washington to sign the deal and share in the formal announcement. The preliminary agreement was so firm that, a day before the signing, HUD officials asked Coleman to prepare the press release. He asked me to do it. I feared jeopardizing my credibility as an objective reporter, but I yielded to Coleman's argument that there was no one else around who both understood the project and knew newspaper style. So I wrote the thing, then made Chattey and Coleman promise never to name its author. Then they stayed up most of the night putting finishing touches on the grant application.

Donald Dodge did not show up at the next day's appointment. Instead, a low-level HUD myrmidon wandered out and began asking Chattey and Coleman basic and ignorant questions about the plan. He made no mention of the grant. Chattey knew the deal was blown instantly. He got so angry, came so close to losing control, HUD officials told me later, that Coleman had to lead him from the room and tell him to wait outside. The attorney then went back in, walked boldly past the little bureaucrat and the secretaries and the rest, and planted himself in the office of Robert Embry to await Embry's return.

This was what had happened:

The same day I was writing the press release, Embry asked his staff to phone around to make sure there was political support in New York for ICONN-Erie. Three calls were made, one each to the governor's resident staff in Washington, the governor's staff in Albany, and the staff of Mayor Ed Koch in New York City.

If Koch had truly appreciated the plan during his ten-minute briefing, either no one had told his aides or the aides had forgotten. That Koch had produced a formal letter of support mattered not. Strike one.

The governor's aides in Washington later told me they were wholly unaware that Carey had publicly endorsed the plan only two weeks earlier. No one had told them, and the only media report they might have seen was my *Times* story, so skillfully buried that even I missed it. Strike two.

And the governor's aides in Albany — these were the invisible people who never appeared in the news, the people who actually ran the government — said nope, New York had no strong interest in the ICONN-Erie Project. Forget what the governor said.

Whether the aides' negative reports were founded in ignorance or conspiratorial maliciousness made no difference at the bottom line: the merits of the plan aside, "we went looking for political support in the state and we couldn't find any," Embry told me. So he sent the grant application off, as had Ruth Davis at the Department of Energy, to the Army Corps of Engineers for "further review."

And Donald Dodge, who had shown Coleman how to make ICONN-Erie qualify as a project for HUD, turned around and wrote to Coleman, explaining that ICONN-Erie did not qualify as a project for HUD. (Later, I spoke with Dodge. He told me his people in fact *had* failed to figure out how to make ICONN-Erie qualify as a HUD grant program, and he cited another reason for HUD's flagging interest in the project: "There just wasn't any crescendo of support from the Army Corps.")

I began to have trouble maintaining objectivity at that point. Chattey really *was* insane, I thought, not because there was anything wrong with the project, but because he honestly believed he would conquer such a system.

"How in the world can you keep on with this?" I asked him once. "What on earth sustains you?"

"I've asked myself that," he said, "and I have to admit that only some of the primeval forces in man can generate this sort of drive. It has to be fear, one of the primordial fears, and I think I can name it: fear for survival. Survival not only of my country; survival of my family unit.

"And one thing more . . . sometimes I honestly think I am playing to a grander design than even I know. It's just a feeling, I have nothing to base it on, I don't believe in the ordained — but I have a terrific feeling of historical order. If it wasn't me doing this, it would be someone else.

"It's almost as if I am in a river, and it's carrying me somewhere. There's the course of this state and the course of this nation, and there's the course of this project. Something in me tells me they are going to converge at some point, perhaps sometime very soon. I just want to keep the water out of my canoe until then so I can be in the goddamned confluence," he said.

Chattey decided to back-burner further approaches to state and federal bureaucracies in the early fall of 1980 ("To hell with that," was the way he put it), reasoning, first, that the agencies were established to implement ideas of government and had learned to cope with ideas of industry but were sadly ill-equipped to deal with ideas of regular people; and second, that precious few of the bureaucrats — too few where the project was concerned — were inspired to promote any prosperity beyond their own.

Chattey then came to believe that funding for his studies, like funding for the Tennessee Valley Authority, would require special legislation and an act of Congress. Broad-based, grassroots support would be needed to achieve that goal, so he packed up his story boards and movies and the rest and hit the road, planning to do as many as three presentations a day to local industries, chambers of commerce, university faculties, economic development authorities and regional planning councils in every consequential village, town, county and city from Buffalo to Albany.

"That's going to be a *lot* of work," Eristoff told him.

Chattey laughed, though not with amusement. He had recently, under my influence, I think, taken to reading about the promoters of the original Erie Canal. "Going back to history has been a Godsend," he told Eristoff. "It took those people *fifteen years.* I can put up with anything now."

Chattey decided against further entreaties to Hugh

Carey as well. Instead, he said, he would brief everyone he suspected might seek the governor's job in 1982.

Meanwhile, U.S. Representative Frank Horton of Rochester, after a briefing arranged by Francis Coleman, invited Chattey to address the Northeast-Midwest Coalition of Congress, a bipartisan group with perhaps power enough to pass ICONN-Erie legislation. Inflation, and the continual refinement of the plan, led Chattey to re-estimate the cost of the feasibility studies at $26 million, about the amount spent since 1970 to study "Westway," a proposed 4.2-mile highway in Manhattan; about the cost of a single state-of-the-art fighter aircraft. Construction of ICONN-Erie, he supposed, would cost tens of billions.

At about the same time, the AFL-CIO and the ILA began promoting the project as "the TVA of the North."

PETER WILES WAS RILED when he learned of HUD's treatment of Chattey, so he devised a plan of his own. The crusty old hide possessed a native genius for lopping off great chunks of complicated matters and isolating their roots. The project was stalled, he concluded, for two reasons: the numerous people who had to agree to make the thing happen had never come together, all at once, for the few minutes needed to hash it all out; and most of them did not know what they were missing — they had never *seen* the Erie Canal. He decided to give them the chance to do both.

In October of 1980, Wiles invited seventy-five VIPs to come on a very special cruise. He invited every cabinet-level secretary in the U.S. Government, every commissioner in the governments of New York and New Jersey, every mayor of every city from New York north to Albany and west from there to Buffalo. He invited bank managers, industrialists, canal personnel, shipbuilders, tow boat operators, oil executives, tourism officials, heavy freight shippers. He invited several state congressmen and both New York senators, also the candidates seeking those offices. He invited Hugh Carey. He invited Nigel Chattey. And he invited all of their spouses.

The cruise would be "no big deal," he told me. "Nothing formal." The food would be free. The drinks would be on the house. Financially, 1980 had been a very good year for Mid-Lakes Navigation.

"It occurs to me that the people who share interest in or responsibility for the canal system may have never experienced it as I do," his letter of invitation read. "I think perhaps a concept is being lost." The cruise, he wrote, "may broaden all of our perspectives. If you see the value of the gathering but are unable to attend, your representative will be welcome. Please be my guest for as much of the day as you like." Passengers could board or debark in mid-morning, before lunch, after lunch, in mid- and late afternoon.

The invitations were sent special delivery.

It seemed to Wiles entirely proper that he should host such a function. I had come to understand that he saw *Emita II* less as a means to step back into history as a means to be part of it. "We make our living on the canal," he said. "We do it the same way they always did. We use the same kind of advertising. We know how the thing works. We know the lock tenders, the guys on the dredgers. We're known in the communities we go through — the people, the lady hanging her wash says 'Hi, good to see you again.' There isn't anybody else in New York State who knows all that or can say all that. What the hell . . . if you're the *only* one, you've *got* to be authentic."

Wiles did not honestly expect many of the dignitaries to show up. "But this way they can never say they didn't have the opportunity," he said. He did expect a few of their representatives. He was correct in the first speculation, incorrect in the second. Not a single public official attended, not one of their aides. The businessmen came. And the tour people, and the shipbuilderss, and the canal personnel. And Nigel Chattey.

During that, their first meeting, Wiles and Chattey had a wonderful time, poring over topographical charts, deciding which towns the new Erie should go through, which it should bypass. The place with fewest options, they agreed, would be Little Falls, a community which all but filled a narrow valley between a pair of thousand-foot mountains. No problem, they concluded. The canal might skirt one of the mountains on the far side of town, might run in a tunnel cut right through the other.

AN INTERVIEW WITH THE GOVERNOR was at last arranged in December of 1980, eleven months after I made the initial request. Carey, at the time, was city-hopping around the state, chairing public hearings on the proposed 1981 state budget. Snyder, the press aide, told me we could meet following such a session in Utica. I assumed Carey and I would go off somewhere and sit down. I had no such luck.

As it happened, Snyder had briefed Carey neither about what I knew nor what I wanted. I was never sure if the governor knew he had an appointment to speak with me at all. Snyder introduced me as a *Post-Standard* reporter, though I had been gone from that job for nearly a year.

The circumstances were unfavorable. Carey had spent the afternoon listening to angry taxpayers in Watertown, then had flown to Utica and spent the evening listening some more. When that session broke at 10:30 P.M., Snyder pulled Carey aside. The interview was to take place in a small office outside the hearing chamber, an office crowded with at least thirty other people, many of them reporters who listened quizzically and got huffy when Snyder forbade their interruptions. One member of the governor's party, an overweight woman, tugged at his sleeve, urging him to leave, throughout our conversation.

It was not my place, I thought, to take cheap shots at or to make value judgments about the governor of the State of New York, so I decided to report the interview verbatim. This was it:

EHMANN: "Governor, in September you called for the funding of studies of the ICONN-Erie Project, yet . . ."

CAREY: "The high velocity rate at which I throw out ideas sometimes gets people to concentrate on the major import of my function to lead the government. In other words, I have to be careful, because some of the ideas — like 'I Love New York' was my idea, I won a personal preference on it — but some of the ideas come to fruition, like that music concert in the Mall, which was probably the 'establishment Woodstock' of all time, which . . ."

EHMANN: "Governor, do you think ICONN-Erie will be studied?"

CAREY: "It *is* being studied, it's . . ."

EHMANN: "Not on *any* formal level at this time."

CAREY: "It's being studied by the Department of Transportation, a very competent planning group under Bill Hennessy. He and I talk on it almost daily. And I reserve the right to my inputs to him. He's an expert, he's . . ."

EHMANN: "What do you see the state's role as becoming, then, as more and more of your front-line commissioners . . ."

CAREY: "The triple-thrust method that I've developed in the state: instead of the public sector going it alone, the state going it alone — for that matter, the federal government *and* the state going it alone — we involve the academic or 'expert' field, we involve the private sector, business *and* labor. And don't get the idea, for instance, that we're going to do what Governor Clinton did when he dug the canal, to do it all with state resources [just] because it was a great idea and we had the manual laborers to do it."

EHMANN: "Let me tell you why I ask, quickly . . ."

CAREY: "We're talking about using the possible two-way traffic on the canal, you know . . ."

EHMANN: "Governor, I *understand* the project."

CAREY: "All right."

EHMANN: "Right now the ICONN people have before HUD a one-million-dollar grant request which will live or die depending on whether or not the state is interested in the project."

CAREY: "Of course we're interested in the project."

EHMANN: "I've spoken with Bob Embry about it and he said that he had no indication *at all* that the state is interested — he even sought it. I don't know yet who he contacted, whether he spoke with someone in Albany, or one of your people in Washington, but . . ."

CAREY: "First of all, we have a delegation down there, and I have worked for Senator Moynihan down there, Senator Moynihan on this project, he and I have talked endless hours on this project, and it is amazing to me that a secretary over in HUD wouldn't understand that we have a definite interest in this, and when a project application goes to him, he hasn't heard what Senator Moynihan and I have been saying."

EHMANN: "Apparently not."

CAREY: "Maybe that's why he's leaving town." (As a political appointee, Embry had been pink-slipped when voters had pink-slipped President Carter the month before.)

EHMANN: "Do you see a place, Governor, for Nigel Chattey in the developmental process of this . . ."

CAREY: "Well, I'm not — we're not going to deal with, or specify, individuals in whatever we talk about here. The chief of transportation in our state is the best in the country in his field. He's Bill Hennessy. He received the award of the National Governors' Association as outstanding commissioner of transportation in the country. It's in his shop. I work with him. Then I talk to experts in the private sector. And when our time is ready, and we have the plan in good shape, *then* we'll involve the feds. Because I don't expect, given the Reagan administration's approach to budgetary matters, that we're going to be able to qualify for a lot of planning help."

EHMANN: "You see this as originating in the state, then, rather than in the federal government or the private sector?"

CAREY: "Well, the federal government did make a commitment to put in about $2.6 million dollars for dredging in Louisiana, to open up the port of Baton Rouge, to bring larger vessels in there. They'll probably have to dredge more at Hampton Roads. We've got a very good delegation down there, with Hank Noak of [the] Public Works [Committee], and we have Pat Moynihan who'll see to it that when they start talking about rivers and harbors, *our* rivers and harbors are not forgotten. The last money we've gotten around New York was to clear up some debris — very little for dredging, very little for harbor maintenance . . ."

EHMANN: "Or for modernization."

CAREY: "Or modernization, right. That day is gone, because the first thing I did when I sat down as governor was to call in Ray Schuler, who was the transportation commissioner, and I said 'This state's ports *must* be redeveloped.' And the Port of Albany's been improved, the Port of Buffalo's being improved, but the Port of New York is lagging. Some of the things we're doing might better be done by the Port of New York Authority. But we'll join with them, kind of wake them up."

The fat lady on Carey's sleeve won out at that point. Her sighs of impatience had grown heavier with each of my questions. That was that for the interview.

If there was a single straight answer in any of it, I missed it.

As was the case when first we spoke, the governor's remarks seemed to me to be claptrap. I had spoken with Bill Hennessy, who did not know how much tonnage a barge could carry, and with four top aides to Senator Moynihan, including his press secretary, none of whom believed that Carey supported project funding. They were not even sure he knew what the project was.

So I wrote to Carey, explaining that the interview had been insufficient, and detailing, in advance, the questions for which I sought answers. I sent copies of the letter to Snyder and to Snyder's boss, Carey's press secretary, Mike Patterson.

None of them answered the letter.

Within a month, Patterson would resign. Before leaving he told another reporter, concerning another matter: "Some of what the governor says could just be his own vision of the future. Not everything he says should be taken as a forecast of imminent action.

Sometimes, it's like he forgets he's governor — and then people feel everything he says is totally scenarioed out. It's just not that way."

I could relate to that.

Within the same month, Snyder would be promoted to the post of Director of Communications, which paid $57,000 a year and included the use of a state car. Snyder said he would, in his new job, concentrate on promoting the governor's positive side rather than on responding and reacting to the press.

Also in the month to come, Carey would find a new belle, one Evangeline Gouletas, whom he would later wed. Prior to the ceremony, she was asked by reporters to describe the governor. "He has a fantastic sense of humor, he thinks wonderfully and he's a great dancer," she said.

Just for the record: Governor Hugh Carey cost New York's taxpayers $1,075,308 every year, very nearly $3,000 a day. He was by far the highest paid governor in America. There was his salary, the cost of maintaining his mansion, the salaries of the mansion's twenty servants and the salaries of his security personnel, his use of state autos and airplanes, his personal expenses, and the costs of his official functions. Carey was outraged by such reports in the media. In the private sector, he said, he would be worth between $2 million and $5 million a year.

Chattey, by the time of the governor's wedding in April of 1981, had made more than 250 ICONN-Erie presentations. Carey had attended none of them, had never even spoken of the plan with Nigel Chattey.

SHORTLY BEFORE THE 1980 PRESIDENTIAL ELECTION, before the ICONN-Erie principals learned that Robert Embry at HUD would abandon the grant request, Chattey and Petty and Eristoff felt another magic moment. In a campaign speech, President Carter promised to attack inflation, increase productivity, revitalize industry and promote both energy security and job development, which sounded like the same old jive until he mentioned — in general terms, of course — the means. He called for "a modernization of our transportation system and ports to make American coal a powerful rival of OPEC oil."

A week later, Carter narrowed the idea further, noting that the federal government was going to "place a special emphasis on facilitating transportation, a traditional federal role that goes back to the inland canals of the early nineteenth century."

That sounded to me like a whopping hint of an announcement-to-come, especially in light of the remarks made the same day by Charles Schultz, chairman of the President's Council of Economic Advisors. Schultz said the United States should increase "spending on infrastructure — canals, highways and perhaps a deepwater East Coast port to spur exports of coal to Europe."

Curiosity got the best of me, so I tried to reach Schultz. I was transferred to Susin Irvin, his special assistant. I posed my question. She answered testily: "Charlie is involved in looking at what makes sense in a large economy on micro-economic grounds, but not on a particular does-this-project-make-sense basis. I'm sort of *amazed* at your taking his comments as referring to something specific."

Okay. "If someone *had* something specific to offer," I asked her, "something which sounds just like what Mr. Carter and Mr. Schultz are advocating, what should he do?"

"You could tell him to write a letter to his congressman," Irvin said.

At the same time that Washington was reindus-

trializing its rhetoric, New York officials moved on
something specific. I thought it ironic that their plan
had been to some extent inspired by the pressures
Chattey had created, and at the same time held real
potential to stop the Chattey project. The players in
the affair were members of William Hennessy's Department of Transportation and the Army Corps of
Engineers.

The Corps' Great Lakes-to-East Coast waterway
study had considered four possible routes — including
the Delaware and Susquehanna rivers — and incremental modifications for each of them, ranging from
shallow drafts to deep. Of the thirteen plans exam-
ined, only three, on paper, produced benefits exceeding costs: a rehabilitation of the Erie Canal from Albany to Buffalo, still limited to one barge at a time in
the locks; a like plan for the Erie from Albany to Three
Rivers, in mid-state, and from there down the Oswego
Canal to Lake Ontario; and a minor modernization of
the Albany-Three Rivers-Oswego route to accommodate two barges at a time in each lock.

The cost-benefit ratios for Chattey's sugges-
tions — modernizations ranging from a four-barge capacity at the present channel depth to a jumbo barge
capacity in a depth of twenty-nine feet, all were found
to be overwhelmingly negative.

Where the Corps study was concerned, Chattey
hoped only to demonstrate that the Albany-to-Buffalo
route was the single sensible possibility. "That way
we'll have a cost estimate for the canal, at least," he
said. The benefits of ICONN-Erie could not be estimated until the canal and the island and the synergies
between them were studied all at once.

It took Chattey less than two minutes to discover
the argument he would use to challenge the Corps'
findings at subsequent public hearings. "Ah-hah!

They've sucked themselves into their own vortex," he said. "Now I'll hoist *them* with their own petard." (Fortunately for our conversation, his and mine, Chattey was not expert in all things. He had used that phrase all his life, believing a petard to be a dirk or a dagger. In fact it was an explosive device used to blow holes through castle gates. " 'Tis sport to have the engineer hoist with his own petar[d]," Hamlet had said. "Oh, dear," Chattey said. "I'm an engineer. I hope this isn't an omen." "Don't worry," I said. "They're a whole corps of engineers.")

The reasoning behind the flaw Chattey found was this: While the four inner Great Lakes lay at more or less the same level, Lake Ontario lay the height of Niagara Falls beneath them.

Therefore, were a canal cut through Oswego to reach Lake Ontario, *another* canal would be needed to connect Ontario to the others. People had been discussing such a LELO Canal (Lake Erie to Lake Ontario) for years. The only alternative was continued use of Canada's Welland Canal, which was forecast to overload by 1988.

Therefore, the Corps could not rely on the Welland: first, because it would be saturated: second, because the sister congressional mandate to the Corps specified an "all-American" route.

Therefore, the Corps would have to add to the costs of any Albany-to-Oswego route the costs of a LELO canal. The cost-benefit ratios for a system of any size would become instantly, thoroughly, negative.

There were other arguments:

"The most serious objection to the Ontario route is that it will inevitably enrich the territory of a foreign power, at the expense of the United States," exactly as the St. Lawrence Seaway had done. That argument was Clinton's, not Chattey's. And for once, they were not alone on their side of the debate.

Joe Stellato, who ran the Erie Canal, asked at public hearings that *at least* a four-barge capacity — the ICONN-Erie base case — be considered.

John Tobin of the New York State Waterway Association asked the same thing, if only to encourage the construction of new barges. The existing units were old. "Otherwise," he said, "the day will soon come when there will be no equipment available to work on any of these canals."

Richard Van Derzee of the Buffalo Port Authority asked the same thing.

Arthur Sambuchi of the United Steelworkers of America demanded specific study of ICONN-Erie, and he lashed out at the representative of the National Railroad Association, who had spoken before him against all of the plans. "When I find Conrail and Amtrak saying they want to buy Japanese and German steel, I know just what I can say to the lobbyist who wants to defend the American railroad." The railroad rep objected. Sambuchi offered to meet him outside.

And George Wyatt of the consulting firm of Alexander & Associates challenged, as had Chattey earlier, the very foundations of the Corps' study. "So-called 'ancillary' benefits, which may, in fact, *dwarf* the benefits to shippers, are never investigated unless a favorable benefit-cost ratio appears. This is the historic approach used by the Corps and it has historically produced unfavorable recommendations."

Certainly no one, 150 years earlier, knew a way to gauge the scope of "ancillary" benefits the Erie would produce, the number of dry docks, sawmills, boatyards, coal terminals, livery stables, general stores, insurance firms, rope manufacturers, pump manufacturers and the rest that would locate at canal-side; to say nothing of the major new industries; to say noth-

ing of all the grocers, carpenters, plumbers, barbers —
all those folks whose trades were needed by the folks
the industries brought in; to say nothing of the Gos-
pel boats and circus boats and museum boats and
floating amusement parks and saloons and brothels
which found homes on the Erie Canal. One entrepreneur, as a matter of fact, made a fortune, the odor notwithstanding, charging admission to see the whale
carcass he carried on a barge from Albany to Buffalo.

A century and a half later, things were no different. *Emita II* had been purchased not to run canal trips
but to do dinner cruises on Onondaga Lake, near Syracuse. On his way to central New York after purchas-
ing the vessel from Casco Bay Lines in Maine, however ("We just sailed out of Portland Harbor and turned
right"), Wiles made a deal with a promoter in Connecticut who wanted to use *Emita II* during a Bicen-
tennial celebration on the Connecticut River.

"Since I was a cheap son of a bitch anyways, I
said, 'Jeez, it's going to cost a lot of money to get back
up there.' So we put an ad in the *Post-Standard*, just
a little classified, that said 'Anybody who wants to
take a canal boat ride, call this number.' Well, the
phone fell off the wall. We left six days later with
thirty-five passengers. So we tried three more Albany
trips in the fall, then looked at what we made on that
and compared it to our dinner cruises and said, hell,
let's go into the long-haul business."

John Petty described ancillary benefits like this:
"When you're improving infrastructure, it doesn't
matter what it is — you can build a highway into the
jungle, and all of a sudden everything pops up along
the way. That's what entrepreneurs are for. Fifty percent of it at least is stuff the planners never imagined."

Yet no such stuff, nor any estimate of such stuff,
went into the Corps' formula.

Moreover, I feared no such Erie Canal would survive to produce any benefits, ancillary or otherwise, by the time the Corps finished its studies. "How long before your final evaluation of these three routes will be done?" I asked Charles Fox, the civilian engineer who directed the studies, before one of the public hearings. "Six or seven years," he said.

Then, during the hearing, John Tobin of the waterway association asked him the same question. "Just as soon as we can," Fox answered.

I mentioned the discrepancy to Chattey, and he laughed. "It doesn't matter," he said. "They will finish a lot sooner than they think." I asked him to explain. "We're firing battery rounds at Albany now from so many different hilltops they've begun to think they're surrounded. The state will move. It will have to." By then, Chattey had quite a collection of educational institutions, planning associations, labor unions, public officials, assorted politicians and of course the powerful Marine Midland, all lobbying on behalf of ICONN-Erie.

(Perhaps not by coincidence, Chattey had used the same strategy during the Kashmir wars in 1947. With six comrades and one howitzer, which they dragged from hilltop to hilltop, he had managed to create the impression of commanding a far larger force than he had, giving a full Indian regiment "a good reason not to advance," he said.)

"The point," Chattey continued, "is that we have now raised such a ruckus that Albany has no choice but to react to us. We appear to have touched them to the quick. If Carey hopes for reelection in 1982, the state must do one of three things, and do it quickly. They must either endorse ICONN-Erie; destroy my credibility; or come up with an alternate plan. I believe they will choose Number Three — not because they necessarily intend to *build* anything, but because the debate will carry Carey through the '82 election.

"Now, a better idea will beat us, and it should, because the dollar investment in ICONN-Erie would be so great that we cannot afford to make a mistake. But not a lesser one — it was never our intention to become spoilers, but if it comes to that, we will be.

"I'll tell you, I *welcome* this firefight. If I can now retire from the fray honorably by reason of having been shot to hell, it won't bother me a bit; in fact, after six years, it will be something of a relief. And if not, that too will be a Godsend. We'll be able to quit this dog-and-pony activity and get down to some real work. If I'd known when I started that 5 percent of my time would be spent technically, 5 percent on administration and 90 percent on dog-and-pony activity, there is no way I would have done it.

"The only horrible possibility with an alternate state plan would be a stalemate, so I'm wishing them every success in the world."

If Chattey was a visionary, he was seeing clearly. In fact the state *did* have an alternate plan in the works, though neither he nor I would know it for another six months. Following the Corps' public hearings, the state DOT asked Army engineers to add to their final study the possibility of a canal for tows of four barges from Albany to Oswego *and* a new LELO canal. The Corps agreed, then altered its original cost-benefit estimates to include some of that grain and coal movement Chattey was predicting.

I learned of the plan, indirectly, through Peter Wiles. The same lead, thank goodness, at last led me to an enemy of the ICONN-Erie Project. I wanted to write both sides of the story, after all.

WHILE NO ONE SAW FIT TO SPEND A NICKEL to study the Chattey solutions, millions were spent studying the problems they addressed. The International Energy Agency, for example, produced a study concluding that its earlier forecasts were wrong; problems predicted by 1990 would appear by 1985, with demand for foreign oil exceeding supply by at least 2 million, perhaps 4 million barrels a day, the study said.

And a study by the Congressional Budget Office concluded that, despite all efforts at conservation, the United States would import at least 3 million, perhaps 4 million additional barrels of oil a day by 1990.

And a study by the U.S. Senate Energy Committee concluded that America had paid too little attention to the geopolitics of oil. It stressed the fact that oil had become a potent political weapon for those who controlled the reserves — exactly as Chattey had told Petty it would, seventeen years earlier.

And a study by the U.S. Department of Energy under the Reagan administration concluded that DOE policies under the Carter administration added up to less than zero, that the policies themselves, if pursued through 1990, would increase the nation's import needs by 200,000 barrels a day.

And a study by the Library of Congress concluded that research into extraction of oil from shale and production of natural gas from coal was probably a waste of money.

And the National Energy Transportation Study concluded that by 1990 the United States would have to double its capacity for moving coal to export.

And two State Department studies concluded that American oil companies were not apt to produce many solutions. The studies called them, collectively, "the marketing arm of OPEC."

And a study by Conrail indicated that the railroad, which only survived because of a $1.8 million daily subsidy, would turn a yearly profit of $3 million in 1985. Conrail then asked for an additional $3 billion in loans to see it through to 1982. President Reagan's people, who were no dopes at arithmetic, responded with plans to sell off the whole operation.

For fun, I think, I wrote to Senator William Proxmire of Wisconsin, famous for his "golden fleece" awards. I wondered what sorts of things qualified for federal study money while ICONN-Erie did not. The list he sent me included:

• A study by the Air Force to determine if an officer's "combat ready" image was impaired when he carried an umbrella.

• A study by the Federal Aviation Administration to catalogue the body measurements of stewardess trainees.

• A study by the U.S. Postal Service to determine if its $3.4 million ad campaign, which encouraged people to write more letters, had worked.

• A study by the Department of Labor to determine the pet population of Ventura, California.

• A study by the National Institute on Alcohol Abuse to measure aggressive behavior in drunken sunfish.

• A study by the National Highway Traffic Safety Administration to design a prototype motorcycle with rear-wheel steering — the administration then built such a thing, though the best of the test drivers managed to stay aboard only two seconds.

• A study by the Department of Labor to determine the Samoan population of Orange County, California.

• A study by the Law Enforcement Assistance Administration to design a prototype do-anything cop car — they came up with one (at a time when municipal budget cutbacks were forcing police layoffs all over the country) which cost $49,000 per unit above the sticker price.

• A study by the Federal Highway Administration

to determine whether or not people driving little cars liked sharing the road with big trucks.

• And, among dozens of others, a study by the National Endowment for the Humanities to determine why people lied, cheated and were rude on tennis courts.

There were hundreds of studies underway at any given time in Washington. The collective cost of just the ten mentioned above was $3.8 million, more than twice the amount needed to begin ICONN-Erie.

"Maybe you were born in the wrong century," I once told Nigel Chattey.

"No, I don't think so," he said, laughing sadly, "but on the wrong planet? Perhaps."

THE AFFAIRS OF MEN made no more sense in De Witt Clinton's day; justice was no easier to find.

Consider this: after three times refusing aid to the project, the federal government, upon completion of the Erie Canal, imposed a tax on the freight it carried, supposedly justified under the Coastal Navigation Act.

To hell with that, Clinton said. "The canals are the property of the state, are within the jurisdiction of the state, have been constructed by the state and can be destroyed by the state," and would be, he said, before any such tax would be paid. He told federal tax agents to shut up and go home, which they did.

And consider this: on the eve of the canal's completion, Clinton's adversaries actually tried to steal from him its lasting glory — and they very nearly succeeded.

Clinton, as I said, was an easy man to dislike. The Erie Canal project notwithstanding, his popularity in 1823 was so low that his own Republican Party chose not to run him for reelection as governor of the State of New York. Martin Van Buren was in Washington at the time, serving as secretary of state, but the people looking out for his interests in Albany saw an opportunity and seized it: they hoped to capitalize on the governor's unpopularity, disassociating the names De Witt Clinton and Erie Canal once and forever.

Directing Van Buren's Bucktails in his absence was Judge Roger Skinner. The power of Bucktails had risen significantly in New York in 1823, and Skinner was convinced he could muster votes enough for legislation to kick De Witt Clinton off the New York Board of Canal Commissioners, a group Clinton had chaired, without pay, for fourteen years. No reason was cited. Motivation for passage, Skinner reasoned, was this: with Clinton both out of the governorship and off the canal board, every other politician in the state could claim a piece of the accolade which was certain to greet completion of the Erie Canal.

Whether or not politicians have always been a gutless tribe, I cannot say. They certainly were then. The bill was introduced in both houses of the state legislature only twenty minutes before the end of the year's session, and almost all the lawmakers — because they hoped for extolment, because they feared Bucktail retaliation, because they did not want their vacations delayed, whatever — went for it. The notable exception was an assemblyman named Cunningham. He had already put on his coat and was heading for the door when the bill came up. He returned quickly to his seat, took the floor and lambasted his colleagues.

"Gentlemen," his ten-minute speech began, "when the contemptible party strifes of the present shall have passed by, and the political bargainers and jugglers who now hang 'round this capital for subsistence shall be overwhelmed and forgotten in their own insignificance; when the gentle breeze shall pass over the tomb of that great man, Clinton, carrying with it the just tribute of honor and praise which is now withheld; the pen of the future historian, in better days and in better times, will do him justice."

Grassroots saved historians the trouble. The vote which removed Clinton from the board backfired horribly, incinerating, for the time, any Bucktail pretension to power. The public was outraged.

Rallies were held to denounce the move across the state, from Buffalo and Syracuse to Albany and New York. Colonel William Stone, editor of the *New York Commercial Advertiser* (the *New York Times* of its day), reported that the angry assemblage in Central Park was the largest gathering in the city's history. So great was the general outcry of "Foul!" that the Republican Party changed its collective mind and ran Clinton for reelection as governor in 1824. He won his fourth term by the largest margin in his career.

Roger Skinner was with Van Buren in Washington when the election returns filtered down.

"I hope, Judge, that you are now satisfied that there is such a thing as killing a man too dead," Van Buren said.

Skinner was overwhelmed. He collapsed on the spot and soon afterwards died in Van Buren's arms.

Medical science was not refined in those days, so a lot of people supposed that Skinner had died of grief over having made a profound mistake.

Of that, and simple shame.

As GOOD AS HIS WORD, John Dyson resumed his lobbying efforts on behalf of ICONN-Erie when his troubles with the coal-fired power plant on Staten Island eased. He asked no kudos for himself when he tried to sway the governor. At least, I think he asked no kudos.

"I told the governor that if it's a success, he could call it 'Carey's Canal,' " Dyson said. "If it fails, he could call it 'Dyson's Ditch.' "

At about the same time, I suggested to Chattey that if his project were funded and built, he might become a national hero. He stared at me oddly for a moment before beginning his response. The look told me my comment was that of a fool.

VIII

CAVALRY RIDING IN TO ASSIST the ICONN-Erie Irregulars arrived in two waves. The first consisted of a single horseman. The second was a massed intellectual force — strong enough, Chattey hoped, to decide the fate of ICONN-Erie, one way or the other, once and for all.

The first was Francis Coleman, the Rochester attorney who had put Chattey in touch with Robert Embry at HUD. Any number of people, upon hearing of ICONN-Erie, voluntarily devoted time and energy to advance the cause, but few, if any devoted more than Coleman; perhaps none did so with such dash, passion and verve. Through much of the time I chased Nigel Chattey, Coleman was his shadow. Interesting, he was another expatriate Englishman, though, having emigrated when only six years old, he retained no obvious trace of his origin. Still, as I watched these two former subjects of the Queen running around, working to save the former colonies, I had the feeling

I was seeing the American Revolution rerun, upside down and sideways.

("It may be that only the first-generation immigrant truly understands the possibilities in this country," Chattey told me once.)

Coleman was either forty-two or forty-three, he could never remember which. He looked ten years younger. He worked in the Environmental Affairs Office of Rochester city government and, on the side, he operated a lucrative export business which sold heavy construction equipment all over the world. "I grew up in a funny old-style English house where my father always said, 'If you are blessed with a brain, if you are blessed with health, if you should ever be blessed with comfort or even wealth, remember this: imposed on *all* of that is a public trust,' " Coleman said. "ICONN-Erie satisfies that sense of civic duty in a way nothing else ever has."

In the summer of 1979, Coleman learned of the Chattey plan through an article in the Rochester *Democrat & Chronicle,* and it rang all of his bells. He held degrees not just in law, but in history and engineering, besides. "Perhaps the most selfish reason I got into this is I want to *do* something with my life," he said. So he phoned John Petty and volunteered. Petty gave him Chattey's number, and Chattey, to Coleman's surprise, said he would be glad to fly up for a personal briefing if Coleman could put together a good enough audience for a formal one. And that was that. Chattey would later describe his red-haired and freckled compatriot as "the 'Patton' of ICONN-Erie. He is my field commander." Not that it mattered, but Coleman had eyebrows enough for them both.

If Eristoff was good at reacting to political machinations, Coleman was expert at creating them. He demanded that Chattey conduct no briefing without first knowing what it was he *wanted* from the audience. "One of the problems is you never *ask* for anything," I heard him tell Chattey once. That was essentially true. Chattey's sense of propriety led him to expect that people charged with the public trust would offer assistance if they thought the project made sense. Another blind spot.

So Coleman did the asking. We want *you* to be the channel for information about ICONN-Erie in this industrial sector. We want *you* to give us a letter of endorsement. We want *you* to put us in touch with the president of thus-and-such, who we happen to know you play golf with on Wednesdays. And so on. Chattey resisted many of Coleman's ideas. I regularly saw them scrap like siblings, but never saw either leave such an engagement anything but the better for it.

Eristoff, meanwhile, had engineered the inclusion of an ICONN-Erie endorsement in a state senate study entitled "Improving the Economy of New York." Coleman used that endorsement to inspire the bill in support of the project which awaited introduction in both houses of the legislature, and he lined up the sponsors, too: Joseph Pisani, a Republican senator; and Roger Roback, a Democratic assemblyman. He even wrote the bill jacket for them.

If ICONN-Erie could be advanced through traditional channels, Coleman would do the dredging.

"Everything was going swimmingly," Coleman told me, but then Brian Smith, an aide on Roback's staff, "tipped me that reservations kept trickling down from the governor's office. The governor had professed to be pro-ICONN, but his staff was giving out the feeling that they would veto such a bill. I asked why. They'd tell Brian their concerns, and he'd tell me. I'd shoot them down — they just were not intelligent questions, they showed a real lack of knowledge. Anyway, Brian would give them my answers.

"But I began to strongly suspect that what the reservations were *really* designed to do was to string us along until the governor put together a proposal to take barges down the Oswego route and across Lake Ontario. The plan came through in bits and pieces from persons I think should go nameless.

"So I started putting strong pressure on the governor's staff. I said, 'Look, what you have to understand is that sitting on the fence and taking no position on ICONN-Erie is *not* a safe course. The subject of energy costs in New York is becoming a highly political question for which scapegoats will be sought and found. There is a growing awareness that our energy problems are not only man-made, they are *American*-made, the result of inaction, among other things, by our political leadership. Now, it's fairly common knowledge in some circles that the governor's family is deeply involved in the oil business, is moving oil by little tiny barges, has a vested interest in the present highly inefficient system; also that those barges are using the Oswego Canal. I'm not going to be the one to do it, but when the governor hatches this neat little alternative to ICONN-Erie, if the wrong people go public with it, he's going to get crucified.

" 'So the governor's course is *extremely* dangerous. He should be running scared, and if he's not, then his staff is letting him down badly.' "

The pressure worked. Thus Chattey's first meeting with the governor's personal minions was arranged. The session was hot and heavy. Chattey lost his temper and got into a bad argument with Hugh O'Neill, the assistant to Robert Morgado, the governor's secretary, when O'Neill challenged his coal-export forecasts. People on both sides got their feelings hurt.

Nevertheless, Coleman had known in advance what he wanted from that audience, and he came away with it: a list of the state's threshold concerns, its reasons for withholding support for ICONN-Erie. They were presented as questions, and Chattey was invited to answer them in writing. These were a few of them:

• Is it likely that New York State will consume large quantities of Western coal?

• What are the realistic chances that the Port of New York will become a coal-exporting center?

• Why would traffic divert to the canal from the St. Lawrence Seaway?

• Would people on Long Island be fearful of ICONN's use as a site for sewage disposal?

• Would people in New York City be fearful of ICONN's use as a site for nuclear plants?

• And, since storage facilities for coal require a great deal of space, where might such facilities be located in the vicinity of the Port of New York?

As with most of the questions Chattey was asked — thousands and thousands of them after almost three hundred presentations — the state's inquiries fell into three groups: those already answered in the project prospectus (Chattey had long since updated the Blue Book, replacing it with the Green Book, which contained, among other things, copies of his letters of endorsement); those which were the very questions the feasibility studies were needed to answer (for them, speculation would have to suffice); and those which were founded in either economic or technological ignorance.

In his response to the governor's staff, Chattey patiently explained that the state would consume large quantities of Western coal only if it had access to

Western coal, the same holding true for all the North-east; that New York would become a coal-exporting center only if it built an exporting facility; that the canal was not intended to divert Seaway traffic (he noted in passing, however, that Japan, the major U.S. coal importer, was a thousand miles closer to the mouth of the canal than to that of the Seaway, an eight-day sailing difference): that, anything but fear-ful, executives of both Long Island counties supported the studies; that ICONN was not intended as a site for nuclear plants; and that ICONN itself, for heaven's sake, would be the coal storage facility.

These were others of the questions, and Chattey's answers:

• *Since salt water damages underground trans-mission lines, what would happen to under-ocean transmission lines?*

"Any transmission system will be installed within a 'double tunnel' which itself will be *under* the sea floor."

• *Have speed limitations on the canal been fig-ured into the cost equations?*

"Speed is seldom a controlling factor in bulk commodity movement. Use of a steady stream of the largest transportation units possible assures a shipper of the inventory cost-benefit of 'floating storage.'"

• *Can ICONN-Erie be ready in time — say, within fifteen years — to service the projected demand for coal exports?*

"Several alternatives exist to bring major portions of both the ICONN and ICONN-Erie projects into use even within six years, phasing in additional usable elements later. This is very much like building a shopping center, with additions being added as needs develop."

For the canal, for example, "Initially, a single lock

system can be built, the locks deeper than the channel connecting them. Subsequently, the channel can
be widened to allow two-way simultaneous passage,
then deepened to increase annual throughput." The
three-step system "can then be duplicated by a parallel lock system, dual locks, to provide another three
increments in annual cargo throughput."

• *Is there enough water in the state to feed a
larger canal?*

"Yes, the water is sufficient. The Finger Lakes
now drain north via Oswego to Lake Ontario. The
modernized canal provides an opportunity to improve
water management in the Oswego, Genesee *and* Mohawk watersheds. This is a significant major by-product of the project.

"Those who need further encouragement," Chattey wrote, should consider the Ludwig Canal through
the Alps. "The Germans are achieving this with *no*
natural water reservoirs lying *above* them, unlike the
Erie which, in its western section alone, has *eleven*
natural reservoirs lying above it."

(In Holland, Jene Langevoord explained for me
numerous new lock designs which husbanded water
supplies. One was for side-by-side locks to fill and
flush simultaneously; the water dumped to lower
vessels going in one direction on one side would
raise vessels going in the other direction on the
other side. Another was to raise and lower the lock
chamber itself — a "bathtub" lock, it was called —
to effectively stop the flow-through of canal waters
at every upstream lock gate. There were a lot of
possibilities.)

• *And finally, are there realistic cost estimates for
any part of the project?*

Chattey enjoyed answering that one. He cited cost
estimates made in the Army Corps' Great Lakes-to-
East Coast preliminary study, then compared them to

the combined cost estimates for the state's favored plan, the Albany-to-Oswego route combined with a LELO canal. A two-barge system on the old Erie route would cost $2.2 billion; on the other, $5.1 billion. A four-barge system would cost $4.5 billion in the first case, $6.3 billion in the second, the Corps reported. Cost ratios for any size of new canal network would follow the same curve of increase.

It would take the governor's staff some time to react, Chattey and Coleman knew, so they returned their attention to the creation of grass roots support for the project throughout the state. And, with a new administration setting up housekeeping, they looked once more to Washington.

Coleman imagined lots of possibilities. For example, at the EPA: "The 'superfund' legislation to tax chemical companies to make money available to process toxic wastes says that two years from December 1980 — when the 'superfund' was passed — the administrator of EPA must report to the Congress on a nation-wide study of toxic waste management sites. The study must be done in coordination with states, regions and *non-governmental* agencies, and it must consider regional, interstate and intrastate approaches. And it *must* solicit and evaluate proposals, *must.* They have no choice. They have got as a matter of law to listen to us. And not only do they have to, they are going to want to."

And on the regional level, Coleman had lots of things cooking. He just happened to chair the environmental law committee of the state Bar Association. The committee just happened to be working on a study to determine if mega-projects, given the complexity of modern environmental law, were still possible in the State of New York and, if not, what would have to be changed to make them possible. The test case just happened to be ICONN-Erie.

Coleman was one of the few people I met who shared Chattey's sense of urgency. I asked him why.

"I have a profound fear of war," he said, explaining that his earliest memories were of London, during the blitz. "I grew up in a world where the stock phrase was 'before the war.' Before the war you had something called oranges, before the war you had something called bananas, which were long and yellow. Before the war you had gasoline. Before the war you had ice cream, raw milk, fresh eggs.

"I remember running down in the basement when the bombers came over. They eventually got our house," he said.

"I believe you're fairly formed by the time you're six. My psychology was that war was the norm. All of existence consists of war, with interludes of peace. People who have grown up in peacetime don't understand that — it's not enough to have fought in a war; to understand it you must have lived in one. War is something that happens unless you fight to prevent it. It's going to happen unless we stop it.

"If the flow of Persian Gulf oil stops, our economy shuts down. It's not a question of price anymore. If the Persian Gulf shuts down, given our present system, it won't be a question of if we will be fortunate enough to pay seven dollars for a gallon of gasoline. There *won't* be any to buy.

"And the average American thinks, well, hell, we'll just run our oil wells in Texas around the clock, and what about the Argentinian supplies? They don't realize that the IEA (International Energy Association) treaty, which we committed ourselves to in Paris, means that Paris becomes the headquarters for the rationing process. On the books, oil will flow to the IEA, and we'll get the national share, and then the White House farms it out as is necessary to keep the vital functions going.

"The vital functions will not include shopping in your car. They will not include commuting in your car. They will probably include a National Guard truck to pick you up and take you downtown to work. It's a scenario that is so alien to our thinking that we just don't face it, yet the sequence of events which needs to be triggered to make it happen is so close — improbable, I hope, but *so* close. And so simple. And so cheap. ICONN-Erie addresses that issue in spades."

(A related tidbit: "We must modify our concept of civilization," wrote Jacques Cousteau, in warning, at about the same time. "Today, our *only* response to an oil boycott would be military.")

Not long after Coleman and I spoke, he used a personal connection to bring ICONN-Erie, for the first time, to the Reagan White House.

(An unrelated tidbit: I once thought it would be interesting to have a sample of Chattey's handwriting analyzed. He had three handwritings, it turned out — one an artist's block printing, one a free-flowing script, one a compromise between the two. The phrase he chose off the top of his head to produce in all three for my examination and comparison was this one: "In the West Wing.")

A VICIOUS WIND drove stinging sleet and whipped great dervishes in the drifting snow on the night in January of 1981 when Peter Wiles heard his first ICONN-Erie presentation. Chattey had been invited to address academicians and anyone else who cared to listen at Eisenhower College, near Seneca Falls on the western shore of Cayuga Lake. Wiles by then knew as much about the ICONN-Erie thesis as almost anyone — he had just never seen the show. He gave me a lift to the session.

Wiles swung into the school's parking lot and toyed with his Ford wagon, spinning ovals and eights on the glaze of ice, then slid expertly into the parking space closest to the door of the auditorium. The space was marked with a blue and white sign which held the image of a man in a wheelchair.

"Handicapped parking," I said.

He considered the fierce weather only briefly. "Yeah, right," he said, then got out and faked a tremendous limp all the way to the building.

Though I had seen the presentation dozens of times, that one was new for me, too. Coleman had gone so far as to restructure the ICONN-Erie argument itself. "You don't start out by telling people about an island and a canal," he said — too many chances there for them to write the whole thing off as science fiction. "You start off by telling them what their problems are" — energy costs, pollution, waste disposal, inflation, a declining economy, national security and the rest — "and *then* you present the solution."

I did not think Chattey's presentations in that format were ever as good as those in the original, but that may have been because he had done the thing so many times that he had trouble remembering, on any given occasion, what he had already said and what he was saving for later. Or it may have been because by then the notion of ICONN-Erie had grown so large it overwhelmed even him. "I can't drive for ten minutes upstate anymore without seeing *something* that relates to the project," he said. In his 1981 presentations, Chattey overlooked core elements of his 1976 approach entirely. "My biggest problem these days," he said, "is front-end erosion. There are only so many neurons in the brain."

Attendance at the college presentation was better than I expected, given the weather. Only the day before, Chattey had done a full briefing for only three members of one county's board of supervisors, the three who braved a blizzard to attend. They turned out to be the *right* three, however, and their influence carried an ICONN-Erie endorsement by the board.

As a matter of fact, Chattey had yet to miss formal approbation of his plan by any assemblage he addressed as he worked his way from Buffalo, east, in the grassroots effort. He and Coleman had generated the proper support in Niagara, Orleans, Genesee, Monroe, Wayne and Ontario counties, and were then working Cayuga. The thing they attempted had never been done before: to ally all the federal A-95 community development regions in a single request for a single project. It appeared to be working.

Wiles left the session that night more convinced than ever. Canallers had time on their hands in the winter, so in the days that followed, when he was not making new oaken benches for *Emita II* in the basement of his Skaneateles office, he ran a letter-writing campaign. His voice ought to carry some weight, he reckoned. By 1981 his company had carried more than 60,000 passengers on the canal and was becoming, in its own right, a major tourism force. Almost half of the passengers — from twenty-nine states and eleven foreign countries — had joined *Emita II* in 1980 alone.

"I used to feel that I had to *sell* the idea of the canal to state officials," he told me. "Now I get a sort of inner joy, because it no longer has to be sold. The poor bastards are going to have to accept it, there's nothing they can do about it. It's just coming, like the floods."

Most of the missives Wiles sent — there were fifty, at least — went to the political types who had failed to attend his VIP cruise. As a body, the responses formed an interesting compendium of the kind of nonsense elected officials told their constituents. Wiles understood the idea better than anyone he wrote to, yet the majority responded by thanking him for his interest and promising that when more was known of the project, they would be sure to let him know. "Hah," Wiles said.

(The skipper was so taken with the plan, in fact, that he tinkered with its design. He figured out, for example, that he could fit into an existing canal barge 105 tractor-trailer bodies — the "containers" which carried the bulk of imports at the Port of New York — and then use a deck-mounted crane to swing them ashore onto waiting flat-bed trucks. That would allow enormous east-west traffic, from New York to Chicago and beyond, he thought. "I almost called Chattey, I really did, I got so fucking excited when I worked that out," he said. "The idea was so good I thought I could patent it.")

One of the responses to Wiles' letters proved to be of particular interest, the reply from the office of Governor Carey. "We are not convinced that the ICONN-Erie proposal represents the best possible plan of action," it said in part. "Other, more modest improvements of the canal are, however, being seriously considered by the State and the Corps of Engineers. These proposals are being pursued. Interest in ICONN-Erie should not be allowed to obscure the other proposals, which might provide a more realistic alternative and a more immediate benefit to the state."

The letter was signed by Hugh O'Neill, deputy to the governor's secretary, the man with whom Chattey had fought at his meeting with the governor's staff.

That letter sent me looking for the "more modest improvements," which were explained to me by the Corps to be the four-barge Albany-to-Oswego route, coupled to a new LELO canal. It also left me wanting to speak with Hugh O'Neill.

PERHAPS BECAUSE THEY WERE GENTLEMEN, perhaps because they were very cautious, politically, none of the ICONN-Erie principals would name for me people they believed were enemies of the project, and I had certainly met none in the field. I was an eavesdropper, however, and I eventually had no doubt about two names on the Enemies List. One was Ray Schuler, the state transportation commissioner who preceded William Hennessy. The other was Hugh O'Neill.

O'Neill, as I interpreted his remarks, had three basic problems with ICONN-Erie. First, the project would be costly. Second, if Western coal were going to be used in the East, somebody besides Nigel Chattey would be making the same prediction. And third, if the canal were the right means for moving the coal, somebody besides Nigel Chattey would have had the same idea. He did not mention the island at all. The state's more modest proposal included no offshore island.

"The fundamental objection is that it is extremely costly and extremely complicated," O'Neill told me.

"The economic justification is at best shaky. Potential benefits of the project only remotely approach justifying the costs.

"Nobody who has seriously looked at the issue, outside of the ICONN-Erie organization itself, has found that there is any economic or engineering sense at all in meeting coal export demands by moving Western coal across the Great Lakes and the canal to New York.

"And even if it did make sense, it would probably make *more* sense to use the St. Lawrence Seaway.

"Nobody other than Nigel Chattey thinks there is going to be much movement of Western coal to the East. It verges on fantasy to suggest that ICONN-Erie makes sense.

"I'll have more faith," O'Neill said, "I'll be more willing to contemplate the possibility of the ICONN-Erie Project, when the people who would benefit from the execution of the project come forward and put some money into it."

That was the same chicken-egg problem — which comes first, state support to inspire industry, or industrial support to inspire the state? — that Petty and Dyson had failed to resolve six years before.

I asked O'Neill if he would identify for me the gubernatorial aides who had killed the DOE and HUD grant applications when Davis and Embry had called. "I don't know who it was," he said. "It wasn't me."

I generally attempted to avoid forthright editorializing as I wrote this story, but I chose to make an exception here. Concerning O'Neill's objections:

First, he was right. The project was complicated, and it would be costly, but only the feasibility studies could determine if benefits would justify costs.

Second, if no one but Nigel Chattey had thought of using the canal for coal movement, it may have been because some people did not feel they had to wait to have an idea until somebody else had the same idea.

And third, there were in fact lots of people who imagined use of Western coal in the East.

Prior to the passage of amendments to the Clean Air Act in 1977, the use of clean Western coal in industrial boilers required no scrubber installation at all, and a great many people connected in one way or another to the coal industry had been saying for years that the reason for the amendments had nothing to do with the environment. It was a straight political shot. For one of the first times in their turbulent history, Eastern coal company operators and the United Mine Workers union — the members of which worked almost exclusively in Eastern fields — joined lobbying forces and forced passage of the amendments, which were so strict as to require scrubbers at *all* coal plants. Scrubbers were expensive. Without that legislation, the miners and operators feared, low-sulfur Western production would put them all out of business.

Before passage of that legislation, Commonwealth Edison in Chicago replaced some of its Appalachian suppliers with producers in the West. Soon afterwards, Detroit Edison invested millions in a major experiment: Could Western coal, with the cost of a 1,500-mile water-borne shipment included, produce power in Michigan more cheaply than could Appalachian coal, shipped 150 miles by rail?

Detroit utility officials in 1975 signed a contract with the Decker Coal Company of Montana, and with the Burlington-Northern, which ran unit trains through the coal fields. They built the ingenious Ortran transshipment facility at Superior-Duluth (the hopper cars had rotatable couplings; the cars were clamped in place, then whole sections of track were inverted to dump the coal). And they built two giant lake colliers, the *Bel River* and the *St. Clair.*

"It's worked out well," I was told by Robert Lundgren, a Detroit Edison vice-president. "In fact you'd have to say it's worked out *very* well." It had worked out so well that Lundgren refused to cite statistics. Just then, Detroit Edison was in court fighting a rate increase proposed by the Burlington-Northern, "and if the railroad knew exactly *how* well we're doing, they'd argue that we could easily afford the increase," he said.

Lundgren did tell me that in 1981 the utility planned to begin construction of a new power plant designed exclusively for Western coal. And Detroit Edison did, in 1980, end a contract for 2 million tons of coal a year from the North American Coal Company, an Appalachian producer, in favor of more Western coal. And a letter-to-the-editor of the *New York Times* from David Alberswerth of the Western Organization of Resource Councils said that had the utility used Montana coal exclusively in 1979, savings to consumers on fuel costs would have totaled $111 million. Had no scrubbers been required, the savings would have been greater still.

I asked Lundgren if he foresaw movements of Western coal further east than Detroit. His company's St. Clair plant, which received Western coal, stood only a spit and a whistle from the westernmost shores of Lake Erie.

"Depending on the rates of the Burlington-Northern, sure," he said, "as far east as Buffalo, at least." Prior to the 1977 Clean Air amendments, in fact, the Niagara Mohawk Power Corporation had planned to use Powder River coal in a plant it was building just south of Buffalo.

Lindgren had doubts about shipments east of Buffalo. There was no way to take it further, he said, except the Welland Canal in Canada, which was already congested. Purposefully, I had not told him about ICONN-Erie.

"But if your basic question is 'Are *we* making money on Western coal,' " Lundgren said, "there is no question — we *are* making money. We're kind of proud of it."

A BIG, FLASHY MODEL OF ICONN'S FIRST POLDER was an occasional prop in Chattey's traveling show. The polder sat on a scale ocean bottom visible under a blue-tinted Plexiglas sea; it was served by an eight-inch LNG tanker and a tug pushing a tiny tow of coal barges through the supposed waves; it was protected by facsimile dikes covered with hundreds of quarter-inch plastic cubes, representatives of the seven-foot concrete blocks Chattey hoped one day to see armoring dikes on a somewhat larger ICONN.

The model was designed as an eye-catcher, mostly. It was the centerpiece of a portable display Chattey used at industrial fairs here and there, a collapsible aluminum framework which opened to form a show wall and counter-space combination, nine feet high and twenty long. It held the model, twenty or so ICONN-Erie and historical placards, and piles of Chattey's promotional material. He no longer handed out Green Books at random, they were too costly to produce, so typically he used instead a stapled sheaf of Xeroxed newspaper clippings, project endorsements and maps. The display was conceived for possible use at the New York State Fair in the fall. It was designed and built by Alexis Oleinikoff, husband of Chattey's eldest daughter, Anna; with a limited operating budget, ICONN-Erie was largely a family affair.

The problem was that both the model and the mate-able halves of the show booth were bulky and heavy — each piece approached one hundred pounds — and Chattey still spent most of his time on the road alone. Thus I found him in the early spring of 1981, sleeves rolled, sweating, struggling to move the contraption to a waiting rented truck at the close of a trade exhibition in Rochester.

The exhibition was secondary; he had come to town principally to speak with people of Coleman's choosing as the attorney worked to establish the ICONN-Erie Development Council of Rochester, a satellite non-profit group, intended to pressure Albany. Coleman hoped it would be led "not by a good board of directors, but by the best possible board," a collection of the most powerful men in the region —

utility chairmen, industrial chairmen, bank chairmen and so on. Chattey had done thirty-six presentations in the Rochester area alone.

At the same time, William Paxon, an Erie County legislator, worked to create the ICONN-Erie Development Council of Buffalo, and Paul Lattimore, the feisty mayor of Auburn, New York, prepared to command the ICONN-Erie Development Council of Central New York. The ICONN-Erie Development Council of Long Island was also in formation; the ICONN-Erie Development Council of the Mid-Hudson Valley was already formed. "Do you see it?" Chattey asked me, beaming over the strategy. "It's a pincer movement. We're moving in on Albany from both sides."

At the same time, two articles about the project — the most comprehensive reports to date — appeared in national magazines. The first, in *Next*, was an essentially straightforward outline of the ICONN-Erie thesis by John Sedgwick, a *Next* staff writer. The greatest strength of the piece, to my mind, was the inclusion of a pair of gorgeous artist's conceptions, commissioned by the magazine and overseen by Chattey — one of Chattey's Island, the other, a new Clinton's Ditch. The only real weakness was the format itself; *Next* was a futurist publication, and Chattey still had trouble convincing people that the project concepts were time-tested, time-honored, nothing new. An editor at *Next* put this headline on the story: "Nigel Chattey Has Power Surges, Then He Macrothinks." ("The last thing I needed," Chattey told me, "was to be made out to be the guru of the Hudson Valley.")

The second article appeared in the spring issue of the prestigious *Wharton* magazine. It was the first account of the project which went beyond simple description of the idea and its author. Freelance writer

Donald Sutherland took in the plan in a snappy, up-beat style and, to my relief, he included interviews with people I had overlooked. That came as no surprise. I had long-since concluded that a writer could spend the rest of the century speaking with the people who had spoken with Nigel Chattey. Sutherland quoted Dr. Frank Davidson of the MIT school of engineering: "We agree that the implications for Europe and for the international trade position of the western world are enormous and promising." He quoted an official of the Port Authority of New York and New Jersey: "I'd sure hate to see the rail lines that parallel the canal get obsoleted."

The only thing I found disturbing about the report was this: Sutherland had researched and written his piece in 1979, before I ever heard of ICONN-Erie. He had intended it for *New York* magazine, but a coup there had changed editorial leadership and the story was dropped from the budget. It had taken Sutherland a year and a half to connect with another editor who understood the stupendous project potentials.

At the same time, back-to-back editorials in support of ICONN-Erie appeared in the *Democrat & Chronicle.* "The governor and the DOT may be short-sighted," the first said. "Dramatic results rarely come without dramatic initiatives and risks," the second concluded. "A feasibility study is essential."

Newsday, meanwhile, had apparently modified its skepticism of 1977; it used a pair of ICONN-Erie pieces as the cover stories in one Sunday's business section. And my old paper, the *Post-Standard,* began running more or less regular reports on the project. One mistakenly carried a head shot of some minor public official in Oswego County over the slug-line, "Nigel Chattey," but Chattey took that in stride. "At least in the picture I had more hair," he said.

The growing grassroots support and increasing

media attention did nothing, however, to give Chattey hands-on assistance or to lessen the weight of the ICONN model and the display assembly, so I helped him lug them from the trade fair to the truck. Outside, we had trouble seeing much more than the dirt being blown through the streets. The National Weather Service that day reported winds of thirty-five miles per hour — a "fresh gale," Force 8 on the Beaufort Scale. While we wrestled with the aluminum framework, a gust caught the model, lifted it free of the dolly on which we had left it, and dropped it, overturned, on the sidewalk. Chattey's dikes survived the storm. The ocean did not. "Well, I've wanted a new model anyway," he said. "I've been working on one that will move."

The growing grassroots support and increasing media attention also did nothing to "dent the shield wall in Albany," as Chattey put it. No action came from the state.

Some people thought they could force it. "We're not here to join the debating society on this thing," said an angry Paul Lattimore, the Auburn mayor, when he formed his ICONN-Erie development council. "We're here to find the people who don't tell you why it can't be done but who can figure out how to do it."

As he spoke, Irregulars with the same gut belief in the project laid the groundwork for development councils of their own in Connecticut, Schenectady and southern Michigan.

Dan Curl of the New York Chamber of Commerce and Industry, ICONN-Erie's first convert, explained: "For all the great projects in the world, there was a leap — there were people who said, 'Okay, we've looked at this thing, now let's just do it.' You could have gone to the traffic managers in the 1940s and said, 'What if we had an interstate highway system?

Would you ship 75 percent of your goods by truck? Would you locate a plant in Kansas?' And they'd all have said 'no, no, no. The *only* way to go is by train.' But later we had a *general* who was the President — he was used to deciding, he decided about D-Day and things like that — and he looked at a map and said, 'Yeah, this would be pretty good. Let's *do* it.' So we did it, and once we did, it sure attracted a lot of business.

"So what we've got to find are leaders, people who'll just do it. History had proven that if you give the job to planners, they just fuck it up. To do something like ICONN-Erie, *some*body has got to take a leap of faith."

Behind the scenes at ICONN-Erie, however, the original faithful grew weary. After six years, Chattey still ran the project from his basement; there was still no support from the State of New York; there was still no financial backing save that of Marine Midland — the bank's contribution by then totaled about half a million dollars — and John Petty's duty to his stockholders continued to haunt him. The bank could not carry ICONN-Erie forever. Despite the new support and fresh publicity, Chattey told me later, the project in the spring of 1981 came closer to turning belly up than it ever had before.

"The truly remarkable thing," Eristoff told me once, "is that with a wild and woolly idea, somehow, we've gotten this far."

I thought so. The core of people who had moved the Chattey plan would have fit into a school bus, with seats to spare. Two of the principals, certainly, were Chattey's wife and their middle daughter, Bonnie. Maria Chattey not only managed the household and family affairs for the six years Chattey spent running all over creation, she both put up with and covered for him, over and over, and brilliantly, when his energy failed. And Bonnie, throughout the affair, had worked unpaid as the project's only full-time secretary. There was something both inspirational and touching in that. An umbilical tangle at birth had robbed her of oxygen for a time, had left her different from other children. Educational and psychological authorities later agreed that she would never learn so much as reading and writing. Maria Chattey would hear none of it. She tried one curriculum after another and finally designed her own. Through sheer force of will, I think, she *made* it work.

So Bonnie, for whom the experts offered no hope at all, became Chattey's round-the-clock telephone receptionist and answering service. With strict business manners, and grace, she meticulously recorded thousands of messages; she became a mainstay of a plan to change the world. "There has never been funding for a staff," Chattey told me. "I'm not saying this because she's my daughter but because it is true. Without her, we'd *never* have made it this far."

For all the proud effort, Chattey doubted they would make it much further, perhaps no further than the next city on his eastward sweep of New York, the city where I lived, Syracuse. There a force grand enough to determine the fate of ICONN-Erie — that second wave of cavalry — stood waiting.

In Washington, meanwhile, Francis Coleman made his first approach ("the first torpedo run," Chattey would say) to the Reagan White House. A friend put him in touch with Danny Boggs, a special Presidential assistant. This was the pitch:

"Reagan could sponsor it — here would be a Western governor solving the energy crisis in the East," Coleman said. "He could take the lead where there is currently no leadership, he could hold the

Northeast's feet to the fire. He could say, 'Look, the federal government won't fund this project, but we'll make it possible — we'll give you the permits, we'll slash the red tape, whatever.' " Boggs agreed to be the White House conduit for policy papers on ICONN-Erie. At the same time — this was May of 1981 — U.S. Representative Barber Conable of Rochester took Vice-President George Bush aside when he visited that city to talk to the Boy Scouts and to make political speeches. Conable was a fan of the project. He explained it and Bush was intrigued.

The interest of Boggs and Bush, Coleman believed, would open doors everywhere.

THE OTHER SUPPOSED ARCH-ENEMY of the ICONN-Erie Project was Ray Schuler, former transportation commissioner and, in 1981, the executive director of the New York Business Council. When we spoke, he took me quite by surprise.

"I don't know who told you I'm not a fan of the project," he said. "I think it's a great idea, one that we should *find* investment money for, to do the feasibility studies. These are the kinds of studies government *has* to start, *has* to move on."

I was baffled. There was no question that the ICONN-Erie principals counted Schuler among their deadliest foes. They went out of their ways to avoid him.

Then it occurred to me that the same failure at routine communication among intelligent men which had wrecked the deal with Dyson years earlier remained in effect. I considered both sides responsible. All that Hugh Carey knew of the project, he had learned second hand; and Schuler was adjudged an adversary, I later discovered, on evidence which was not just second hand, but third.

There were many other examples. ICONN-Erie promoters, after the business with Dyson, assumed the "shield wall" was up at the state Department of Commerce, even after Dyson moved on. When I spoke with William Hassett, the new commissioner, however, he told me he would be glad to put up some of his department's money to get the studies started. "Then why don't you?" I asked. "Nobody's asked me to," he said. It just may have been that a lot of governmental perimeters were less fortified than Chattey imagined — that behind many of the "shield walls" were neither opponents nor conspirators, just regular folks who needed more of his time and patience and understanding, more education about ICONN-Erie.

That much was my speculation. Schuler flat-out told me, however, that he knew of many pockets of support for the plan in Albany. "Then why is the project stalled?" I asked.

"Well, let's look a little bit at the reality of the last several years," Schuler said. "In the mid-seventies, when this thing broke, New York was fighting to establish that it *had* an economic future. We were losing jobs, we were losing industry, businesses were closing. The project came on the scene at a time when we were trying to save forty-two jobs here and fifty there. That's what the attention and focus have been on. Now we've finally gotten that stuff; we haven't recovered, but we're reversing the tide. *Now* we can start striking out and looking at some of the bolder things that need to be done. Like ICONN. The idea has enough obvious merit to be pursued to the next stage."

"Fine," I said. "Tell me how."

"Well, I don't mean to seem critical, but I don't think there is a mechanism here at the moment that can do it. You'd need something like a mini-cabinet, combining commerce, economic development, energy, transportation, the Public Service Commission, the power authority, environmental conservation. And that can only be formed if the governor were to run to one of his commissioners and say, 'You — put this together.' "

"The governor does not seem so inclined," I said.

Schuler hesistated a moment, then said: "Then it sounds like the project needs you. Maybe it's you who'll put people together. It may be that what you're doing now — stirring, pollinating — will be what kicks it off."

I had heard that sort of reasoning before, from Dyson's people, among others, and I did not like it at all. The idea that the leaders of government were incapable of so much as speaking with each other until the press gave them an excuse to do so offended me deeply. And the possibility that the idea was also the truth simply scared me to death.

"If I were to try it," Schuler continued, "if I were to start jumping up and down and shouting about this great project that's going to be the renaissance of New York, the re-creation of the Empire State, all the people here would say, "Hell, here comes upbeat Schuler with his positive games again. He must be running for office.'

"What the project needs now," he said, "is someone who is not suspect of using the media for his own advantage. It needs an ass-kicker. It needs a cheerleader."

AFTER CHASING CHATTEY for more than a year, I felt qualified to draw some conclusions. I settled on five. Four of them were horrible.

First: That many of the people in power who ignored ICONN-Erie, to the possible detriment of millions of their countrymen — and to the conceivable detriment of the nation itself — ignored it not because they disliked the idea but because they disliked Nigel Chattey.

Second: That many of the people in power who ignored ICONN-Erie because they did not understand it had never tried to understand it.

Third: That there was nothing blocking immediate implementation of the feasibility studies that could not have been resolved by a dozen of the right people, sitting around a conference table, in a single day of polite conversation.

Fourth: That the people who tried so valiantly to arrange such a meeting — the ICONN-Erie crew — did not know how to do it.

And fifth: That the people who did know how neither bothered nor could be bothered to do it.

"I used to think there was a conspiracy, I thought so for a long time," Chattey told me one night when the project seemed doomed. "What I think now is worse. It is very simple. The ingredient consistently missing in the people we've gone to is *any* ultimate concern for the rest of us. I find it nowhere. They do not care," he said.

SYRACUSE UNIVERSITY was the eleventh institution of higher learning to host ICONN-Erie presentations. Many of the others had expressed interest in working on the final feasibility studies, but none offered help in reaching that point. In Syracuse, however, things started clicking for Chattey. Cavalry for sure. Cheerleaders, maybe.

Members of the metropolitan and regional planning associations liked the idea, so they swung an invitation for Chattey to address the University Roundtable, an invitation-only discussion group comprised of many of the community's leaders. Chattey charmed that conservative crowd. Richard Oliker, a dean at SU, met with him afterwards and gathered enough data for his transportation studies department to consider. Department members concluded that the idea warranted further study and so, for the sake of comparison, Oliker went looking for other large-scale economic development possibilities for the state. He found none.

So he arranged for Chattey to brief his faculty, and that of the State of New York College of Environmental Science and Forestry, which shared the campus. The faculty consensus was positive. "So what can we do for you?" Oliker asked.

"You could test the thesis," Chattey said, proposing a "concept" study — less of feasibility than of credibility — a does-it-make-sense study. That would end the crazy-man problems at last; it would generate the national media attention needed to educate everyone at once. A report by a disinterested and respected third-party would send academia and the fourth estate to shake the Albany fences. Industries would have to reconsider. The Reagan administration would have a sufficient excuse to jump in. "And the other universities will *flock* to get a piece of the larger feasibility," Coleman said. "The pot will just boil and boil."

And such a study would forever end speculation that Buck Rogers had somehow assisted in the project design. It would make ICONN-Erie real.

All that was in the offing, *if* the findings were positive.

"They might not be, you know," Oliker told Chattey. "Are you sure you are willing to trust us with the fate of all this?"

"If you can find something significantly wrong with it," Chattey said, "then do it, please, so that I don't spend *another* six years doing this. Negative findings will free me to go and do something *useful.*"

Paul Brennan, head of SU's Department of Civil Engineering, volunteered to direct the study. "It will be an adventure," he said.

Syracuse University officials did not dislike Nigel Chattey. The six-week evaluation would cost $144,000, they said, but the university itself was willing to assume the $56,000-overhead charge. SU thus would become the second largest contributor to the ICONN-Erie Project.

So Chattey lay his child on their altar, asked that they try to cut its throat, then went out to raise the money to buy the knife. He had little time. The nineteen professors of engineering, economics, business, transportation, forestry, resource management, government and environmental science would be available only during the summer sessions. The study would have to begin by mid-May.

Chattey scurried. Chattey hustled. Chattey met precisely the same short-sighted resistance he had met all along, and precisely the same success. When the deadline for coming up with the cash drew close, John Petty and the Marine Midland Bank came through with the requisite $88,000. The opportunity was too good to pass up.

The SU and ESF professors designed their inquiry to evaluate future use of Western coal; potential for coal export from the Port of New York; alternatives for east-west bulk commodity shipment; availability of water resources; the pollution and anti-pollution consequences of ICONN; the technology of island and canal design; the possibilities for securing joint federal, state and local support; the impact of ICONN-Erie on foreign trade and foreign relations; and the overall need for the project.

The credibility study would be preliminary, but

technical. It would give Chattey one thing he had never had before: numbers. He could begin weighing people's desks down with paper.

Perhaps the faculties at SU and ESF were more visionary or more curious than those Chattey had met with before. And perhaps events in the world at last had caught up to the ICONN-Erie thesis. The problems it first addressed in 1975 had only grown worse, in some cases orders of magnitude worse. To cope with them, the mood of the country had changed — for example, the Clean Air Act was up for revision in 1981, and most political observers expected repeal of the 1977 scrubber amendment, to encourage the use of low-sulfur coal. And specific dilemmas for which ICONN-Erie was a possible solution had appeared all over the region. Even as the study began, for example, New York officials announced plans to build a toxic waste treatment plant north of Syracuse at Sterling. Both communities were up in arms. People in Sterling wanted no such thing in their back yards, and people in Syracuse challenged the wisdom of siting the plant so close to the Lake Ontario lines through which the county drew much of its drinking water. ICONN had not been considered as an alternative.

"Yet here's an *obvious* alternative," Dean Oliker told me. "Instead of building at Sterling, you just put all that shit on barges and ship it down to the ICONN. There are other alternatives, but not many as safe as ICONN would appear to be."

Soon after the study began, the professors realized that ICONN-Erie "was even bigger than the goddamned great auk's egg they'd imagined," as Chattey explained it. Assembly of the necessary research data was taking longer than expected, so the academicians proposed an extension of the inquiry: they would spend the same amount of time, do the same amount of work, but stretch both over a longer time frame.

The study would be done, they said, not by the end of
June but rather by the end of August.

That was fine with Chattey. For one thing, it
meant they were doing a proper job. For another, so
far as he was concerned, the ICONN-Erie Wars were
over. If the findings were negative, a surrender was
likely. If positive, only details would remain — a
mopping-up operation, a fight of a different kind entirely.

Moreover, all of the pending ICONN-Erie initiatives — development of the grassroots coalitions, approaches to Washington, the demonstration program
to run grain down the Erie Canal, the lobbying effort
with the Northeast-Midwest Coalition of Congress,
the bill awaiting introduction in the state legislature,
the follow-up talks with the governor's staff — everything was best left alone until SU and ESF published
their findings.

So Nigel Chattey, for the first time in a long time,
had some time on his hands, perhaps time enough to
go riding or sailing, to play tennis — activities he had
put aside when he began the ICONN-Erie Project.
There was certainly time enough for a holiday, so he
and Maria took their first real vacation in years. They
spent a week in the Bahamas.

"We must be unnatural people," Maria Chattey
told me over the phone when they returned. "We get
along by ourselves. We really don't need other people.
We never watched the news. We never read a paper.
We missed none of it."

"Did you get a good tan?" I asked.

"You wouldn't believe how beautiful I look," she
said. "We just sat by ourselves on the beach for seven
days. We did absolutely nothing."

Two days later Chattey flew up to Syracuse. He
stayed for a while, monitoring the study.

EPILOGUE

THE PRE-FEASIBILITY TEST of the Chattey plan pro-
gressed on schedule in June, July and August of 1981.
During that same summer:

• Shipbuilders at Toronto launched the world's
first floating mineral refinery. The plant was towed
3,500 miles to permanent anchorage near the lead and
zinc mines on Little Cornwallis Island in the Canadian arctic.

• The barge-mounted polyethylene plant designed
by Union Carbide was delivered to Argentina three
months ahead of schedule. The Japanese firm which
built it had by then also completed a floating power
plant for Bangladesh and a floating hotel for Abu
Dhabi.

• A 75-megawatt hydroelectric station, built in
France and towed 6,500 miles across the Atlantic and
up the Mississippi and Ohio rivers, was installed on
the Ohio at Vanceburg, Kentucky.

• And Daniel Ludwig, the American who fostered
construction of a power plant and a paper mill on

barges for use in the Amazon, began consideration of floating offshore coal-exporting terminals.

During that same summer, a Japanese collier of 165,000 deadweight tons turned up to load Appalachian coal off Seven Isles in the St. Lawrence Seaway. Most East Coast port officials by then were discussing plans to meet coal-export demands, but none proposed a harbor with sufficient depth to serve such a vessel. The most ambitious called for dredging to fifty-five feet, the requirement for colliers of only 125,000 tons.

And the President's Interagency Coal Export Task Force reported that the initial dredging costs of achieving even fifty-foot depths in the major East Coast ports, all told, would approach $8 billion.

During that same summer, the Consolidated Edison Corporation in New York City released two private studies which indicated a savings to consumers of $4 billion by 1990 were Con-Ed allowed to convert just three of its generating facilities from oil-firing to coal.

And the State of New Jersey revised its Energy Master Plan to include these words: "Even under zero load growth, it is likely that by 1990 all of the region's oil-fired steam electric facilities will need to be retired, or converted to coal. The proposals for siting coal-fired power plants offshore appear sound. The ICONN site would result in air quality degradation [which], under the worst-case conditions of a strong onshore breeze, would be no worse than burning coal in the metropolitan region itself. There can be no question that the option merits examination."

THE GOVERNOR'S AIDES, by the summer of 1981, had reviewed Chattey's responses to their "threshold concerns" regarding ICONN-Erie. I phoned to learn their reactions.

"It would take two hundred years to get a draft of the environmental impact statement," one said. "You can take Nigel's answers and throw them in Lake Erie," said another.

IN ALBANY THAT SUMMER, Peter Wiles and I attended the latest state-sponsored seminar on the developmental challenges facing New York's infrastructure. "Why don't they just say highways and railroads and canals?" Wiles asked me. For him, "infrastructure" was a mouthful.

Three experts on one thing or another, paid well for their time, occupied all of ours on the first morning of the session with speeches. One of them told the audience of two hundred that it was corruption among the private-sector promoters of the original Erie Canal which led government to get into the infrastructure business in the first place.

Wiles was appalled by the dissemination of such misinformation. "Wrong," he said aloud. The canal was a public-sector project from the start, with the governor, for heaven's sake, as its primary advocate.

At the subsequent committee session on ports and waterways, Wiles hoped to call the attention of legislators to those ancillary canal benefits which decision-makers regularly overlooked. The state building industry, for example, was comatose save alongside canal and river banks, where property remained in high demand by developers of hotels and restaurants and shopping plazas and new housing and golf courses. Then there was the business of building pleasure boats. Then there was the business of mooring pleasure boats. Then there was the business of tourism.

The skipper produced a scrapbook thick with clippings about his packet service from newspapers across the nation. "I'm the littlest company represented here," he told officials, "and in one year I've generated seventy-two articles, just by writing letters. Now, if I can do that, what could you do?"

Wiles hoped to propose a state-run marina in Onondaga Lake to attract boaters from the Northeast and Midwest to the State Fair at Syracuse. He hoped to propose display of classy photographs of canal locks, and directions on how to reach them, at all the rest areas on the state Thruway. "Instead," he told me earlier, "if you go looking for a lock, what do you find? A sign that says 'Dead End. Not a Thoroughfare. — NYS DOT.' " Were the state to promote the canal through a marriage of the New York departments of Commerce and Parks & Recreation, "the whole world would come to the reception," he hoped to say.

But he found no chance to voice most of the ideas. The committee session was a raise-your-hand affair, designed to afford various special-interest representatives the opportunity to read the same policy statements they had read at such gatherings for years. There was little real discussion, no talk at all of strategy. Wiles lost patience and left.

On the sidewalk outside the Albany Mall, New York's seat of government, Wiles got to chatting with a hot dog vendor.

"Special session?" asked Joe Ferris, who was thirty years old, as he laid on the mustard and kraut.

"Same old bullshit," Wiles said.

"Tell me about it," said Ferris, a man in the know. "I was a top aide to an assemblyman in there for five years."

"You quit?"

"It was unfulfilling," Ferris said. "Nothing *ever* happens in there." Selling hot dogs, he explained, was a lot more rewarding.

THE PAPER FOR WEIGHING DOWN DESKS stood to crush the weaker among them. In September of 1981, Syracuse University delivered a document seven hundred pages in length. Chattey knew that few people would wade through such a tome, so he asked the professors to go on to produce a concise executive summary of each part of the report. They agreed to do so. Then Chattey and Petty decided against going public with the study until the summaries were in hand.

In the meantime, Francis Coleman loaned me his copy of the full report, and I waded through. The first three parts dealt with engineering, environment and economics. The fourth was strictly political.

The study found that the proposed site of ICONN held "no geological features to make it unsuitable." Moreover, "There are deposits of sand and gravel up to ten meters deep over most of the [New York] bight," providing ample materials for island construction, it said.

The study found that "electric power can be generated safely, effectively and reliably" at an offshore island. The academicians said either AC or DC current, delivered to the mainland through entrenched, oil-filled cables with lead sheaths and steel armor, would produce no radiation harmful to marine or terrestrial life. In a cluster of perhaps ten 700-megawatt power plants, "ICONN might burn 40 million tons (of coal) per year for the 39-state power grid." Even if only half of ICONN's power production replaced power generated by burning oil at $32 per barrel, the island would "reduce the need for [imported] oil by $2 billion" annually, it said.

The study found "no legal restrictions on the use of the New York Bight area for an energy island."

The study found that "atmospheric pollution levels would not significantly increase in the area, nor would the westerly flows to Europe and the arctic," despite the professors' assumption that winds would blow onshore 50 percent of the time.

That finding was all well and good, but Chattey doubted that winds at ICONN would in fact blow toward the mainland half the time. The university based its estimate on reports by land-based weather stations. Much of the wind might have originated somewhere between the coastline and the island site, Chattey said. He told me measurements by wind buoys at the proposed location would be part of the larger feasibility test.

In assessing the canal aspects of ICONN-Erie, the researchers based their calculations on a waterway fourteen feet deep and 250 wide, with a four-barge capacity in each lock. A canal of such size was the smallest of the ICONN-Erie possibilities, but it would still rank among the largest in the world, they said.

The study laid to rest governmental fears that the state's water resource was insufficient to serve a modernized Erie. In a 290-day navigation season, the new canal could handle shipments of 80 million tons of cargo each way, as compared to the total of 3 million tons carried yearly on the existing waterway, the report said.

The route requiring the least excavation, according to the study, was from Albany west to Three Rivers along the existing Erie Canal; from Three Rivers north to Lake Ontario along the existing Oswego Canal; from Oswego west over the lake to Olcott, near the New York-Canadian border; and from Olcott inland, along a new canal, to Lake Erie.

Chattey agreed that such a route might be the cheapest, but he noted, as did the study, that the recommendation was based solely on engineering considerations. A variety of other factors remained to be studied, including the possibly hostile wind and wave action on Lake Ontario, and the political and economic ramifications of bypassing almost all of western New York.

In the study's consideration of canal economics, I found a problem. The professors accepted as given fifty lockings at thirty minutes each to traverse the Erie Canal. But in fact there were only thirty-five locks on the existing canal, and a modernized version no doubt would have fewer still. I did not know, nor could I learn, the degree to which the addition of at least fifteen hours of round-trip travel time skewed the university's findings.

The mistake was made, I suspected, because of the linguistic atrocity Wiles was fond of mentioning. People had come to call the Erie "the barge canal." New York's "Barge Canal System" — again, comprised of the Erie, Champlain, Cayuga-Seneca and Oswego canals — held fifty-seven locks in all.

That error aside, the SU study showed that a new Erie Canal would mean substantial savings for Great Lakes shippers who currently relied on the Mississippi River and the port of New Orleans. In a microstudy, researchers considered the movement of corn and soybeans produced in Ohio, Indiana and Illinois, to ICONN. As compared to the Mississippi-New Orleans route, savings for Erie-ICONN approached $40 million per year in barge transport costs alone.

Moreover, ICONN would lie at least 1,600 miles closer than New Orleans to European markets. Savings on trans-Atlantic grain shipments would be at least five dollars per ton, the study said. Thus, the researchers concluded, "Prospects for expanded exports [of grain] are excellent."

While the professors were unable either to confirm or deny the Chattey contention that supercolliers would eventually handle much of the coal-export trade, they were able to assess the ability of existing ports ever to serve such vessels.

"The ports of Hampton Roads, including Portsmouth and Norfolk, are ruled out because of the tunnel which runs under the bay entrance, restricting depth to a 55-foot maximum," the study said. Philadelphia was ruled out "because of the problems of dredging that far inland." Boston's port "is out of contention because of the absence of inland water outlets." And "Baltimore bedrock prevents 70-foot port improvement."

The study went on to note the periodic loss of channel depth in the Mississippi, affecting New Orleans; the limited facilities for export at Mobile; the high demurrage costs at Hampton Roads; and congestion in the ports of Philadelphia and Baltimore.

The ICONN-Erie thesis "is correct that the other ports cannot, in toto, handle a major increase in exportation of coal tonnages without considerably increased investment in terminals, transfer and blending facilities, and dredging," the study said. All port-expansion proposals "are counting on federal assistance with dredging projects," the report continued. "If federal funding is not forthcoming for dredging, some provision other than dredging, such as ICONN, must be made to accommodate larger ships for the European trade."

In theory at least, using Eastern coal, Western coal, or both, "ICONN-Erie could provide slightly less than one-third of the total steam coal [exported to Europe] from this country," the study said. Without it, "Even at maximum expansions, the ports of the East and Gulf coasts could face a shortage of as much as 37 million tons of throughput potential" per year by the year 2000, the study said. At a conservative $54 per ton, that would translate as an American loss in trade of nearly $2 billion a year.

ICONN "appears unique among the Atlantic Coast ports for the following reasons," the study said. "Location at the mouth of major inland water systems; proximity to a dense population; natural depth of channel; and [potential for] island storage of coal without claiming shorefront land."

While the university study posed many questions about the Chattey plan — future use of supercolliers, for example — it directly challenged the proposal on only two counts.

First, some academician apparently disapproved of Chattey's use of "man-years" in describing employment possibilities, and so replaced it with "person-years" in subsequent discussion.

And second, the study cast serious doubt on the export demand for Western coal which, while low in sulfur content, was also lower than Eastern coals in energy content.

"Only a substantial shift in the relative prices of delivered coal would make it competitive with Eastern coal," the study said. It estimated the delivered price of Western coal to ICONN at $3.21 per million Btu's, as compared to $2.10 per million Btu's for Kentucky coal barged to New Orleans. The spread might narrow when the overestimate of locking time was corrected, I thought.

In any event, the SU calculation "was strictly a cost study," Coleman told me. "There are other factors which affect price." The researchers agreed, and in the study they noted several of them among a number of things which would change the export outlook:

• The mine-mouth prices of Eastern and Western coals might change.

• Worldwide demand for American coal might outstrip the capacity of Eastern mines to produce.

• Loading delays at ports like Hampton Roads, which already added between six and ten dollars per ton to the cost of coal transshipped there, "might quickly void any transportation cost differentials between Eastern and Western coal," the study said.

• The price premium for low-sulfur coal, with environmental considerations in mind, might grow dramatically.

• And Eastern coal might "become undesirable in the future" because of labor conditions, high sulfur content, quality control problems and uncompetitive transportation rates.

Chattey agreed with each of those points, and he added another — not a possibility, he said, but a fact: "Coal from western Kentucky can be profitably moved to the Great Lakes and mixed with coal from the West," in facilities built alongside the canal, "to produce a coal with an acceptably low sulfur content *and* a sufficiently high Btu content."

In theory, the researchers agreed. If the Western supplies were to move at all, "We feel it is possible that only ICONN-Erie would be able to export large quantities of low Btu coal across the Atlantic at competitive prices," the study said. Indeed, while the cost survey found Wyoming coal costing $3.21 per million Btu's upon delivery at ICONN, the same coal cost $3.38 per million Btu's upon delivery at New Orleans. "The availability of very low sulfur coals might open up a market for some Eastern steam coal which might not otherwise have been exported," the study said. Thus ICONN-Erie stood to benefit all coal producers, East and West.

The professors also surveyed domestic potential for use of low-sulfur coal. One New England utility official said this of ICONN-Erie: "It is just this type of innovative program that may be needed to assist in bringing our energy problems into better balance with the economic realities and environmental needs of the nation."

The study contained many such qualifiers concerning its gloomy conclusion about the movement of Western coal. Perhaps the most significant disclaimer was this one: "It is difficult to separate the rhetoric of bargaining from the actual buying behavior of foreign markets," the study said, just as Coleman had said.

Chattey agreed again. Academia "can only study what has happened, not what is going to happen," he said, arguing that the data base needed to assess European interest in Western coal simply did not exist in the United States. So he packed his bags and his charts and the rest in September of 1981 and boarded a Concorde, bound for Europe. In the week that followed, he explained ICONN-Erie, at meetings arranged by Marine Midland's overseas staff, to energy officials in Brussels, Rotterdam, Milan, Madrid, London, and Paris. His aim, he said, was "to unravel the European positions, and composite them."

"TWO PROPOSITIONS ARE PARADOXICAL but nonetheless arguable," began the university's political assessment of the Chattey plan. "The ICONN-Erie idea is so big that it is not politically feasible. Or, the ICONN-Erie idea is so big that it is clearly politically feasible. The point is that estimating the political feasibility of ICONN-Erie cannot be done by looking at any other specific case."

Political scientists at SU noted Chattey's problem with bureaucracies. "Those who are against have yet to become visible," the study said. "The principal barrier at the moment is indifference and skepticism on the part of certain government officials at both the state and federal levels. One would think the Arab oil embargo of 1973–74 would have induced New York State leaders to turn this crisis into an opportunity, but there has been no sense of urgency."

The study went on to quote U.S. Senator Daniel Patrick Moynihan. "The [New York] Department of Transportation," fearful of lessening traffic on the state Thruway and losing the tolls, "insists that the canal has disappeared," Moynihan said. "We have a real conspiracy to return upstate New York to the condition in which Fenimore Cooper found it. The effort is going well, I must say."

In considering the future of ICONN-Erie, professors wrote, "Nothing is as certain as the uncertainty of political action. Such action can give rise to worthwhile as well as worthless projects. We do not know into which category ICONN-Erie will ultimately fall. But we would judge it is sufficiently promising to be worthy of further study.

"Perhaps the greatest challenge of all to proponents of ICONN-Erie is that of gaining the support and cooperation of the parties at interest in the enterprise," the study continued. At the top of the list of "parties at interest" was "the entire population of the Northeastern U.S."

"A citizens' association for ICONN-Erie is a sine qua non for its success," the study said. "This association should span all the geographic area to be impacted. It should be the principal spokesman, the explainer, the pleader, the central advocate."

Maybe so, but Chattey thought otherwise following his trip abroad.

The response of foreigners to the plan was "overwhelming," he said. "To find people suddenly talking in such a logical and sequential manner about energy supply could have *such* an effect on me," he said. "I might suddenly burst my seams."

The public sector had responded. In Paris, New Jersey's Governor Brendan Byrne introduced Chattey at a session of the International Energy Association.

ICONN-Erie fit neatly into the IEA's long-range plan for energy supply. Robert Duncan, a member of the U.S. embassy staff in Paris, later described the association's response to the project as "very, very positive." Chattey began to believe that the first governmental investment in ICONN-Erie might actually come from overseas.

And the private sector had responded. "In Belgium, they showed me a coal terminal where a rock *this big*," he said, spreading his arms wide, "and a piece of steel as long as that table had come in with the coal. They tore the entire conveyor system to pieces." That coal had come from small mines in Eastern fields and was shipped via Newport News.

Such contamination was all but unheard of in strip-mined Western coal shipments, and it would be far less likely to occur in Eastern coal supplies processed or blended at a modern transshipment facility like ICONN.

Private and public officials alike, "They *all* understood," Chattey said of the Europeans. He had experienced less luck with the American public sector, of course, so upon his return to the United States he refocused his energies on business and industry. The growing interest in coal export and the numerous private studies of the possibilities — Daniel Ludwig's, for example — convinced Chattey that he could form a consortium of coal suppliers, commodity traders, shippers and exporters to do the final planning and design studies of ICONN. The effort would include all work needed to apply for construction permits. A small-scale island, costing less than a single nuclear power plant, might then be built. Chattey believed the very existence of the first offshore element would prompt funding for the overall ICONN-Erie studies.

The bank, he said, could not be expected to finance the project beyond its conceptual stages. "Now I've got to interest the people who'll be *using* the thing." In so doing, he expected to make some money. Chattey prepared to establish a for-profit group called "Hydro-ICONN." He planned to manage Hydro-ICONN and ICONN-Erie simultaneously.

When Coleman learned of the new direction, he thought Chattey had suddenly burst his seams. He called the plan "a major strategic error." The private-sector approach would undo past efforts to form citizens' councils in Rochester and elsewhere, Coleman said, by destroying the project's long-standing non-profit pose.

He and Chattey argued about it, and the argument, I later learned, became both angry and personal. Coleman subsequently dissolved the ICONN-Erie Development Council of Rochester and resigned from the ICONN-Erie promotion.

"The object of the development councils was to create a level of awareness to influence Albany," Chattey said. "Coleman's approach was extremely logical, and his effort for two years was superhuman, but it did not succeed. Perhaps formation of development councils was simply not the correct approach. No one labored harder than Coleman. Yet Albany remained un-influence-able."

Chattey believed the same could be said of Washington. Budget cutbacks proposed by the Reagan Administration left legislators so fearful of losing the federal monies they already enjoyed that no one was about to ask for more. Chattey's approach to the Northeast-Midwest Coalition of Congress would best be left for another day, he reckoned. The logical approach had worked in a week in Europe, "but I am convinced logic will not sell the project [to government] in the U.S. Here, it will be built only in the crisis atmosphere," he said.

Clearly, more than that was said in the altercation between Chattey and Coleman. Eristoff wrote the argument off to "a misunderstanding" and told me later that one of his highest priorities was to figure out a way to bring Coleman back onboard.

In the meantime, yet another strategy was underway and yet another ally was offended. Whether either was for the best remained to be seen.

Once I asked Chattey about all that. Was it possible that flaws in his own judgment, or flaws in his personality, had undermined ICONN-Erie? "Of course I have flaws," he said. "All people have flaws. Where the project is concerned, however, the question is this: Are my flaws *fatal* flaws?"

TACIT APPROBATION of Chattey's acid-rain hypothesis came in September of 1981 when the Environmental Protection Agency granted the Allied Corporation a permit to dump 59,000 tons of hydrochloric acid into the ocean each year. The acid would be neutralized upon contact with seawater, the EPA said.

That same month, Chattey explained the plan to the President's Intergovernmental Scientific Energy & Technology Advisory Panel, and panel members were intrigued. "What had been slated for an hour and a half, with movies and slides," Chattey said, "ended up four and one-half hours, without movies, without slides, without lunch."

In October, New York City environmental groups, still unaware of ICONN-Erie, suggested that perhaps the best option to the dumping of toxic sewage sludge twelve miles offshore would be to dump it one hundred miles offshore, instead.

In November, the U.S. House of Representatives

committee on energy and commerce gave interested gas companies approval to finance a 4,800-mile trans-Canada natural gas pipeline by charging their customers for gas they had yet to receive. The approval was needed because private investors turned up their noses at the plan. Gas industry analysts said the Alaskan natural gas would reach consumers costing four times as much as other domestic supplies, the equivalent, per million Btu's, of oil priced at $120 per barrel. Nobody would buy it, the analysts said.

That same month, the Reagan Administration denied to the promoters of coal-slurry pipelines the right of eminent domain.

At the same time, West Germany's deal with the Soviets to purchase Siberian gas broke Germany's energy future free of the Western Economic Alliance and tied it to the Communist Bloc.

In December, the International Energy Association warned a complacent world that the recent oil glut could disappear as quickly as it had arrived. The next oil emergency would appear by 1986, the IEA reported. "Unless ICONN is in place by then," Chattey said, "the fates of Japan, Israel and all of Europe will be in jeopardy."

That same month, the Reagan Administration said it would provide no more handouts for the dredging of East Coast ports.

And the Organization for Economic Cooperation and Development predicted an unemployment rate of 9.2 percent for the United States in 1982, the highest level since the Great Depression.

The Port Authority of New York and New Jersey, meanwhile, paid $6 million for a 131-acre railyard in Jersey City, for possible use as a coal-storage site. Jersey City Mayor Gerald McCann was "unequivocally opposed" to the plan because of the horrendous environmental impact, he said.

All of which augured well for ICONN-Erie. The "crisis atmosphere" was building. The American process of political decision-making "just might work," Chattey said, "if one lives long enough."

In January of 1982, Sheik Yamani of Saudi Arabia warned that the oil glut of 1981 "will not continue" because of Saudi willingness to cut oil production, prompting new shortages and higher prices. The Saudis had nothing to lose, he said. Though they were engaged in a development program which would cost $800 billion by 1985, the nation had earned so much on oil sales in the 1970s that it could continue the effort even if it produced no oil at all between mid-1982 and early 1984. Yamani told Americans that "the only way to defuse the oil weapon" would be "to solve the Arab-Israeli problem."

Chattey saw another possibility, natch, so that same month he again tapped his personal financial resources and turned his basement into a bindery. He hoped to combine a revised ICONN-Erie prospectus with the SU executive summaries, for distribution to coal exporters, coal importers, the U.S. Commerce Department and the U.S. Department of State.

The document would also contain the findings of a computerized econometric model, developed by Pace University and the Wharton School, of the economic and employment impacts of the Chattey plan on the Greater New York Metropolitan Area. That study was late. The initial computer run had shown benefits of ICONN-Erie so immense "that they thought something must be wrong with the model," Chattey told me, "so they're tinkering with it now, to make it more precise."

Meanwhile, WCNY-TV, the Public Broadcasting Station in Syracuse, secured funding to do a thirty-minute documentary about ICONN-Erie. The program, part of the award-winning "U.S. Chronicles" series, was slated for broadcast in the fall of 1982 on at least forty-nine PBS stations nationwide.

CHATTEY SEEMED INSUFFERABLY PLEASED, and I could understand why, when I phoned him in the early evening of January 15, 1982 to discuss the news of the day. He was delighted. "I've had two strong drinks" in private celebration, he said, "so bear with me."

The news of the day was this: Hugh Carey surprised political observers throughout the state by announcing that he would not seek reelection to the governorship in November. The man Chattey had often described as a "non-governor" in essence was soon to become a non-governor in fact. The initial impediment to the advancement of ICONN-Erie, and perhaps the principal impediment throughout, was simply to pass from power.

"I have decided," the governor said, "to devote all of my strength to finishing the work of these past seven years; to achieving a program that sets a certain, safe course for this state's future; to seeking a victory more enduring and more important than any personal triumph at the polls." Aides told me later they doubted that the rhetoric referred to ICONN-Erie.

A leader of Carey's party said this: "Hugh Carey will be known as the governor who led this state through some of its most perilous times." A leader of the opposition party said this: "Carey's tenure led to a precipitous decline in the quality of life for the people of the State of New York."

(Two weeks later, in a report commissioned at the national Conference of Manufacturers Associations, the Chicago firm of Alexander & Co. concluded that New York's industrial climate was the second worst among the forty-eight continental United States. Twenty-two criteria were considered. New York was twice distinguished, leading the nation in state and local taxes, and leading the nation in per capita expenditures for welfare. The most attractive states for industry were Florida and Texas, the report said. The only state ranked below New York was West Virginia.)

Carey's decision to step down, and what it might mean for ICONN-Erie, brought to mind something John Petty had told me of the project years earlier. "You get things like this primarily by working at them. If you read histories and biographies, you find things get done through persistence."

Concerning the Carey announcement, Chattey voiced a similar sentiment as we spoke in January. "We've outlasted the bastard," he told me. Chattey knew most of the people who would seek Carey's job, "and I'd have no problem going to *any* of them," he said.

At least two of the contenders were apt to need no convincing. One was Mayor Ed Koch of New York City, who had long since called for funding of the ICONN-Erie studies. Another was the first public official to understand the project, the first to try to promote it, the man who four years earlier had offered Chattey almost a quarter of a million dollars in fees and services to further develop the concept. John Dyson became a candidate for governor.

In approaches to other candidates — Republicans and Democrats together, there were more than a dozen by the end of January — Chattey was counting on Constantine Sidamon-Eristoff to arrange the meetings and fine-tune the politics so that ICONN-Erie became no one's campaign issue and remained a non-partisan project.

Regardless of the outcome of the November election, Chattey knew that future problems in Albany would be of small consequence as compared to those past. Carey's abdication gave the bold dream and the dreamer "a new lease on life" in the halls of state government, he said. So he went on, as zealous as ever, insisting that a troubled New York might yet become the capital of a re-created world.

There was precedent, after all.

ACKNOWLEDGMENTS

I want to thank Peter Allen, Anne Bagamery, Jared Emery, Steve and Betty Galante, Ron Trinca, Richard Wright and especially Patricia Cappon, Michael Connor and Michael Fish, each of whom, in a different way, made this work possible.

Much of it would have been impossible but for the detailed notes on the early ICONN-Erie years recorded by Constantine Sidamon-Eristoff. He graciously gave me free access.

I also owe a considerable debt to Tom Beardsley, first mate of the M/V *Emita II*. When my typewriter fell apart, he loaned me his.

There were dozens of other initiatives and intrigues in the ICONN-Erie promotion. There were also a number of people I neglected to mention whose labor and faith helped to keep the project alive — a few who come to mind immediately are James McAllister, William Yost, Ron and Mitzi Wertheim, Peter Hoffman, Francis Pinnella, and Chattey's part-time secretary in the later years, Denise Fast.

Some of the omissions I am sure I made through ignorance. Other details were purposefully sacrificed to simplify the narrative. In both cases, I apologize to the people behind the ICONN-Erie Project if in any way I have presented their collective effort as anything less than it was.